Tradition and the Critical Spirit

9/15/91

Dear David,

Your generous and expert help at crucial points was essential in making this this book possible. I'm deeply grateful to you. Let's hope it will help to bring Tyrrell to the attention of a new generation of scholars and students.

Warm thanks,

Jim

FORTRESS TEXTS IN
MODERN THEOLOGY

IN THE SERIES

FORTRESS TEXTS IN MODERN THEOLOGY

Tradition and the Critical Spirit

Catholic Modernist Writings

George Tyrrell

**Selected and Introduced by
James C. Livingston**

Fortress Press   **Minneapolis**

TRADITION AND THE CRITICAL SPIRIT
Catholic Modernist Writings

Cover design: Jim Churchville.

Library of Congress Cataloging-in-Publication Data

Tyrrell, George, 1861-1909.
    Tradition and the critical spirit : Catholic modernist writings /
  by George Tyrrell ; selected and introduced by James C. Livingston.
        p. cm.—(Fortress texts in modern theology)
    Includes bibliographical references.
    ISBN 0-8006-3210-9 (alk. paper)
    1. Modernism—Catholic Church—History—Sources.
  2. Theology—19th century. 3. Theology—20th century. 4. Catholic
  Church—Doctrines—History—19th century—Sources. 5. Catholic
  Church—Doctrines—History—20th century—Sources. I. Livingston,
  James C., 1930– . II. Title. III. Series.
  BX1396.2.A72   1990
  230'.2—dc20   90–47206
                                                                        CIP

The paper used in this publication meets the minimum requirements of American National Standard for Information Sciences—Permanence of Paper for Printed Library Materials, ANSI Z329.48-1484.   ∞™

Manufactured in the U.S.A.   AF 1-3210
95   94   93   92   91   1   2   3   4   5   6   7   8   9   10

Contents

Preface

This book was born of the conviction that it would be a service to teachers and scholars, both senior and junior, to bring together under one cover George Tyrrell's most important and representative writings. Some of these are little known and/or difficult to come by. The timing of such a collection, moreover, coincides with the current interest in Catholic Modernism and in Tyrrell as perhaps the most characteristic of all the Catholic Modernists. Tyrrell's writings deeply reflect the questions that preoccupied and troubled theologians at the turn of the century. They are also surprisingly prophetic of concerns and themes in Catholic—but also Protestant—theology in recent years. Tyrrell's theological interests and quandaries largely remain our own.

I am indebted to the College of William and Mary for a summer research grant that allowed me to work uninterrupted on this book. David Schultenover, S.J., and Nicholas Sagovsky were generous in advising me about my plan for the volume and about my selections. I am especially grateful to David Schultenover for his meticulous reading of my introductory essay. His advice, based on a deep knowledge of Tyrrell, greatly improved my effort to summarize Tyrrell's life and thought. Lorraine C. Corporon's accuracy and efficiency in preparing the typescript spared me much work, and I express my appreciation to her.

Introduction.
George Tyrrell: His Life, Thought, and Significance

George Tyrrell (1861–1909) is, after John Henry Newman, the most significant English Roman Catholic theologian of the nineteenth century. Tyrrell was not, it must be said, a systematic theologian. His religious writings are the passionate expression of the man, the fruit of his own spiritual and intellectual struggles.

Many of Tyrrell's friends believed that in his almost obsessive dedication to writing after 1899 ("I can write all day long from morning till night. . . . It is the only narcotic that is strong enough to make me forget myself and my imaginary woes") and in the turn that it took, he had missed his true vocation as a spiritual director and healer of souls. That may be true. Tyrrell's most important writing, however, is not found in his spiritual meditations and essays, although much of this work is wise and searching. All of his religious writings are, finally, the product and the testing of spiritual experience.

It has been said that George Tyrrell's mind was not theologically original. That is true only if the word original is reserved for a scholar or a thinker whose work initiates, in a singular way, a revolution or paradigm change in our interpretation of texts or doctrine. Tyrrell was thoroughly trained in scholastic theology and well read in the continental scholarship of his day—both German theology and biblical scholarship and the best in French thought. His own late writings especially reveal his most current intellectual tutelage, in addition to his unique and creative mind and sensibility and his lucid, lively, often witty and ironic style. Most significantly, they express the existential passion of a profoundly spiritual man deeply engaged by the swift currents of modernity which threatened the traditional foundations of faith. Tyrrell often said that his preoccupation was with the Church's traditional teaching and "with the problem of reconciling it, on the one hand, with the exigencies of the inward life; and on the other, with the recent results of critical Church history."[1] He spoke of himself as "a weaver of materials gathered from many quarters"— but what a superb weaver he proved to be! Ronald Chapman quite rightly remarks that in comparison with Newman, Tyrrell probed more deeply into *our* problems. He is, simply, more "a man of our own time, questioning everything, courageously following the truth wherever it might lead."[2] The religious concerns that preoccupied and often troubled George Tyrrell persist today.

Tyrrell is unquestionably the most important English exponent of Catholic Modernism. For this alone his work will be of lasting value. But his own Modernism is, again, distinct. His critics have often failed to read him closely, if at all, and have misrepresented his subtle and complex thought, not infrequently and unfairly tarring him with the excesses of Loisy and others. Tyrrell was—as he described himself— a "hopeless tangle," and his writings resist simple categorization. Both the man and his essays remain elusive, paradoxical, unfinished— never fixed or at rest. If these are faults, so be it. Many Anglican Modernists, such as Dean Inge, found him too Catholic; some Catholics declared him a Protestant. He was a priest who kept a Buddha image under his crucifix. To some he was a mystic; the Vatican denounced him a rationalist, another Voltaire or Strauss. Tyrrell called himself a revolutionary but, like a true conservative, he worked in the service of the ancient and the traditional, the fruits "of life and experience." Here was a man who, on the same page, was capable of writing stinging polemic and cool, detached self-analysis.

In the years immediately following his tragic death, which cut short a brilliant career marked by mutual alienation from the Catholic Church, Tyrrell's writings were regarded with suspicion—by some friends as well as foes. The "stormy petrel" of Modernism was too volatile and unpredictable but also far too subtle for most churchmen's comfort. He was indiscriminately declared a pragmatist, imma-

1. George Tyrrell, *Medievalism: A Reply to Cardinal Mercier,* 107.
2. Ronald Chapman, "The Thought of George Tyrrell," in W. W. Robson, ed., *Essays and Poems Presented to Lord David Cecil,* 166.

nentist, agnostic, individualistic Protestant, even a skeptic by, among
others, Roman Jesuits and Vatican authorities. None of these dis-
missive epithets can stand the test of time, at least without significant
qualification or clarification. A half-century later—and after the
Nouvelle Theologie and Vatican II—Tyrrell's reflections on such
matters as revelation, the nature of dogma, development, authority,
and ecclesiology are not only highly relevant to contemporary theological discussion but, in many cases, appear to lie within the main-
stream of progressive Catholic theology.

In any case, the time has arrived for a reconsideration of both
Tyrrell's historical and continuing significance. The reevaluation of
Catholic Modernism has gained considerable momentum in the past
quarter-century through the work of Alec Vidler, Emile Poulat,
Thomas Loome, Lawrence Barmann, and others, including members
of the Roman Catholic Modernism Group of the American Acad-
emy of Religion. Brief and instructive essays on Tyrrell have
appeared in books by Vidler, Gabriel Daly, and others within the
past decade, and book-length studies of Tyrrell have been published
by Loome, David F. Wells, David G. Schultenover, S.J., Ellen
Leonard, and Nicholas Sagovsky (see the bibliography). Nevertheless,
much work on Tyrrell—his life, letters, writings, and influence—
remains to be done, although some has been begun. This volume
is intended to bring some of Tyrrell's essential, but often not easily
accessible, essays to the attention of a wider audience of scholars
who are interested in modern religious thought and contemporary
theology.

LIFE AND CHARACTER

Baron Friedrich von Hügel wrote to his friend George Tyrrell, "You
are a German brain, an Irish heart, a most fruitful but costly and
adventurous combination."[3] Tyrrell was, indeed, such a rare hybrid.
His life experience, character, and personality are crucial to an
understanding of his writings and his often turbulent involvement in
the events of the Modernist era. His life's pilgrimage, as is true of
most thinkers and scholars, was a largely interior one of mind and
heart. The public aspects of Tyrrell's life were quite unexceptional
until 1904 when he came into increasing public conflict with ecclesi-

3. "Father Tyrrell," *The Hibbert Journal* 8 (January 1910): 242.

astical authorities and faced both dismissal from his order, the Society of Jesus, and minor excommunication from the Roman Catholic Church. In the last five years of his life, he achieved a certain notoriety.

Tyrrell was born in Dublin on February 6, 1861, the last of four children of William Tyrrell and his wife, Mary Chamney. His father, a respected journalist for the Dublin *Evening Mail*, died two months before his youngest son's birth. The family suffered constant financial strain, and moved a good deal. Under the direction of his Protestant evangelical Aunt Melinda, George endured tedious church services and, he recalled, Sunday became a "day of dreariness and funereal solemnity."

In 1869, Tyrrell was enrolled in the Rathmines School in Dublin, where he proved an indifferent student but came under the generous and compassionate influence of the headmaster, Dr. Charles Benson. Benson also gave Tyrrell his first taste of the High Church, liturgical religion that, Tyrrell later wrote, "helped me on towards Catholicism." In 1875, Tyrrell came under the influence of the devout High-Churchmanship of Father Maturin of Grangegorman and, shortly thereafter, of Robert Dolling, who later became a noted Anglo-Catholic priest and social reformer. Dolling had great sympathy for Roman Catholicism but disliked Vaticanism. Later, he was to wean Tyrrell away from Father Maturin's narrow Anglican, Tory High-Churchmanship.

In 1878, under Dolling's encouragement, Tyrrell entered Trinity College, Dublin, with Anglican ordination vaguely in mind. Soon, however, he followed Dolling to London, but with the secret purpose of testing out his desire to become a Roman Catholic—and even a Jesuit priest. On May 18, 1879, he was received into the Roman Catholic Church and forthwith became a candidate for admission into the Society of Jesus. Tyrrell was advised, however, to serve a year's apprenticeship at the Jesuit colleges at Cyprus and, later, in Malta. In 1880, he entered the Jesuit novitiate of Manresa, outside London. In Malta and Manresa, Tyrrell's romantic notion of Jesuit life received its first cold dose of realism. In 1882, however—and contrary to Dolling's prediction—he took his first vows and was sent immediately to Stonyhurst to study scholastic philosophy. Tyrrell proved that he was one to be reckoned with and threw himself, as he was to recall, "wholly into the task of mastering and defending the scholastic—or, rather, Thomistic—system of philosophy and theology." He recognized St. Thomas as "essentially liberal-minded and sympathetic" in contrast to "the narrow spirit" of the zealous neo-Scholastics and their arid manuals. Tyrrell emerged from his studies in 1885 profoundly influenced by John Henry Newman but also an ardent disciple of St. Thomas. He entered a period of fairly rigorous orthodoxy which was to last until 1896. The frictions with his order, however, were to continue.

In 1885 Tyrrell returned to Malta as a schoolmaster, where he taught for three happy years. This period was followed by four years of theological studies at St. Beuno's College in North Wales. On September 20, 1891, he was ordained a priest. He returned to Manresa to complete his final year of priestly formation and to prepare himself for his apostolate. In 1893, Tyrrell was sent for a short time to do mission work in Oxford and then went to St. Helen's in the coal country of Lancashire. He soon gained the affection of his poor and untutored flock. This pastoral work proved only a brief interlude, since he was assigned, against his wishes, to teach philosophy at Stonyhurst. From this time on, his struggles with the authorities intensified. At Stonyhurst, he defended "pure" Thomism against the prevailing Suarezianism of his Jesuit colleagues and soon won the allegiance, as well as the affection, of his students. This was too much for his faculty peers, and in August of 1896 Tyrrell was removed from Stonyhurst and assigned to the literary staff of *The Month* at the Jesuit headquarters in Farm Street in the heart of Mayfair, London.

Transfer to a more sophisticated residence did not dilute the strength of Tyrrell's dissatisfaction with what he increasingly came to view as the limitations—indeed, the "heresies"—of Scholastic "theologism" and ecclesiastical "Vaticanism." It was at this critical time that he made the acquaintance of Baron von Hügel, who introduced him to the work of contemporary Catholic philosophers, such as Blondel and Laberthonnière, who had already broken with Scholasticism and were developing a religious philosophy along Augustinian and voluntarist lines. Later, von Hügel was to initiate Tyrrell into the labyrinth of late nineteenth-century German biblical criticism. The period 1897 to 1900 was a time, however, when Tyrrell explored what he called "meditating liberalism," a position more akin to Newman than to St. Thomas. However, his newly discovered critical studies soon alerted him to Newman's critical-theological limitations.

Tyrrell's Modernist period can perhaps best be dated from the publication, in November 1899, of his essay "The Relation of Theology to Devotion." It contains *in nuce,* as he later was to remark, his new understanding of revelation, theology, dogma, and authority—themes that were to remain dominant in his subsequent writings. This essay marks a turning point in his theological experience. Tyrrell's testing of official ecclesiastical accommodation reached a crisis with the publication of "A Perverted Devotion" in December 1899. His call for a "temperate agnosticism" regarding the traditional Catholic view of Hell raised a storm. Roman officials declared the article "offensive to pious ears," and Tyrrell was removed from the staff of *The Month,* barred from publishing outside the journal, and sent into retirement ("exile") to the Jesuit mission house at Richmond, in remote Swaledale, North Yorkshire. There he lived in seclusion for more than five years, the remaining years of his life as a Jesuit.

His time in Richmond was richly productive. Of the books written during these years—*The Civilizing of the Matafanus, Religion as a Factor of Life, Oil and Wine, The Church and the Future, A Letter to a University Professor*—all were published anonymously, pseudonymously, or privately. Only *Lex Orandi* received an imprimatur. *Lex Credendi* and most of the critically important essays that were gathered in *Through Scylla and Charybdis* (1907) were also written during these years of "exile." Relations with his order continued to worsen during the Richmond period as relations between the Modernists and the authorities became increasingly unsympathetic and, finally, irreconcilable.

Letter to a University Professor (1904) was reissued anonymously as *A Much-Abused Letter* in 1906. Tyrrell admitted to its authorship and was given the option of repudiating the essay or being removed from the Society of Jesus. On February 19, 1906, he was dismissed from the order. The following year Pope Pius X issued his broadside condemnation of Modernism in the encyclical *Pascendi dominici gregis.* The main target was Alfred Loisy, but Tyrrell clearly was among those condemned and associated with heresy. He replied to the encyclical in two vigorous letters of rebuttal to *The Times.* His friend von Hügel found Tyrrell's riposte "real and substantial" but also "very hot, vehement, and sarcastic." A letter followed from the Bishop of Southwark, who informed Tyrrell that he was henceforth deprived of the sacraments and that his case was reserved to Rome.

Tyrrell spent his last two years living with close friends in Clapham and in Storrington, Sussex. He continued to write articles and completed two books, *Medievalism* (1908) and *Christianity at the Crossroads* (1909). The latter was his most radical reconception and defense of Catholicism, and was completed only two weeks before his death. Early in 1909, Tyrrell fell ill and was diagnosed with Bright's disease. He died at Storrington on July 15, 1909. He was refused Catholic interment and so was buried in the Anglican parish churchyard in Storrington. The funeral was attended by about forty friends; the Abbé Henri Bremond, a French diocesan priest and former Jesuit, offered prayers, a eulogy, and a blessing over the grave. For doing so, Bremond was suspended from his priestly office.

Tyrrell's early disillusionment with the Jesuits and with the dominant Scholasticism and Ultramontanism of his time has caused some to question the depth and sincerity of his conversion and his allegiance to Catholicism. Today, students of Tyrrell's life and work are in little doubt about either the depth or the integrity of his Catholic faith. However heterodox or idiosyncratic his theological views, Tyrrell could never find a spiritual resting place in Anglicanism or Protestantism—or in Romanism as he saw it developing after 1870. Romanism or Vaticanism were not, he insisted, Catholicism. Tyrrell wrote to an Anglican vicar: "I feel my work is to hammer away at the great unwieldy carcass of the Roman Communion and wake it up from its medieval dreams. Not that I shall succeed, but that my failure and many another may pave the way for eventual success."[4]

Those who are uncomfortable with ambiguity, paradox, and dialectical openness will not find George Tyrrell the man, the seemingly contradictory "hopeless tangle," easy to understand. Nor are they likely to have an immediate or easy appreciation of his writings, which are ambivalent, subtle, often merely tentative or suggestive, and yet also hard, polemical, assertive, and at times bitterly ironic. Tyrrell will denounce Romanism and yet insist that Roman Catholicism is the most perfect vehicle of Christ's spirit. He scorns "externalism" in religion and yet argues that religion demands embodiment in obviously weak and fallible earthen vessels. He criticizes theology, yet defends its imperative role. And yet there is in Tyrrell—as in Luther and in Kierkegaard—a spiritual harmony and a compelling witness to truth which shines through all the contrariety and paradox.

Tyrrell's thought is a mirror of his own passionate struggles and

4. Maude D. Petre, *Autobiography and Life of George Tyrrell*, 2:373.

his changing ideas and moods.[5] His writing, he came to understand,
was a necessary act of clarifying his own mind but, even more, of
purging his soul. His essays represent—and for this they are invaluable—a convergence of the inner life of the man and the stormy
events in the life of the Church at the turn of the century. He was
compelled to probe the facts, the truth of the case, be it Newman's
theory of development, William James's *Varieties of Religious Experience,* or Johannes Weiss's *Die Predigt Jesu von Reiche Gottes.* "I do
not 'fight down' my doubts," he wrote, "as I should in some cases
advise others to do. Rather, I go deliberately in search of every
difficulty in that line lest I be haunted by the thought that new revelations might rob me of my faith, or that those who deny have reasons for their denial that I have not *felt.*"[6] He confessed to von Hügel
that he could not bear the thought that he owed "his stability to any
sort of ignorance or half-view."[7]

Tyrrell's scrupulosity and ruthless honesty were not rooted in
intellectual concupiscence, and yet his public candor was, it can be
argued, reckless and imprudent. Prudence he regarded as a moral
fault. It cannot be denied that he enjoyed combat, and he plunged
into areas where others feared to tread. He was, however, indifferent
to his personal safety, and his combativeness and impetuosity were
innocent of personal vanity. Gabriel Daly rightly concludes that the
unifying principle of Tyrrell's character was his courage,[8] which he
regarded as the "very rarest of all virtues."[9] For that reason, he was
often hard on his confrères in the Modernist cause, especially those
friends who he felt were willing to straddle or evade or were hesitant
to speak out. Tyrrell admitted that his "whole life was a continual
process of adjusting and readjusting." He wrote, "I am too miserably
honest to stick my head in the sand and be comfortable."[10] He had, in
fact, a puritan suspicion of comfort and ease, but, mercifully, he did
not allow his misery and isolation to descend into self-pity. His self-
deprecating humor usually broke through on such occasions. But, as
Maude Petre observed, it was "the humor of the tragic . . . tempera-

5. For a perceptive account of Tyrrell's character, on which I am here dependent,
see Gabriel Daly, "Some Reflections on the Character of George Tyrrell."
6. *George Tyrrell's Letters,* ed. Maude D. Petre, 158.
7. Petre, *Autobiography and Life of George Tyrrell,* 2:96.
8. Daly, "Some Reflections on the Character of George Tyrrell," 265.
9. *George Tyrrell's Letters,* ed. M. D. Petre, 164.
10. Ibid., 159.

ment," of the "sad clear vision of those who gauge the puny efforts of man in comparison with the vast universe in which he moves."[11]

Despite his faults, Tyrrell's character as reflected in his writings is attractive to us because we can see in him a man of our own times. So are his thoughts on religion.

TYRRELL'S RELIGIOUS THOUGHT

Tyrrell, as noted, was no systematic theologian. His method of communication—even when one excludes his several books of meditations—was the essay and review. Between 1886 and 1909, he published close to two hundred reviews, articles, and introductions —many of them long essays. Of his twenty books, only about a half-dozen are whole works; most are edited collections. While it has been said that Tyrrell's vast literary outpouring lacks any scheme or system, the reader of the books he published in the last decade of his life will recognize that Tyrrell was preoccupied with four or five cardinal themes that give his theological reflection a definite coherence. He does not provide many solutions, and his essays often lack a satisfying closure which we—perhaps unconsciously and wrongly— find satisfying in the work of a more systematic thinker. But Tyrrell's essays are usually probing and suggestive.

The key to Tyrrell's religious philosophy is his acute suspicion of "a priorism," of rationalism and system. His sense of religion is practical and experimental. Everything is to be tested by experience— how it works. "That the religious life of the Church is the source and criterion of doctrinal truth; that experiment is the criterion of theory as the fruit is of the tree, is a point that I will not even discuss. It is a truth that theological pride hates and kicks against but which it dares not deny in the teeth of the Gospel."[12] Tyrrell continually warns against "a certain narrow, cock-sure orthodoxy"; the religion of those for "whom everything is clear and common-sense, and obvious; who can define a mystery but have never felt one."[13] External religion, as such, offers us not bread but a stone. Following Matthew Arnold, Tyrrell defined faith as necessarily "rooted in some kind of experience and not merely in propositions and principles accepted on hear-

11. Petre, *Autobiography and Life of George Tyrrell,* 2:9–10.
12. Tyrrell, *Medievalism,* 39.
13. George Tyrrell, *External Religion: Its Use and Abuse,* 125.

say." "It rests," he continued, "upon the evidence of a Power in myself and in all men 'making for righteousness.' "[14]

For Tyrrell, the root religious experience is located in the will and in conscience—and in this Tyrrell was one with Newman. "We are nothing else but wills," Tyrrell writes, quoting St. Augustine. Our relation to other wills is what makes for our humaneness and our unique spirituality. Primary among our will-relations—of agreement and disagreement, love and hate, for example—is our relation to that divine Will that is the transcendent yet immanent center and limit-point of the entire will-world. Our will-relation to God—which, with twentieth-century theologian Karl Rahner, Tyrrell regards as a primordial, prereflexive, human intuition—is the foundation of those sentiments or feelings that regulate all our other relations. While our religious sentiments are not all of life—since life includes our thinking and our acting—religion is nevertheless, for Tyrrell, the principal element in the life of our affections. Our religious feelings and efforts do therefore govern and control all other aspects of life, including the rational and ethical. Perceptions may precede and actions follow, but our religious sentiments, our will-attitude, is the valuating and energizing center of life. Religion, then, is simply the movement of our will-attitude in relation to God's will, and its measure is the extent that God's will is understood, loved, and acted upon. Our understanding cannot, however, as we shall see, reach God in himself, but only in his effects and manifestations. Because we are essentially social beings, our knowledge of God's being and will is mediated to us through our social experience. Through the accumulated wisdom and experience of the ages, God does not leave us without true, compelling witnesses to God's will and way.

Until 1899, Tyrrell conceived of divine revelation in scholastic fashion as an instruction of the mind. Thereafter he came sharply to distinguish revelation, as supernatural experience, from theology, the after-reflection and statement of the experience. For Tyrrell, theology is a science, an exercise of the human intellect. It is the fruit of our philosophic reflection on the facts of religious experience. The granting to theology of a divine or infallible status—a tendency of ultramontane theologians—Tyrrell branded "theologism." "We know," he constantly reminds his reader, "more theology than St.

14. Letter to Bremond. Cited in David Schultenover, *George Tyrrell: In Search of Catholicism,* 190.

Peter or St. Mary Magdalene or St. Paul, but do we believe more or hope more or love more?"[15] "Revelation," Tyrrell came to insist, "is a showing on the part of God, a seeing on the part of the receiver. Prophecy is but the communication of this vision to others. Theology must take prophecy not as statement, but as experience."[16] The prophet's aim is to kindle in others the direct, existential experience of revelation—"a spirit answering to Spirit." Here Tyrrell is working independently with an idea similar to that developed by Kierkegaard in the *Philosophical Fragments.* Every revelation, whether to Christ or to the humblest believer, is of the same kind—"the showing of God." Every true revelation is equidistant to the Eternal.

There is, according to Tyrrell, a "derivative" sense in which the word revelation is also used. It is represented in the halting efforts of the recipient to give expression to and to communicate the inner preconceptual experience and vision to others—to evoke the same spiritual experience. But all such efforts require "a certain translation of inward vision into outward language and symbolism—a translation that can never be exhaustive or adequate, but at most suggestive."[17] Again, unless the prophet's word kindles a spirit to answer the Spirit, the communication

> may present concepts to the understanding and pictures to the imagination, but no real spiritual content. It will, if anything, rather puzzle, perplex, and annoy, than illuminate and kindle; for it will be estimated as theology or history . . . as statement and not as experience.[18]

It is revelation as divine "presence," as experience "that we answer by the act of Faith, recognizing it as God's word in us and to us. Were it not already written in the depths of our being, where the spirit is rooted in God, we could not recognize it."[19]

While revelation "is a perennial phenomenon," the revelation experienced by Christ remains for Tyrrell the summit and norm of all divine disclosure:

> As the spirit did not cease with the apostles, so neither did revelation and prophecy. But a peculiar character rightly attached to that which was the effect of immediate contact with Christ, and of the spirit as it

15. George Tyrrell, *Through Scylla and Charybdis,* 325.
16. Ibid., 289.
17. Ibid., 303.
18. Ibid., 304.
19. Ibid., 305.

was breathed forth from his very lips. This has rightly been regarded
as alone classical and normative, as the test by which all spirits and
revelations in the Church are to be tried. As a fountain cannot rise
above its source, so neither can the waves that circle out from that
central and original disturbance excel or even equal it in intensity.

They may manifest the same spirit, "but they do not complete it
organically or develop it."[20]

Tyrrell became convinced that it is a "patent fallacy" to speak of
the development of revelation. There is no more advance in revelation than there is in poetry or art. "There is no progress in goodness,
i.e., in the *love* of what is right; but only in ethics, i.e., in the *understanding* of what is right. There is no progress in religion, i.e., in the
spirit of Faith, Hope, and Charity; but only in theology, i.e., in
the *understanding* of things divine."[21]

For Tyrrell, it is what he came to call the "Spirit of Christ" that is
the normative revelation, the *depositum fidei* or deposit of faith—with
all of its implications. He rejects the prevalent notion in the Church
that the relation of the *depositum* to its subsequent history in the
Church is to be likened to that of an acorn and a mighty oak. At this
time, his view of Christ drew heavily on the Liberal Protestant picture of the historical Jesus. However, his Christology was soon to
reflect the serious tension found in the most advanced late nineteenth-century discussions of Christ, namely, that between the "return
to the historical sources" and appeal to personal, largely moral, religious experience. Tyrrell's historical radicalism brought him face to
face with the earthy, yet otherworldly, apocalyptic Christ and thus
with the necessity of repudiating the Jesus of Liberalism. Neither
Harnack nor Loisy could help him now.

Tyrrell's response was to appeal to the "Spirit of Christ" as the
depositum fidei and, paradoxically, to reject the forms of the earliest,
primitive New Testament picture as not being fully adequate to
express that Spirit. The sectarian Bible-thumping literalist may, in
certain externals, appear to be more in accord with the milieu of
New Testament apocalypticism. Yet, for all the palpable differences
in historical context, Tyrrell boldly insists that the spirit of St. Francis,
for example, is immeasurably truer to the "Spirit of Christ" than is
the biblical literalist. Tyrrell's radical modernity is revealed in part in

20. Ibid., 292.
21. Ibid., 295–96.

his awareness that our knowledge of the details of the life and psychological development of Jesus is made uncertain by historical criticism. His christological reflection finds a solution akin to that taken by Ernst Troeltsch, whom he had read at about the same time. It is, Tyrrell now insists, the total historical phenomenon of Jesus that is capable of being established as historical fact, and this allows the Church to maintain that the "idea" or the "Spirit of Christ" is rooted in reality—and is, in Troeltsch's words, "the support, center, and symbol of [the church's] religious life."[22] This fundamental "Spirit of Christ" is experiential, corporate, and cultic. Fire is kindled from fire. "This," writes Tyrrell, "it is that distinguishes Christianity from the following of a teacher or prophet. . . . Jesus Himself was the great sacrament and effectual symbol of the Divine Life and Spirit . . . a personal influence, fashioning the soul to its own divine nature."[23] The Spirit of Christ touches our own "internal sympathy." But the historical vehicles and sacramental symbols are not the Spirit itself. "The human frame and mind of Jesus, His local and temporal limitations of thought and knowledge, were but the sacramental elements through which the influence of His Divine Spirit was mediated. To our age He would have spoken differently; but the spirit would have been the same."[24] So it is that "we have long since outgrown those apocalyptic forms of religious thought in which the Spirit of Jesus first uttered itself. . . . But the spirit itself we have not outgrown, and in us it seeks ever new forms wherein to clothe the same revelation."[25] For Tyrrell, Christian theology entails a return to neither outmoded apostolic forms nor a doctrine of the development of revelation, for example, from implicit to explicit.

Tyrrell was ever grateful to Newman for offering him an alternative to the theological Scholasticism then ascendant, but he departs from Newman on the question of the development of the *deposit of faith.* For Tyrrell, *custodi depositum* (guard the deposit) is the sum of the Church's commission, the custodian of the original New Testament deposit; it must never claim to have developed the original *depositum.* The Church rests satisfied to preserve and protect, not

22. Ernst Troeltsch, "The Significance of the Historical Existence of Jesus for Faith," in *Ernst Troeltsch: Writings on Theology and Religion,* trans. and ed. Robert Morgan and Michael Pye (London: Gerald Duckworth & Co.; and Atlanta: John Knox Press, 1977), 202.
23. George Tyrrell, *Christianity at the Crossroads,* 264–66.
24. Ibid., 266.
25. Ibid., 267.

develop "this concrete, colored, imaginative expression of the Divine mysteries, as it lay in the mind of the first recipients," for that expression "is the rule and corrective, both of popular devotion and of rational theology."[26] But, Tyrrell insists, God's revelation to fisherman and peasant, to the *profanum vulgus,* is the *depositum* itself, already once removed from the original vision. It remains for us "a translation of supernatural experiences into the terms of the natural; that is, its truth is the truth of analogy, not of exact scientific equation."[27]

Here Tyrrell's discussion tends to confusion because of his imprecision regarding revelation and the deposit. He often appears to equate the two, but then he will speak of revelation or prophetic truth as God's self-revelation, which lies outside the world of ordinary experience and expression, a step removed, it would appear, from the language of the New Testament. In any case, prophetic truth as it is given in the deposit is, for Tyrrell, "directly practical . . . approximative, and only indirectly speculative."[28] To look for some perfect adequation between the language of revelation and theology—between prophetic and scientific truth—is for Tyrrell the root error of theologism. That is, the deposit of faith is never simply doctrine or creed; it is more directly a *lex orandi* than a *lex credendi,* a law of prayer than of belief. The former is always the test of the latter.

Theology, like biblical criticism, is a science, a function of human reason. Just as science is removed from the province of the prophet, so is the claim of divine authority withdrawn from the theologian. "Christian Revelation is 'the same yesterday, today, and for ever.' " The work of the theologian, on the other hand, "is as variable as his intelligence and information; today different from yesterday; tomorrow from today."[29] Nevertheless, Tyrrell insists that theology has a necessary role and that "revelation viewed as experience, is rightly and profitably made the subject matter of theological reflection."[30] Furthermore, "theology, like any other science, must develop itself freely under no other limitations than those imposed by its subject-

26. Tyrrell, *Through Scylla and Charybdis,* 95.
27. Ibid., 131.
28. Ibid., 210.
29. Ibid., 345.
30. Ibid., 353.

matter and the laws of thought."[31] In his essay "The Rights and
Limits of Theology" (1905), Tyrrell fully defends the rights of theology and acknowledges that "the Christian revelation is largely
expressed in the language of theology."[32] Doctrine, creeds, and formularies are, after all, the creation of the collective religious experience of Christians. But their function is protective of that experience.
"The Church's teaching-office is simply to guard the Apostolic Revelation identically for all ages and capacities . . . consequently her
dogmatic decisions possess a protective but not a scientific or philosophical infallibility."[33] The language and concepts of theology may,
for example, be Neo-Platonic, Aristotelian, Cartesian, Hegelian, or
Existential, as the particular time may require.

Tyrrell expresses very nicely the interdependence of the *lex
credendi* and the *lex orandi*:

> Not every devotion of Catholics is a Catholic devotion, and the Church
> needs to exercise her authority continually in checking the tendency to
> extravagate, and in applying and enforcing the original *lex orandi*. In
> this work she is helped by a wise and temperate theology. But theology
> is not always wise and temperate; and has itself often to be brought to
> the *lex orandi* test. It has to be reminded that, like science, its hypoth-
> eses, theories, and explanations, must square with facts—the facts here
> being the Christian religion as lived by its consistent professors.[34]

Dogma must, finally, be judged by the *lex orandi*, that is, by its
prayer-value:

> Beliefs that have been found by continuous and invariable experience
> to foster and promote the spiritual life of the soul must so far be in
> accord with the nature and laws of that will-world with which it is the
> aim of religion to bring us into harmony; their practical value results
> from, and is founded in, their representative value.[35]

Later doctrinal developments—dogmas associated with Mary, for
example—are to be understood and tried by the *lex orandi*. They are
practical and protective of the deposit of faith and the spiritual life.

For Tyrrell, dogma occupies a middle position between natural
knowledge and spiritual truth. In relation to our understanding of

31. Ibid., 353–54.
32. Ibid., 229.
33. Ibid., 354.
34. Ibid., 104.
35. George Tyrrell, *Lex Orandi, or, Prayer and Creed*, 57.

the outer, natural experience, it "is a necessary fallible approximation," and in relation to the order of divine realities "it is an infallible
approximation":

> The Spirit of Christ seizes from the chaos of current beliefs—theologi-
> cal, ethical, historical—those that are most appropriate for its own
> embodiment and progressive expression, and weaves them into a gar-
> ment adapted to the present state of its own growth. If the choice and
> the weaving is its own, the matter chosen is the work of fallible man in
> his quest for truth.[36]

Tyrrell thus insists that if Christian belief should prove mistaken in
matters of philosophy, history, or science, "it matters as little as the
discovery that Dives and Lazarus never existed."[37] And so it is that

> certain concrete historical facts enter into our creed as matters of faith.
> Precisely as historical facts they concern the historian and must be
> criticized by his methods. But as matters of faith they must be deter-
> mined by the criterion of faith, i.e., by their proved religious values as
> universally effectual of spiritual progress.[38]

Beliefs fruitful of the spiritual life are, Tyrrell insists, rooted in
fact; they put us in touch with reality. Here we see a theme of modern theology which runs from Hegel through the British Idealists and
the Catholic Modernists to Bultmann and Existentialist theology,
namely, the effort to conserve the facts of spiritual life from the
corrosive work of the scientific historian and critic. As Ronald
Chapman strikingly puts it in the case of Tyrrell, "The object was to
place the ark of God beyond the reach of impious men. Strictly
speaking, there is no such thing as a liberal theory of revelation because no one makes plans for saving what is considered as
already lost."[39]

According to Tyrrell, true belief and doctrine are the work of the
collective spiritual labor of the Christian community. His understanding of authority thus follows naturally from his charismatic view of
revelation and his experiential conception of the role of theology and
doctrine. He writes, "The authority of the collective over the individual mind as being the adequate organ through which truth,
whether natural or supernatural, progressively reveals itself, has

36. George Tyrrell, *The Church and the Future*, 89–90.
37. Ibid., 90.
38. Tyrrell, *Lex Orandi*, 169.
39. Chapman, "The Thought of George Tyrrell," 153.

always been the fundamental assumption of Catholicism—*Securus judicat orbis terrarum.*"[40] For Tyrrell, authority rests in the *consensus fidelium.* The teaching office of bishops, councils, and popes is that of interpreter of the collective mind of the Church. They are "witnesses to, not creators of" the Church's belief and practice. To claim that spiritual authority rests in "the people of God" does not contradict its divine origin; rather it is to insist that

> God's highest and fullest manifestation is given, not in the clouds, nor in the stars, but in the spirit of man, and therefore most completely in that completest expression of man's spirit which is obtained in the widest available consensus and is the fruit of the widest collective experience.[41]

Tyrrell believed that democratic authority in the Church had come to stay; "any other conception of authority will be simply unthinkable."[42] The priesthood must therefore ever remain receptive to, and, indeed, obey, the general mind; "if they assail it, if they fling themselves against that rock . . . they shall be bruised." Tyrrell perceived the democratic principle, then defended by the American Catholic Church, as the way of the future. Change, of course, can rightly come only through the workings of the Holy Spirit in the Church. And how the "Spirit of Christ" works its will is never easily discerned. Tyrrell was certain, however, that following one's own private judgment is always wrong. Nevertheless, he wrote, "when it is clear that a counter-belief is gaining ground in such a way that it represents a 'consensus' of the future," that is, reached independently and simultaneously by various thinkers,

> one may, and at times one ought, to follow the belief that lives in the spirit (however small the number of its supporters) . . . for in so doing one departs from the dead letter only to conform oneself to a truer, higher, and more authoritative expression of the living spirit.[43]

Authority rests, then, in the widest, most enduring consensus regarding the manifestation of the Divine Spirit as God revealed *in* man. The locus of authority is never "an external influence streaming down from heaven like a sunbeam through a cleft in the clouds . . .

40. Tyrrell, *Through Scylla and Charybdis,* 355.
41. Ibid., 371.
42. Ibid., 381.
43. Ibid., 369.

singling out God's arbitrarily chosen delegates." Authority is something inherent in and inalienable from the people of God. "It is the
imperativeness of the collective conscience."[44] Tyrrell, as I have
noted, did not disdain the externals of religion, including the visible
Church—only their abuse. Christ lives on, actually and effectively, in
the visible Church and its sacramental life, despite all of the Church's
"beggarly elements." The Church's ecclesiastical apparatus, too,
is essential, so long as it does not exist for its own sake but as an
instrument of spiritual service. The priest has "received power and
authority to teach and govern the religious community, and to
administer its sacred rites,"[45] but this power is from the Spirit,
through the community. He "stands above the layman solely as the
representative of the whole organism of the Church."[46] It is important to stress that Tyrrell does not wish "to laicise the Church but
only to recognize the participation of the laity in that sovereign
priesthood and authority from which those of the official hierarchy
are derived."[47]

The bishops in Council do not rule a "passive Church from outside, as a shepherd rules his flock" but rather as the head "in which
the whole Church becomes self-conscious and vocal."[48] And so it
follows that "the infallibility of the Pope is not other than that which
belongs to the whole Church"—his *ex cathedra* pronouncements
being the expression of the general mind of the Church whose vicar
and spokesman he is. The Pope is no *alter Christus,* "a distinct
personality outside and above the Church" but rather "the inherent
head of an organism, a part of that whole which is the spouse of
Christ."[49]

Tyrrell's doctrine of authority was branded "Protestant" by the
Catholic authorities. Although most of the essays collected in
Through Scylla and Charybdis had been published earlier with the
approval of duly appointed censors, the book appeared in 1907, only
weeks before the Vatican's condemnation of Modernism in the sylla-
bus *Lamentabili sane exitu.* The condemnation was followed within
the year by Cardinal Mercier's Lenten pastoral letter of 1908 in which

44. Ibid., 369–70.
45. Ibid., 361.
46. Ibid., 371.
47. Ibid., 384.
48. Ibid., 380.
49. *George Tyrrell's Letters,* ed. M. D. Petre, 69.

Tyrrell's "errors" were singled out specifically for censure. Tyrrell's answer was *Medievalism: A Reply to Cardinal Mercier,* a passionate, eloquent, ironic polemic in the form of an open letter. It was one of Tyrrell's most popular and provoking books and was immediately translated into French and Italian. The book not only countered the prevailing Vatican misconceptions regarding Modernism and its relation to Protestantism but is, especially in the retrospective distance of our own day, a compelling critique of the Ultramontanist conception of the Church, its constitution, and authority.

Typically, Tyrrell closes this parting shot with an expression of his persistent love for and allegiance to Catholicism. He writes,

> The very word "Catholic" is music to my ears. . . . If the Roman Church still holds me it is because, in spite of the narrow sectarian spirit that has so long oppressed her, she cannot deny her fundamental principles; because, as a fact, she stands for the oldest and widest body of corporate Christian experience; for the closest approximation, so far attained, to the still far-distant ideal of a Catholic religion.[50]

Despite Tyrrell's protestations against Cardinal Mercier's caricature of Protestantism and Tyrrell's own "veneration" for its "great truths and principles," he could not blind himself to what he considered its defects, "its naked severity, its relentless rationality." "If it feeds one half, perhaps the better half, of the soul, it starves the other. The religion of all men must be the religion of the whole man—Catholic in depth as well as in extension."[51] Tyrrell's *apologia,* "Reflections on Catholicism" (1907)—included among his essays here—is as beautiful and as persuasive a defense of the Catholic religion as may be found. Of Tyrrell's love and loyalty to his Church, Dean Inge remarked, "Happy, and yet unhappy, the Church which can afford, and endure, to trample upon such devotion."[52]

Tyrrell's reflections on Christology, God, and eschatology may appear conventional in liberal theological circles today, but they were advanced and even shocking at the turn of the century—not only to traditionalists but to Protestant Liberals and many Anglican Modernists as well. Again, he offers no systematic treatment of these themes but is original in the way that he sets out some of the issues that have occupied the best theological minds since. These subjects

50. Tyrrell, *Medievalism,* 185.
51. Ibid., 186.
52. William R. Inge, "Tyrrell's Last Book," *Hibbert Journal* 8 (January 1910): 434.

are explored most radically in *Christianity at the Crossroads* (1909), which some regard as Tyrrell's masterpiece, and in the posthumous *Essays on Faith and Immortality* (1914). In the former, he confronts the implications of the most advanced critical-historical New Testament scholarship, especially the work of Johannes Weiss and Alfred Loisy. The book represents Tyrrell's break with traditional Christology and his repudiation of the Liberal Protestant Jesus of Adolf von Harnack and the Ritschlians. His earlier effort to mediate between Harnack's Jesus and Weiss's visionary, apocalyptic Christ had failed. He now had to assert that "Whatever Jesus was, He was in no sense a Liberal Protestant."[53]

Tyrrell did, in fact, retain more of the ethical Christ that he had imbued from Harnack and Matthew Arnold (the Power not ourselves that makes for righteousness), but he also found in the "consistent-eschatology" of Weiss and Schweitzer the otherworldly transcendentalism that was absent from the Liberal portrait of Jesus. Tyrrell wrote to von Hügel:

> Having finished Schweitzer and reread J. Weiss very carefully, I . . . see my way more clearly. . . . If we cannot save large chunks of transcendentalism, Christianity must go. . . . The other-world emphasis, the doctrine of immortality, was what gave Christianity its original impulse and sent martyrs to the lions. If that is accidental, we only owe to Jesus in a great measure what we owe to all good men in some measure.[54]

Tyrrell came to see Liberal Protestantism as an effort to minimize the transcendental heart of the Gospel. Liberalism's blindness to the New Testament eschatological tension and offense tended to reduce Christianity to a set of moral precepts. This was the form of immanence that Tyrrell found truly dangerous, but of which he was not guilty.

Christianity at the Crossroads is Tyrrell's highly original effort to interpret Catholic Christianity in terms of the spiritual meaning of Christ's prophetic apocalyptic vision. He was to carry out this task not by a liberal accommodation and reduction of the *depositum fidei* but by means of a radical reconception that retains the Gospel's alien, transcendental message.

> If we agree with Liberal Protestantism in taking symbolically what the early Church took literally, we differ in taking it all as symbolic of transcendental values and not of the moral order of this life. . . . We

---

53. Tyrrell, *Christianity at the Crossroads,* xxi.
54. Petre, *Autobiography and Life of George Tyrrell,* 2:398.

hold to the transcendent Kingdom . . . hence we claim to be true to the
"idea" of original Christianity.[55]

The way in which Tyrrell works out this symbolic interpretation of
the original "idea," of transcendence, of the "abiding values of
Christ's apocalyptic vision"—the Incarnation, Resurrection, and the
Kingdom—is set forth in the passages from *Christianity at the Crossroads* that appear in this volume.

Gabriel Daly has suggested that the tension between divine transcendence and immanence is the key to Tyrrell's theological reflection and reconception. This is especially relevant in his unsystematic
wrestling with the doctrine of God. Like Newman, Tyrrell could find
no evidence of God in nature; more likely, nature points to the Devil,
he said. God is present to us in conscience, in the intuitive, preconceptual experience of the presence of a Will more than human. In
this sense we all are *naturaliter Christiana.* "If experience gives us a
Power that makes for Righteousness it gives us God—it gives us not
a statement or an idea, but a thing, a term of action, of obedience, of
worship, self-sacrifice, about which we more or less spontaneously
frame ideas and statements. Experience is revelational . . . it reveals
Him not in statements but in the moral and religious impulse that
proceeds from Him."[56]

Tyrrell abhorred the scholastic proofs of God. "If God is what
religion teaches; if He is to man's soul what light is to his eyes, or air
to his lungs . . . is it conceivable that we should hold Him merely by a
slender thread of obscure inference; or that it should be necessary to
prove his existence before we begin to live our spiritual life?"[57] No,
Tyrrell insists, because we, at least unconsciously, affirm God in our
uniquely human moral and spiritual experience. He had early learned
from Newman that conscience is the path to God.

While we experience God in our deepest sentiments and actions,
our understanding of the transcendent Divine Will is mediated to us
only through our human, hence our anthropomorphic, symbolism.
We must be prepared "to submit to the limitation [of imaginative
symbols] consciously; to realize that our best God is but an idol."[58]
Tyrrell reminded undergraduates at Oxford that

---

55. Tyrrell, *Christianity at the Crossroads,* 145.
56. George Tyrrell, " 'Revelation as Experience': An Unpublished Lecture of
George Tyrrell," *Heythrop Journal* 12 (April 1971): 144.
57. Ibid., 143.
58. Petre, *Autobiography and Life of George Tyrrell,* 2:416.

> God is not directly reached by our *mind,* or our *imagination,* but only an idea or picture of God which we ourselves have constructed out of the fragments of our experience—a crude, childish representation at the best. It is not God, but only this rude image of God we set before our mind's eye when we pray to Him or think of Him. . . . No wonder, then, that He seems so far away, so uncertain, so intangible.[59]

Tyrrell shared and may well have been influenced by Matthew Arnold's abhorrence of the brash familiarity and literalism of much theological God-talk—as if one were describing one's next-door neighbor. The scholastic theologians, it appeared, had lost all sense of God's transcendence, of the divine otherness. "Religion dies with the sense of mystery. . . . That is why our theologians are so irreligious. . . . They speak as though the inadequacy of our God-idea were merely quantitative." [60]

Our symbols of God, though finally inadequate, nevertheless do point to and are genuinely representational of transcendent reality. Tyrrell believed that the old scholastic solution to the controversy between realists and conceptualists remained applicable to our own problem of conceiving of God. Our most adequate images are not mere poetic fictions or dreams. "They must be *fundamentaliter in re,*" founded in reality, despite the fact that they are *formaliter in intellectu,* fashioned by the mind. "They are a fiction founded on fact." Tyrrell was not, as charged, an agnostic; his philosophy was a form of symbolic realism: "To say that [our concepts] are symbolic of the transcendent is not agnosticism; since symbols may be representative. Nor is it pure pragmatism, since the degree of their practical utility is just that of their correspondence to reality."[61]

Tyrrell's theism is essentially Christocentric. "All I dare say," he admitted to a friend,

> is that the divine has a human aspect which alone concerns man. . . . It is man's privilege to think of it; to wonder; to hope; to figure it to himself in terms of his own spirit. It is the Divine Will, because it is human nature, that he should do so. . . . We do not know nothing about God; but we know infinitely little. We can have no word of God, no revelation, except the ideal or eternal Man; the Christ. That is as much of God as we can ever *see.* It is only because He presents Himself to us as the Christ, with a human spirit, face, voice, and hands, that we can speak to Him or deal with Him at all.[62]

59. Tyrrell, *External Religion,* 158–59.
60. *George Tyrrell's Letters,* ed. M. D. Petre, 32.
61. Tyrrell, *Christianity at the Crossroads,* 104.
62. Petre, *Autobiography and Life of George Tyrrell,* 2:416.

In a letter to another friend in that same year (1908), Tyrrell remarked that his "imagination [was] quite cured of the outside God." Tyrrell often had been charged with "Immanentism," and this tendency in his work always had worried his friend von Hügel. In 1902, Tyrrell's book of meditations, *Oil and Wine*, failed to pass the ecclesiastical censors largely for this reason. In the preface to his 1907 published edition of *Oil and Wine* and after his excommunication, Tyrrell acknowledged that "in avoiding the false 'transcendence' of Deism, I may have drifted too near the Charybdis of Pantheism in search of the middle course of Panentheism."[63] Gabriel Daly has shown, however, that Tyrrell maintained, with a few pantheistic excesses here and there, the necessary tension between divine immanence and transcendence. This is most evidently the case in the later, more purely Modernist writings. It is especially pronounced in the radical Christocentrism of *Christianity at the Crossroads*.

Tyrrell's most original and panentheist reflections on God appear in a lecture delivered a few months before his death. Entitled "Divine Fecundity," it was published by Maude Petre with other material in *Essays on Faith and Immortality*. The lecture was occasioned by the public response to an earthquake which occurred on December 28, 1908, and devastated southern Calabria and eastern Sicily, killing about 150,000 people. It is a haunting, unflinching reflection on the nature of divine immanence and providence in a world void of any larger, purely future teleology. At the same time, it affirms "a transcendental other-world hope to oppose to this immediate and provisional pessimism."[64] Tyrrell suggests,

> We have made our God in the image, not of the artist but of the artisan or the man of affairs. "What is He going to make out of it all?" Perhaps nothing; perhaps the universe is but His eternal keyboard, His eternal canvas. Perhaps each melody, each picture, may have a worth in itself apart from all the rest. Lost stars, lost species, lost civilizations, lost religions—lost as far as any influence on our own is concerned—may have justified their existence, though they have led to nothing further.[65]

There is, Tyrrell suggests, no plan working itself out, no far-off earthly paradise "into which some far-off generation is to enter."

63. George Tyrrell, *Oil and Wine*, ix.
64. George Tyrrell, *Essays on Faith and Immortality*, 277.
65. Ibid., 260–61.

xxxii   Introduction

Rather, "every generation, every individual life, has an absolute value of its own, and constitutes a world apart."[66] The world

> teems with aims and meanings, although it has no *one* aim or meaning. It is like a great tree, that pushes out its branches, however and wherever it can, seeking to realize its whole nature, as far as possible, in every one of them, but aiming at no collective effect. This is its play, this is its life, this is, if you will, its end.[67]

There is no necessary arrangement in God's garden; it is only for us human gardeners that the universe, conceived as a luxuriant wilderness, appears as a scandal.

Tyrrell also insists that we dispense with our long-accustomed "cheap eschatology" and recapture the Greek sense of the "dark mystery, of a sad mortality o'erswaying man's largest and loftiest undertakings."[68] The Kingdom of God must not be identified with "the Gospel of Progress" or "some socialist millennium." No doubt Tyrrell would scorn the political romanticism of some expressions of present-day theology (what he might call "sanctified worldliness"), but he was no advocate of ethical quietism or world-denial. "Man must," he concludes, "obey the life impulses of his nature, and go on building and toiling. . . . He may not sit down in oriental listlessness and despair." He would agree with Troeltsch that the Christian ethic—like none other—keeps the proper tension between the *Dieseits* and the *Jenseits,* between world-affirmation and world-denial.

We are reminded by Tyrrell that life has its pathos but also its divine dignity; that we do share in a divine life and a divine sympathy.

> It is not as a self-centered, self-seeking individual organism, but as the son, the infant son no doubt, of God, that he wakes to a sense of the tragedy and mystery of existence and of the nothingness and unreality of all that is not God. God alone is the substance that gives meaning to all this shadow-play. And thus we are drawn back to Kant's great intuition, that there is nothing really or absolutely good, no end on which man may fix his whole heart, but good will. And good will is just God's will. To be one with that will, to enter into and cooperate with God's struggle in the battle of life, that alone is the inspiring motive, the justifying end, of all our endeavours.[69]

Tyrrell's reference to the Creation's "nothingness and unreality" and "shadow-play" is disturbing, but his eschatology affirms that,

66. Ibid.
67. Ibid., 259.
68. Ibid., 270.
69. Ibid., 272.

despite the fact that we face no inevitable worldly success, there remains the joy that "we are sharers in the Divine fecundity." That, for Tyrrell, is the true, eternal life. "The true Kingdom of God consists, not in a final solution of the insoluble . . . but in the multiplication of the sons of God, of wills reconciled and atoned with the Divine will in its endless joys and sorrows."[70] In this essay we can hear echoes of Bergson and of William James, philosophers he read diligently and whose influence he acknowledged. Clearly Tyrrell shares James's vision of a world unfinished, in process, a world of risk and real losses as well as glorious joys and victories.

We do not, Tyrrell concedes, have any knowledge of our *post mortem* state. But in our devotion to the divine will we have all the light we need. It is, finally, "with this Heaven and Hell of the present that we have now to concern ourselves; with that little corner of the battle in which our destiny has placed us. The rest we leave in the hands of God."[71] Tyrrell's eschatology, like the best of contemporary process thought, leaves many theological questions unresolved, but we also take leave of him, at the end of this deep yet problematic essay, strangely satisfied.

TYRRELL'S SIGNIFICANCE

George Tyrrell's importance for an understanding of Modernist theology at the turn of the century is enormous. First, better than any other figure, he represents the aims, themes, and converging historical influences and circumstances that together make up that very distinctive movement called Catholic Modernism. The encyclical *Pascendi* called Modernism "the synthesis of all heresies"; Tyrrell saw his own writings as a "synthesis" of Modernism. On the discussion of revelation, the nature of theology and the function of dogma, on the relation of belief and practice, on authority, and on the effort to conjoin Catholicism and science, Tyrrell best represents the Modernist position. This is not to suggest that his views are those of Loisy, LeRoy, or others—on some matters they most definitely are not— but rather that he best exemplifies the general aims of those in the Modernist movement and the concerns with which they wrestled. Furthermore, nowhere can one study the Modernist "apology" for Catholicism to better advantage than in the writings of George Tyrrell. The eminent historian Karl Holl wrote,

70. Ibid., 273.
71. Ibid., 276.

> Among the Modernists, George Tyrrell is pre-eminent—the noblest
> expression of the whole movement. He makes a special appeal to our
> sympathy [in] that the religious motives are with him at their purest
> and strongest. . . . To his strength of thought there is added a wonder-
> ful simplicity of language . . . a homely beauty of form.[72]

Holl goes on to point out how Tyrrell joins a deep knowledge of
the Catholic theological tradition with a profound dependence on
and appreciation of the currents of nineteenth-century critical Protestant thought. The student interested in exploring the converging
streams of thought at the turn of the century—of Blondel, William
James, and Bergson; of Weiss, Harnack, Schweitzer, and Loisy—will
find Tyrrell a critical source. Historically, he remains a significant
figure as both thinker and prophet.

After his excommunication, Tyrrell came increasingly to realize
that the Modernist cause soon would spend its force and that it had
accomplished all that it could under the then-existent circumstances.
His own work was done. He had long sensed this and had written in
his breviary: "Thou shalt see the land before thee which I will give to
the children of Israel, but thou shalt not enter into it."[73] He was,
nevertheless, confident that the current Ultramontanist expression of
Catholicism was only provisional and would pass. If not, Catholicism
would itself perish for its failure to live by the laws of spiritual and
intellectual growth. He believed that "fragments of the ruin would be
built into some new construction"—the Church would slowly and
quietly adapt and assimilate what once were the sources of bitter
controversy. To a perplexed correspondent in 1908, he wrote:

> Catholicism means a belief in that living, continuous body of Chris-
> tians called Catholic—a belief that it is the organ by which an ever
> truer idea of Christianity is slowly but infallibly worked out through
> many errors and blunders and fluctuations and contradictions, by all
> sorts of costly experiences good and evil; that God leads it much as He
> led the stupid and recalcitrant people of Israel from Egypt toward a
> Land of Promise.[74]

In hindsight, we can see that the results of Vatican II prove Tyrrell
partly correct about the Church's ability to assimilate and change
"into some new construction," one that would little resemble its
"medieval" triumphalist form. Current interest in Tyrrell is due, in

72. Karl Holl, *Modernismus* (Tübingen, 1908), 29.
73. Petre, *Autobiography and Life of George Tyrrell,* 2:450.
74. *George Tyrrell's Letters,* ed. M. D. Petre, 249.

part, to the striking similarities between his ideas and the theology, even the language, that emerged from the documents of Vatican II and post–Vatican II theology.[75] These comparisons include their common views on the mystery of revelation and on the need for a more "reverent agnosticism" concerning our human, historical apprehension of the divine mystery; their common sacramentalism and understanding of the relation of the natural and supernatural; their focus on the religious consciousness, its natural, intuitive knowledge of God, which Rahner calls the "supernatural existential"; their common assertion that all religions are—however vaguely and feebly—searchings and glimpses of the divine truth, "anonymous" proximations of the Church's complete truth.

The most striking convergences are to be found on the theme of ecclesiology; on the Church as the "people of God," not a hierarchical, juridical institution; on the "pope as servant"; on priests and bishops as "the servants of the servants of God"; on the collegiality of pope and bishops; on the Church as a "servant" in the service of the world; and on the apostolate of the laity. The whole tenor of the Constitution *De Ecclesia* appears to be the expression of Tyrrell's wish "to invert the hierarchical pyramid carefully balanced on the Pope as its apex, and to set it firmly on its base again."[76]

Our purpose here is not, however, to elaborate on the affinities between Tyrrell's portrayal of Catholicism and the new Catholic theology of the past two or three decades but simply to call attention to Tyrrell's relevance to contemporary theology. The same can be said, to a degree, of his relevance to post–Liberal Protestantism, its ongoing struggle with the God-question, especially with the question of evolutionary process and providence; its concern with history and demythologization; and its attention to language and the metaphorical character of theology. Few, if any, religious thinkers at the end of the nineteenth century touch so many of our concerns, our questions, as forcefully or as courageously as does George Tyrrell. He remains for us a vital resource of theological and spiritual reflection.

<hr>

75. For a discussion of this, see Michael Hurley, "George Tyrrell: Some Post–Vatican II Impressions," *Heythrop Journal* 10 (July 1969): 243–55; Ellen Leonard, *George Tyrrell and the Catholic Tradition;* and David F. Wells, *The Prophetic Theology of George Tyrrell* (Chico, Calif.: Scholars Press, 1981).

76. Tyrrell, *Through Scylla and Charybdis,* 382.

Select Bibliography

BOOKS BY GEORGE TYRRELL

1897

Notes on the Catholic Doctrine of Purity. Roehampton, Eng.: Manresa Press.

Nova et Vetera: Informal Meditations for Times of Spiritual Dryness. London: Longmans, Green & Co.

1898

Hard Sayings: A Selection of Meditations and Studies. London: Longmans, Green & Co.

1899

External Religion: Its Use and Abuse. London: Sands & Co.

1901

The Faith of the Millions: A Selection of Past Essays. 2 vols. London: Longmans, Green & Co. The third edition (1904) deletes chap. 20, "An Apostle of Naturalism," and introduces two others, "Religion and Ethics" and "Vita Nuova."

1902

A Handful of Myrrh: Devotional Conferences. London: Catholic Truth Society. Published anonymously.

[A. R. Waller, pseud.] *The Civilizing of the Matafanus: An Essay in Religious Development.* London: R. Brimley Johnson.

[Dr. Ernest Engels, pseud.] *Religion as a Factor of Life.* Exeter: William Pollard & Co.

Oil and Wine. N.p. Reprint. London: Longmans, Green & Co., 1907. The book was first printed without title page and "for private circulation only" by Manresa Press, Roehampton.

1903

[Hilaire Bourdon, pseud.] *The Church and the Future* (L'Eglise et L'Avenir). Abridged and rearranged. Reissued under Tyrrell's name as *The Church and the Future.* Preface by Maude D. Petre. Hampstead, Eng.: Priory Press, 1910.

Lex Orandi, or, Prayer and Creed. London: Longmans, Green & Co.

1904

A Letter to a University Professor. Published anonymously. Reissued under the author's name as *A Much-Abused Letter.* London: Longmans, Green & Co., 1906.

The Soul's Orbit; or, Man's Journey to God. Compiled with additions by M. D. Petre. London: Longmans, Green & Co. The book was published under Maude Petre's name, but Tyrrell was the principal author.

1905

Another Handful of Myrrh: Devotional Conferences. London: Catholic Truth Society. Published anonymously.

1906

Lex Credendi: A Sequel to Lex Orandi. London: Longmans, Green & Co.

1907

Through Scylla and Charybdis: or, The Old Theology and the New. London: Longmans, Green & Co.

1908

Medievalism: A Reply to Cardinal Mercier. London: Longmans, Green & Co.

1909

Christianity at the Crossroads. London: Longmans, Green & Co. Left in manuscript form at Tyrrell's death. Prepared for publication by Maude Petre with the assistance of Friedrich von Hügel.

1912

Autobiography and Life of George Tyrrell. 2 vols. London: Edward Arnold. Vol. 1: *Autobiography of George Tyrrell, 1861–1884,* arranged, with supplements, by M. Petre. Vol. 2: Petre, M. *Life of George Tyrrell from 1884 to 1909.*

1914

Essays on Faith and Immortality. Arranged by M. Petre. London: Edward Arnold.

STUDIES OF GEORGE TYRRELL

In addition to this list, a list of unpublished Ph.D. dissertations on Tyrrell appears in the Schultenover bibliography, below.

Books

Daly, Gabriel. *Transcendence and Immanence: A Study in Catholic Modernism and Integralism.* Oxford: Oxford University Press, 1980.
     The chapter on Tyrrell is a valuable study.
Leonard, Ellen. *George Tyrrell and the Catholic Tradition.* Ramsey, N.J.: Paulist Press, 1982.
     Tyrrell's contribution to ecclesiology and idea of Catholicism.
Loome, Thomas M. *Liberal Catholicism, Reform Catholicism, Modernism: A Contribution to a New Orientation in Modernist Research.* Mainz: Matthias Grunewald Verlag, 1979.
     A broad, provocative study of modern liberal developments in Catholicism with Tyrrell as a central figure.
Petre, Maude D., ed. *George Tyrrell's Letters.* London: T. Fisher Unwin, 1920.
     Important source for understanding Tyrrell, his thought and spirituality.
————. *Von Hügel and Tyrrell: The Story of a Friendship.* London: J. M. Dent & Sons, 1937.
Ratte, John. *Three Modernists: Alfred Loisy, George Tyrrell, William L. Sullivan.* London: Sheed & Ward, 1968.
Sagovsky, Nicholas. *Between Two Worlds: George Tyrrell's Relationship to the Thought of Matthew Arnold.* Cambridge: Cambridge University Press, 1983.
     In exploring Tyrrell's relation to Arnold, the author sheds valuable light on Tyrrell's epistemology, ecclesiology, and Christology.
————. *"On God's Side": A Life of George Tyrrell.* Oxford: Oxford University Press, 1990.
     The most up-to-date biography, which supplements the specialized studies.
Schultenover, David G., S.J. *George Tyrrell: In Search of Catholicism.* Shepherdstown, W. Va.: Patmos Press, 1981.
     The most thorough and valuable study available on Tyrrell's developing philosophy of religion and apologetic to 1903.

Vidler, Alec R. *The Modernist Movement in the Roman Catholic Church.*
    Cambridge: Cambridge University Press, 1934.
    An old but still worthwhile study of Tyrrell in the context of Modernism.
Weaver, Mary Jo, ed. *Letters from a "Modernist": The Letters of George
    Tyrrell to Wilfrid Ward, 1893–1908.* Shepherdstown, W. Va.: Patmos Press,
    1981.
    Important in understanding Tyrrell's move from Newman and Liberal
    Catholicism to Modernism.

Articles

Scores of articles on Tyrrell were published during the Modernist
crisis and immediately following Tyrrell's death. Schultenover lists
some of the most important ones. In the past thirty years, a few
dozen brief studies of Tyrrell have appeared. Articles through 1980
are listed in Schultenover. While many of these recent articles are
highly valuable, two especially illuminate Tyrrell the man and the
thinker:

Chapman, Ronald. "The Thought of George Tyrrell." In *Essays and Poems
    Presented to Lord David Cecil,* ed. W. W. Robson. London: Constable,
    1970.
Daly, Gabriel. "Some Reflections on the Character of George Tyrrell."
    Heythrop Journal 10 (July 1969), 256–74.

BIBLIOGRAPHIES

The student who wishes to pursue the study of Tyrrell in greater
depth will necessarily want to consult many additional essays and
reviews by Tyrrell, as well as the less available studies on him. Three
bibliographies serve as invaluable resources for further research:

Loome, Thomas M. "A Bibliography of the Published Works of George
    Tyrrell." In *Heythrop Journal* 10 (July 1969): 280–313.
————. "A Bibliography of the Printed Works of George Tyrrell: Supple-
    ment." In *Heythrop Journal* 11 (April 1970): 161–69.
Schultenover, David G., S.J. *George Tyrrell: In Search of Catholicism,* 434–86.
    Shepherdstown, W. Va.: Patmos Press, 1981.
    This volume contains an extensive, often annotated list of Tyrrell's
    published writings, as well as studies of Tyrrell and Roman Catholic
    Modernism.

1

Letters of Counsel
and Meditations

TO A CONVERT*

31 Farm Street, W.
February 14, 1900

Dear Miss W.,

I observe this "formality" with everyone as a protest against the "*Ma chère enfant*" style, which I abominate. Outside my duties as confessor I do not see that I have any commission to "direct" or drive people's souls. If I advise, it is always on a footing of perfect equality, to help people to see and decide for themselves or to read more clearly what their own conscience tells them: but not to dictate or stand to them in place of conscience. There are some things I should consult you about as being better informed or experienced; and there are other things you consult me about for a like reason; but there is no parental relationship created in either case. Outside sacramental matter your priest is not your superior in any way, but only your adviser, whom you choose and listen to or leave *on your own judgment,* and to whom you have no debt of obedience. For some souls the unauthorised tyranny of the "*Père directeur*" may be the less of two evils; for you it will be very hurtful, and lead to violent reaction. My advice to you would be to go often to communion and

*From *George Tyrrell's Letters,* ed. Maude D. Petre, 243–45.

1

seldom to confession; to confess your faults and get absolution, but not to ask advice or direction unless you can find a priest whom you feel to be in sympathy with your character and cast of mind. You will rarely find such an one; but better far to do without a "director" (for it is not an essential) than to have one who tries to force your mind into the mould of his own—a mould in this case far too narrow. As to prayer difficulty, of course we cannot cage the Holy Ghost or bind Him to come at our prayer hours; He "bloweth where He listeth." It is often at meals, or in company, or at the most incongruous moments that the good thoughts come. And the best habit is that of being on the alert, and registering the inspiration for after-rumination. Else the "birds of the air come," etc. But no doubt you have stifled yourself with methods and routines instead of following the lead of your good inclinations. Like many converts you revolt blindly against everything Protestant, forgetting how much good there was mingled with their error and making it plausible—good that Catholics overlook very often. Change as little of that as you can; and supplement it with the riches that Catholicism offers. You cannot abruptly change the whole structure of your mind, nor is there any reason to wish to do so. Go on saying your prayers night and morning as of old, in the same way as far as possible. Don't attempt strait-waistcoat methods of meditation; but take up your Bible or à Kempis or St. Augustine's *Confessions,* and read quietly and think and pray as you feel moved. Begin perhaps with a Veni Creator and end with a Pater—and that will be formality enough. Or, better still, if you know Latin enough, recite *slowly* and *intelligently* some part of the daily office of the Church—the best of all prayers. And in fine, do try to be yourself, and don't try to be *Père* B. or somebody else. Christ's net holds all manner of fishes, even you and me; we are not all sprats or herrings, but each a separate kind. Let us try to know ourselves, and then we shall know God; but if we disguise ourselves in other people's clothes we shall never know ourselves or live, but shall be like mummies swathed from head to foot and spiced, if you will, but dead.

I don't often write like this, and perhaps you will be scandalised at my warmth; but surely you will some day say I was right.

ON PRAYER:
TO MRS. STRACEY*

Richmond, Yorks
November 27, 1905

I do not *know;* and that is the simple truth. As to my practice, I have gradually grown dumb, partly from a sense of the fictitious character of all our notions of the divine and a desire to keep clear of unreality, partly from a conviction that the verbal "externation" of our desires, however profitable when possible, is not the essence of prayer. Overmuch reflection on religious problems is bound to produce this paralysis. To use forms helpfully one must be able to forget that they are forms; to approach God as "Our Father" one must not be *too* conscious of the hopeless inadequacy of the appellation. But this is a subjective defect and has little bearing on your case.

The instinct to pray is too spontaneous, too universal among religious people not to be well founded in the laws that govern the world to which our spirits belong. The outward form, in which that instinctive impulse embodies itself, depends on the form in which we present that mysterious world to ourselves. Christ has taught us to picture the divine as a heavenly Father whose children we all are. Taking things that way, what can we do, how can we embody our love for one another better than by lifting up our eyes to the skies to ask help in our needs? Our Lord would not have been (as He certainly was) "true man" and a man of His *milieu* had He departed from the current religious ideas of his day as to prayer; had He not taught and practised intercessory prayer of the simplest and directest form— prayer not only for the meat that endureth, but also for the meat that perisheth. His *human* mind was that of a little child in simplicity and freedom from our weary modern sophistication. It was in His heart and spirit that He rose beyond the limits of humanity. Yet the inadequacy of the "Father and Child" scheme is proved nowhere more abundantly than in the seeming inefficacy of prayer, its barrenness of all *demonstrable* fruit. We ask and do not receive; seek and do not find; knock and are left knocking. Masses of evidence of answers (mostly temporal) to prayer might be collected; as has been done by the P. R. S. for the existence of ghosts. But I think, if properly sifted and criticised, little would be proved beyond (and this I greatly

*From *George Tyrrell's Letters,* ed. Maude D. Petre, 144–46.

doubt) an occasional and exceptional efficacy in the way of an inter-
ruption of the natural course of events. This would be a most lame
and impotent conclusion; since, according to common religious
teaching, failure should be the exception and not the rule. Moreover,
prayers for grace should never fail, whereas our experience tells us
they nearly always do when we pray for others; so that if it seems
otherwise when we pray for ourselves this must be put down to the
subjective reaction of desire. It is no theory but simply the uniform
testimony of experience, that stands against the literal truth of the
common doctrine as to the efficacy of prayer. In each case there are
always a thousand reasons to give why the prayer failed; but for the
failure of the vast bulk there is no adequate reason forthcoming
except that prayer is not an efficacious means. And yet I feel sure
that the instinct of Christ and His saints, however incapable of analysis, is a right one, and that underneath the literal sense of the prayer-
doctrine there is a sacramental sense. I think we shall find that there
is an organic connection between every member of the spiritual
world; and that, however circuitously and remotely, every sincere
and selfless desire for the welfare of others in general or in particular
will tell in the long run, and that the bread cast on the waters will
return after many days—and this, not by an inversion of law, but in
strict conformity to the laws of Providence that nothing evades, not
even an involuntary sigh. This, of course, is faith and not knowledge;
and will probably be a poor consolation to you in your embarrass-
ment. But its practical upshot is that they do well who can practise
the prayer-doctrine in its crude simplicity untroubled by the contradiction of experience; that they do better, perhaps, who take it at its
sacramental value and can pray with a blind trust that the instinct is
not an idle one; that they do not ill who are content to believe that
love is a potent force in the working out of God's schemes and that
our desires are causal.

ON PRAYER:
TO MRS. METCALFE*

(Date uncertain)

To stop between the several acts of your life, and refer them to
God, is like stopping at every step of the road to remind yourself

*From *George Tyrrell's Letters,* ed. Maude D. Petre, 251–52.

where you are going. It is impossible and quite useless. God has given you instincts and common-sense to tell you what you should do in each detail; and so you should not ask each time for a special revelation on the subject.

St. Paul asked the question, "What wouldst Thou have me to do?" *once,* at his conversion, and received a revealed answer. Our spiritual life is not a chain of sudden conversions. "But the saints have done so," you will say. As a married woman, probably you have once been "in love" and you know how, in that state, the thought of the beloved obtrudes itself and haunts us morning, noon, and night; how all our actions are done in that imagined presence; how all our idle thoughts turn thither, in spite of us; how the room brightens or darkens with that presence or absence. But in all this one is passive and not active; one can't escape from it if one would. Were one not in love with the person, the effort to imitate the effect of love would drive one mad. The saints *were* in love with God, and we are *not.* If you ask me for a recipe for falling in love with God or man, I don't know one. It can't be done by effort of any kind. Let us then accommodate ourselves to the *fact* that, though we should like to be, we are not "in love" with God; we love Him as dutiful servants and sons, but are not carried away by our love. This latter he does not ask from us, for it is not in our power; we may ask it of Him, for it is His to give to whom He wills. To *act* being in love, when one is not, is unreal and untruthful and no good can come of it; while much harm may.

TO THE SAME*[1]

Richmond, Yorks
June 29, 1901

I heard of your illness—first of the worse fears, then of their groundlessness, from other sources. These depressing anxieties are so inseparable from your present state of health that words can do little or nothing to dispel them; they are as much an affliction from God's hands as the illness itself of which they are the necessary sequel. I am not sure that the prayer which asks God to stay the ruthless grinding—as it seems to us—of His will is nearly as good as the prayer which makes us lie still and say nothing, trusting that the

*From *George Tyrrell's Letters,* ed. Maude D. Petre, 252–53.
1. She was dying of cancer.—M.D.P.

seemingly ruthless law is governed by a higher love and wisdom than we can ever comprehend. To ask anything definite might, in some, argue a simpler and a stronger faith; but for you I think there is a higher and more intelligent faith in a certain kind of fatalism, which takes each hour by itself, with its own burden, and studiously refuses to speculate or to look further. Even as a doctor I should say this was almost indispensable for the recovery of your health, just as fretfulness and worry, especially about spiritual matters, are almost fatal to the same end. May I recommend you the spirit that breathes in the poems for Tuesday, Wednesday, Friday, and Saturday of Holy Week in the *Christian Year?* Lines in those poems, as well as others familiar to you, will best serve to keep your soul tranquil and untroubled, while your more formal exercises will serve, at least, as a mute expression of your wish to do and bear all that God wants of you. That these latter should be hopelessly dry and wearisome is of no spiritual significance whatever.

Put interior rest before everything. God does not like fidgets. I will bring your case to the altar.

CHANGE OF FAITH, TO L. R.*[1]

Wimbledon College, Wimbledon
July 9, 1898

On thinking over our conversation I feel sure that it would be premature were you to embark on anything like controversial reading at present. God is undoubtedly calling you to a life of closer union with Himself, and I personally know well that, had you been earlier familiarised with the Catholic religion, it would have satisfied superabundantly all those needs which you now feel unsatisfied. Still the human mind cannot easily and suddenly cast off its habitual ways

---

*The two letters to L. R. are from *George Tyrrell's Letters,* ed. Maude D. Petre, 254–59.

1. The first of these letters to L. R. was written nearly ten years before the later one. Father Tyrrell had seen the correspondent in question at the time of his first letter, and had encouraged her to quiet reflection and delay, before taking any further step. He left London for Richmond in 1900, and saw no more of her for some years. Meanwhile she had fallen under the influence of a very different type of director, and had been hurried into the Roman Catholic Church without much consideration for her particular character and needs. The transplantation was not wholly successful, and gave rise to the later correspondence.—M.D.P.

of thought and begin to look at things from a totally new standpoint; nor could any solid good be expected from such an effort. It would be very hard for us to throw ourselves heart and soul into sympathy with Chinese ways and customs; and I think the Catholic conception of Christianity is almost as far removed from other forms—not excepting High Anglicanism, which resembles it only superficially, and has far less of its spirit than has evangelical Protestantism. All one wants in order to be in good faith and to satisfy God is a sincere and practical desire to know what is true and to be free from all unjust thoughts about the religion of others. If it be a sincere and practical desire you will take a little trouble to find out the truth; you will be slow to think evil of any religion, willing to believe the best. God does not give the full light of religion to all in his life; but to all he gives abundance for salvation, though many shut their eyes and will not see. You need not fear being classed with these latter, seeing your whole trouble at present is lest you should in any way be wanting to the grace of God. If at any time you felt a clear command of conscience bidding you submit to the Catholic Church, it would be then time enough to put yourself under instruction and to consider in detail the many difficulties by which the mind is hindered from following the heart; but the heart must first be drawn. Meantime I think you will satisfy all justice if you strive to clear your mind of those common and almost vulgar travesties of Catholicism which have been current in this country for three centuries and exist in minds otherwise fair, charitable, and cultivated. Before considering the Church's claim to be Christ, it is well to see that at least she is not Anti-Christ, that she is not a monstrosity or an absurdity. I saw no trace of such narrow prejudices in you, but I fancy it is simply because you never thought about Rome, never discussed the subject with any Protestant seriously, so as to draw out the usual flood of calumnies by which we are assailed. Now, however, it may well be that you will get the benefit of all these commonplaces as soon as it is understood that you have really considered Rome as a remote possibility. But were you never to come a step nearer it is a part of Christian charity not to condemn the great mass of one's fellow-Christians, the millions of all generations who have been guided by Rome, without a hearing. For this end I think you should read Newman's *Present Position of Catholics in England;* also his *Anglican Difficulties* (2 vols.). That I think will be quite enough for the present as far as the *mind* goes, unless perhaps you might read his *Apologia* again. For the *spirit* I should recommend to you *The Creator and the Creature,* by Father Faber; *All for Jesus,* by the same; also *The Devout Life,* by St. Francis of Sales; *The Sacred Heart,* by Father Dalgairns; *The Life and Letters of St. Theresa,* and *The Life and Letters of St. Francis Xavier,* both by Father Coleridge. Catholicism is seen at highwater mark in Mrs. Craven's *Récit d'une Soeur. . . .*

Whatever happens it will be well to have read these things and to have lived a little with those strange people called saints. Above all, it is only by silence and tranquility of heart that one can hope to hear the still small voice of Truth. A "visit to the Blessed Sacrament," as we call it—that is, to go to the church when all is quiet and to remain a little in wordless prayer before the "Living Bread" from heaven—will be a source of great spiritual strength. For a prayer, I can recommend nothing better than à Kempis's *Imitation of Christ,* Book III, c. 2.

I told Messrs. Longmans to send you a copy of my meditations, of which some may help you, and the others you can leave. May Our Lord perfect and further your desire to know His truth and to do His will in everything.

TO THE SAME

16 Old Town, Clapham, S.W.
March 17, 1907

I confess I was very angry with Father N. for all his tactlessness and stupidity; but the truer and kinder interpretation is to be found by the recognition that in many respects he is an undeveloped specimen of humanity, and that what would be inexcusable in a grown man is excusable to the naive self-confidence and self-delightedness of a vigorous boy in his teens. He is, I know, absolutely sincere and devoted, and in no sense a charlatan; but the immaturity of his judgment makes him a dangerous guide for those who take him seriously as a grown-up person. Of course this is confidential.

I shall not regret your being in the Church if you can take it for what it really is—a means to serve you, not an end to be served. It caters for every kind and level of spiritual need, and you must find out and use just what suits and helps you; you will find all that the Church of England offered you, and a good deal more; and of that "more" some will nourish you and some will give you indigestion—

so you must use your good sense and not let yourself be hustled and
worried by doctors who know nothing about your constitution, and
make their own stomachs a rule for other people's. I should say:
Communion as often as you like; and confession very rarely and, if
possible, never. And, above all, avoid discussing religious questions
with traditional Catholics, whether priests or layfolk. For your mind
has been built up on a different system altogether, and it will be like
a conversation between a dog and a fish. All their machinery is justified solely as a means of getting where you have got already; namely,
alone with God. Only, if they are narrow in wanting you to use
crutches when you can walk without, you must not be Protestantly
narrow in condemning crutches all round. Protestantism caters only
for the elect and the "converted"; Catholicism for all humanity—
saints, scribes, pharisees, publicans, and sinners; and for all moods
and stages of each individual spiritual life; for its infancy, youth, and
old age; for its healthy and sick periods. You may not want crutches
to-day; but you may sprain your ankle to-morrow. Or if you don't
want crutches you may want spectacles, etc.

Well, I hope we shall soon meet and talk all this out.

THE STABILITY OF FAITH*

Now Faith is the substance of things hoped for—Heb. xi.1.

The recognition of the dominant part played by the will in the
assent of faith furnishes an answer to many difficulties experienced
by believers themselves who are troubled as to the reality of their
faith owing to their inability to explain the natural side of the process
in a way satisfactory to themselves or to others. For which of us does
not almost daily meet with Christians who are seriously troubled as
to the sincerity of their faith, and whose trouble, on examination, is
found to be rooted in the misapprehension—that unless they feel
towards the mysteries of faith, all, and more than all, that sense of
helpless, irresistible persuasion that they feel in regard to their own
existence, there is something wrong, something untruthful and insincere in their professing a certainty which they have not got?

This is a fallacy which occasionally drives people out of the
Church; and far more often prevents their coming into it. It is, of

*From George Tyrrell, *Oil and Wine,* 25–35.

course, by no means the only cause of the rapidly spreading decay of
faith, but it is a sufficiently prominent one to be worth a few
moments' attention.

In this country, the mistake is encouraged by inevitable contact
and intercourse with rationalistic Christianity to which the idea of
faith as a voluntary certainty is unfamiliar; which assumes that to
believe, means, to hold a very firm personal opinion with regard to
some religious question, which mere opinion, especially in such
obscure matters, can never reach the firmness of mathematical truths.
Now many certainly speak as though, in reciting the Creed, they
were giving a summary of their own private opinions, and not rather
making a solemn promise or vow to stand by these truths through
thick and thin; they seem to forget that the Creed is an expression of
a resolve on the part of the Will, far more than an expression of an
intuition on the part of the mind.

Another source of the evil, connected with this, is the prominence
necessarily given in our age and country to apologetic instructions—
oral and written; to controversy and argumentation of all kinds—
whereby an impression is insensibly created that faith depends upon
arguments as upon its cause, and that it stands and falls therewith;
whence again it is plain that no belief so supported can satisfy the
mind as completely as simple axioms and first principles do. No doubt
we are often told that these arguments are but a condition, and that
the will is the real, effectual cause of faith; but this statement is too
occasional, too indistinct, to obliterate the deeper impression created
by the ceaseless din of argument and controversy, and hence comes
the very prevalent disposition on the part of the educated or half-
educated to rest their belief directly upon arguments, and thus to slip
unconsciously from faith into rationalism.

The only remedy for the disease is the clear and frequent reassertion of the part played by the will in the free assent of faith; for it is
not merely that we must will to apply our mind to considering the
motives and grounds of faith, or that certain moral dispositions and
sympathies are needed for the appreciation of the grounds and
motives; but given all this intelligence and appreciation of the
grounds of faith, the act itself is a free assent elicited from the mind—
not passively under compulsion of evidence, but actively under compulsion of the will.

Faith then is not a passive and forced belief, but an actively free
belief. Under the force of evidence our mind is passive and receptive

like a mirror; or, as our eyes are, under the influence of objects duly presented to them. When the evidence is put before us clearly, we cannot resist or withhold our consent, even if we would. But in the case of a free assent like faith, we have to assert ourselves. It is not a case of "letting go," but of "holding on;" not of drifting down stream, but of beating our way up against the stream. It is an occasion for action and energy; for asserting our personality by opposing ourselves to, and resisting natural causes, instead of losing our identity by submitting to them passively and becoming part of the machinery of nature. It is just in these beliefs of our free choice that we are most human and least mechanical; it is in them that we determine our own character and life and end,—in some sort, creating for ourselves the world in which we choose to live; it is by them, and for them, that we shall be judged at the last, as worthy of eternal life or death.

These free beliefs are, as such, the noblest furniture of our mind, far nobler than those forced assents that we have to yield to necessary and natural truths, general or particular. These latter may be compared to those instincts and acquired habits to which we commit the greater part of our conduct, not because semi-unconscious mechanical action is better in itself, but because hereby our attention is liberated for the exercise of those free, conscious, intelligent acts which are proper to man as man, and distinguish him from automata. Similarly, the natural and necessary beliefs that are forced on us by evidence, are wholly subservient to, and for the sake of, those free and self-chosen beliefs, which are the fruit of our own action and mental life.

But what seems so important to observe is that, a certain sense of unreality, one might almost say, of pretence, is the normal and natural accompaniment of these freely-chosen, actively-sustained beliefs; and that this sense of unrest and infirmity is in no wise incompatible with the deepest and most genuine faith. For faith has it in common with opinion, that it does not quiet or satisfy the mind according to the laws of thought, and by motives proper to the mind, although it secures a greater than scientific certainty through the extrinsic influence of the will, supplementing the defects of sense and reason.

While then our necessary beliefs are self-supporting, our free-beliefs need to be supported by the continual exercise of the will; the former are like the things we see, that force themselves on our vision; the latter are like the pictures we construct in our imagination, that depend on our will for their maintenance.

For when (for one reason or another) we *choose* to believe what we are not *forced* to believe, it means that we take and treat as a fact, what, relatively to our perception, is not a fact. It means, not only that we speak and act as though we saw it to be true (for often we do not act up to our faith), but that we think and reason and argue in our own minds as though we saw it to be true. And yet all the while, we do not *see* it to be true, but hold it true by an act of our will. It is somewhat as when a mathematician assumes a certain value of x, and builds up all his calculations on that assumption. So with faith; what my natural reason proclaims to be bread, I freely believe to be the Body of Christ. I not only worship it and receive it as such; but in my reasonings and reflections I build on that assumption; and bring the rest of my mind into agreement with this belief.

Now in all this there seems to be the same element of pretence and unreality that comes into mere fictions and working hypotheses. I seem to be saying from the teeth outwards that something is white, while in my heart, all the time, I know it to be black. Yet the difference is that, in the case of hypotheses, and fictions and other freely chosen beliefs, the motive of our choice is not such as to make it a matter of supreme moral obligation; whereas in the case of faith we hold to the belief in obedience to the command of God as made known by the voice of conscience. And furthermore, we hold to it with that degree of willingness which He commands. Did we see the truth as it lies in God's mind, our intellect would be irresistibly forced to assent to it more firmly than to any natural truth; but since we do not, and cannot, we throw our whole will, without any reserve, into the act of belief, that it may have as much certainty for us as our will can possibly give to it. But all this will never prevent that seeming black to us, which God tells us and which we sincerely believe to be white, which we treat as though it were white in our conduct and in our reasonings; and therefore a certain sense of unreality and fiction is an essential part of the trial of faith.

Nor is this peculiar to truths of faith. It holds equally for those nciples and ideals whose values we accept on testimony : have come to prove it by experience; it holds even of nd scientific truths, so far as we take them on faith, not seeing the reasons for them; for there are numbers, for instance, who believe firmly that they must die, who regulate their conduct, thought, and speech by that belief, and yet to whom it is such a fiction and unreality that death comes in the end as a surprise and shock.

But it must not be forgotten that a free belief which costs us at first some effort to sustain and live up to, in process of time comes to be woven into the very fabric of our thought and life, so that even were our will to change, and our faith to fail, it would need some effort to cast aside the belief and to free ourselves from its influence. To a large extent this is due to the natural growth of mental habits; and the apparent reality and firmness that it gives to our faith is not due to any strengthening of the will to believe, or to what deserves the name of "virtue." At best, it is the removal of a certain natural difficulty in believing for which relief we ought to be thankful; seeing at the same time that we do not turn it to an occasion of slothfulness in faith. Thus manual labour, which at first calls for self-conquest and will-effort, eventually through the mere strengthening of the muscles ceases to make any such demand. This muscular habit must not be confounded with virtue, which means an increased readiness of *will*, a habit of self-conquest. So neither must the negative easiness in belief which comes from custom, imitation, or even thoughtlessness, be confounded with that easiness which comes from an increased goodness and strength of will subduing the mind, in obedience to the Will of God. This latter is compatible with all that feeling of unreality, pretence, and dreaminess which so needlessly disturbs those who hear that "the certainty of faith" is the highest of all certainties, and who falsely conclude that doubt about faith should *seem* to them as impossible as doubt about their own existence; which of course it does not, ought not, and cannot; else, faith were not free.

There is some danger—is there not?—lest we who have for so many years, perhaps from infancy, been accustomed to speak and think and act on the suppositions of faith; who have lived chiefly in the society of those governed by these beliefs; who have had the adventitious support that education, custom, tradition, and example can lend to faith—there is some danger lest we confound this negative facility in believing, due to the removal of difficulty with that positive facility due to the conquest of difficulty,—with that strengthening of the "will to believe" implied in the growth of faith. The strength which these causes add to a belief is no guarantee of its truth; since they operate no less effectually to confirm the errors of misbelievers than the faith of believers, and are therefore a curse or a blessing according to circumstances. These crutches provided for faith by natural habit, education, and example, may spare us from putting too great a tax on our legs, may support us when else our strength would fail; but it is the support of a wooden prop, not the vital support of intelligent virtue; and it may well be that the faith of those who lack the facility is stronger than ours, for the very reason that it needs to be stronger.

The more our beliefs have become customary to us, and have been wrought into the tissue of life and mind, and the more they have become independent of the exercise of our free-will, and of the virtue of faith, the less we are able to put ourselves in the condition of those whose belief is the fruit of faith and of faith alone; still if we cannot feel, at least we can understand their state of mind and soul, and so far minister to its necessities.

GOD IN US*

If you keep My commandments you shall abide in My love—John xv.10.

That our idea of God to some extent determines our love of Him is but a case of the more general principle that will is dependent upon knowledge—"*Nihil volitum nisi cognitum.*" Hence to get to know about God is admittedly one of our first and highest duties. On the other hand, it is no less evident and familiar to us that there is no exact equality between the measure of our love, and the measure of our knowledge; between the clearness of our theological conceptions and the purity of our lives. For often the most ignorant and untutored souls, whose ideas about God are almost as grotesque as the idols of primitive savagery, are full of an effectual and tender love of God, in no way justified or explained by their notions of Him; while a refined, spiritual and altogether philosophical conception of the Deity will as often leave the heart dead and cold as a stone.

Indeed Christ seems to imply that, as a rule, the love of God varies inversely with the power of conceiving Him intelligently: "Thou hast hid these things from the wise and prudent and hast revealed them to babes." Doubtless, if the wood be dry a little spark will start a great conflagration; whereas green wood may be stubborn to yield to the fiercest flame. The simple unspoilt heart of the child may be quickly and strongly responsive to those feebler rays of divine loveliness which beat idly on the callous surface of a heart hardened

*From George Tyrrell, *Oil and Wine*, 203–13.

by worldliness and sensuality, and by infidelity to past light. Hence
the spoken word that falls equally on many ears, is as seed sown over
a tract of varying fertility, yielding here nothing, there thirty, sixty, or
an hundred-fold.

So far then we may regard the word, the notion, the mental image
of God as a cause of divine love whose efficacy, however, is conditioned by the state of the heart to which the word is spoken. It is not
then without reason that, when religious teachers or preachers come
to us and tell us that we ought to, and must and shall love God with
our whole heart and above all things, we demand: Who is He? Where
is He? What is He like, that we should thus love Him on hearsay?
And then they begin, each according to his ability, to describe to us
in lame words, not God, whom they have never seen, but that notion
or image or picture of God which they have laboriously painted in
their own minds, that poor, clumsy skeleton-conception which they
have strung together piece by piece, and joint by joint, and set up for
worship in the shrine of their hearts. And often we could wish that
they had either held their peace altogether or had said less. He, who
came from the bosom of the Father, could have said much, and yet
He said but little; for He knew a more living language than that of
the tongue,—one in which He "showed us the Father" by stretching
out His all-embracing arms and dying, not only, as man does, for His
friends, but, as God does, for His enemies. Hence we are but slowly
and slightly stirred by the spoken word, by the notion of God that is
transferred, through language, from some other intelligence to our
own. What moves us more really in the preacher is, the manner of
one who has found some treasure which he himself cannot rightly
conceive, still less express to us in words; who has found a well of
living water, a secret fount of happiness which he would willingly
share with the thirsty; who therefore excites our curiosity and bids us
come and see and taste for ourselves; who knows that his stammering
descriptions are almost irreverently unlike what personal experience
alone can reveal to his hearers—as unlike as a spoken description of
some wonderful symphony, of which all one ought to say is: "Go and
hear it."

Therefore a deeper reason why, as a rule, a strong and supreme
love of God is quite separable from a clear intellectual conception of
His nature, is to be sought in the truth that, in this life God presents
Himself to us as an object of the heart and will, rather than as an
object of the mind and intelligence; as something to be laid hold of

by action rather than by contemplation, as something to be done, rather than as something to be gazed at or argued about. "This is life eternal," says Christ, "that they should *know* Thee;" and certainly hereafter we hope to see God face to face, not as our mind now sees Him in images and symbols and ideas, even as we see our departed friends in their portraits, or in their letters, or in some work they have left behind them. To have the veil torn away which now prevents the light of God's face shining straight into the eyes of our soul, is indeed what we long and labour for. But meantime the veil is there; and it is not by our mind but only by our action that, in this life, we are brought into immediate contact with God. . . .

He himself is not, in this life, a direct object of our mind; and if here we are to touch Him and be immediately united with Him, it is not in thinking about Him but in acting with Him. For every good action of ours is His also—the offspring of the marriage of our will with His; the seal and pledge of the active union, the union in action, of our soul with Him. From the first suggestion of good, to the wish, the desire, the will, the accomplishment, He is co-operant with every movement of our faculties. . . .

God is that centre of goodness which draws us ever towards closer union with itself, by a continual magnetic attraction. Whether we climb up-hill or run down-hill we are influenced by the earth's attraction, resisting its force in the one case, using it in the other; and similarly, whether we resist the inclination or use it, in every conscious and free action we are under the influence, however dimly acknowledged, of an attraction towards goodness, of a wish, however feeble and ineffectual, to do the right thing; and if we go with the attraction there is a sense of ease; and if we go against it, a sense of unrest. And this attraction is simply the felt will of God, whose presence within us is as essentially a condition of our conscious rational life, as air or light is of our bodily life.

And so when we talk of "union with God" let us put aside all childish pictures of the mind which portray that union as a sort of local relation of two things face to face, or fastened or fused together, inactive and unchanging; and let us rather picture it as the meeting or mingling of two streams reinforcing one another, even as when we run down-hill our own action and that of the earth conspire to one and the same end.

So it is not in standing still, but in movement and action that we are united to God and our life mingled with His. And the closer we come to Him the more strongly He draws us; the more frequently, fully, and strenuously we act with God, the more abundantly does He enter into us; so that action is, in a way, the vessel into which God is received. And like every other appetite, the desire for that sense of rest and peace that comes of yielding to God's magnetism, grows keener with every indulgence, till it comes easily to out-sway every counter-attraction, and till nothing irks us more than the unrest of having resisted.

Thus it is that whereas not God, but only some feeble image or symbol of His nature can be touched by our mind, He Himself can be touched by the heart where His will is felt striving with our will, and His spirit with our spirit; and He can be embraced and held fast in the embrace of action whereby His life and ours are spun together and firmly co-twisted in the union of a single and undivided process. "I am the Way," He says, "and the Truth and the Life"—but principally a Way to be trodden; a Life to be lived. He is also a Truth to be known, an idea to be conceived; yet here, not directly, but through images and shadows—as things distant and absent are known to us. . . .

Often what men deny with their lips they confess with their lives; the sense in which they reject received dogmas is not the true sense, but a travesty thereof—their own or another's; it is not God whom they refuse to worship, but some unworthy idol of the imagination. Of our deepest convictions, our conduct is often the truest utterance; it is just in regard to them that our powers of self-analysis and expression are most apt to fail.

While, then, no man can be saved without faith and knowledge of God, yet there is a truer knowledge than that of ideas and images; a knowledge of direct contact and experiment, a matter of tasting, touching, and feeling. For a musician, a knowledge of Beethoven, means a skill in reproducing his music; not an acquaintance with the details of his biography, though this may be added as a luxury. We know God in the only way essential to our nature and destiny when we know how to reproduce the music of His life in our own. We need to know the sun as that which gives light and warmth and vigour, but its internal composition concerns us but little. . . .

SPIRITUAL EQUILIBRIUM*

Simon Peter saith unto them: I go a-fishing. They say unto him: We also go with thee—John xxi.3.

The instinct which in seasons of strong emotional preoccupation, whether joyful or sorrowful, bids us turn back to the hypnotizing rhythm and routine of our ordinary avocations, is true to reason. At root it is the same which makes an excitable speaker unconsciously seek relief from the nervous tension under which he is labouring, in some sort of fidgety movement or mechanical idling. The unduly prolonged concentration of the entire energy and attention on any one point of interest wearies out the faculties of perception and emotion so engaged, and weakens the rest by under-exercise. As in hysteria, laughter and tears alternately give birth each to the other by way of violent reaction, so it is sometimes observed that an unwisely sustained intellectual or contemplative effort prepares the way for an act of reprisal on the part of violated Nature in the form of a rebellion of the senses and lower affections. The worn-out spirit half slumbers for sheer exhaustion and leaves the starved and irritated senses almost as free to run riot as they would be in the state of bodily sleep. "Thou art man," says à Kempis, "and not an angel." The attempt to anticipate the state of the Blessed in Heaven, and to live as the angels who behold the face of the Father, if pushed far beyond metaphor, can only result in singed wings and a disastrous fall into the mire. Had we been meant to live as angels—we should have had the faculties of angels—a God-seeing faculty, and no body to cumber us; Heaven would have been as near to us as earth, as evident as the things we see, touch, and taste. But we are made to walk by faith, not by sight; by inference, not by intuition. We deal with God, for the most part in and through creatures—as identified with them, not as apart from them; and only occasionally, in the explicit exercises of religion and worship, do we treat with Him directly as distinct from and above all creatures.

Thus, though religion should dominate our whole life, it is not our whole life, but only a part—albeit the head and principal part. It need not ordinarily dominate, in the sense of occupying the greater part of our time and attention:—God reserves but one day in seven;—but in the sense that its claims are paramount and that its obligation in case of conflict take precedence of all others. If it so dominate,

*From George Tyrrell, *Oil and Wine*, 260–65.

then indeed our whole life, so far as it is not counter to religion, may be said to be, implicitly, a continual act of prayer and praise.

But as the body is not all head, so neither should our life be all religion. Neither are the members solely for the sake of the head, nor is the head solely for the sake of the members; but both are directly for the sake of the whole, and indirectly for the sake of each other. Religion is not simply a means to the greater fulness and sanctification of our temporal life; nor is this wholly subordinated to religion. Our natural cares, interests, occupations, and studies do not need to be justified by a direct reference to religion as relaxations, or inevitable interruptions, or necessary ministrations and conditions thereof. They are, of their own right, and co-ordinately with religion, integral though secondary elements in our whole human life.

The organic connection of these co-ordinate factors of our life is such that if one member suffer, the rest suffer with it; and that the undue development of one to the prejudice of the rest on which it depends, eventually issues in the hurt and destruction of that one together with the rest. Religion has therefore everything to gain by the evenly balanced development of those other departments of life over which it should reign, not as a tyrant, but as a constitutional monarch.

An all-round even development of all our capacities is never possible, since many of them are so incompatible, that we must choose one and forego the other. We must fix on some one of the many professions or pursuits of which we are equally capable. Such matters are oftenest determined for us by outward circumstances which will not allow us to choose what would bring out of us the best that is in us. We may not bury the talents that we have been told to use, but God Himself buries most of our talents in the disposition of His Providence.

But even where the matter rests with ourselves, the limits of any one life are too narrow to admit of the successful development of even all those talents whose development is compatible. We must make a selection in such wise as to get as much out of ourselves as circumstances will allow. But though with a view to this, specialization, wholesale exclusion and sacrifice are the conditions of any sort of excellence and fertility; yet there is a point at which one-sidedness and narrowness become deadly. Common-sense suggests that we should make one interest central in respect to the time and attention we give to it; and should develope such others as either minister to it, or else harmonize with it, were it even by way of contrast and difference, so as to preserve the soul's balance.

To make religion not only dominant in point of dignity and influence, but also central in point of time and attention, is a special vocation granted to the few who are drawn to live before God more consciously and explicitly than others, to give Him their whole mind as well as their whole heart, and who therefore withdraw themselves from the conditions that would make such concentration morally impossible and even indiscrete.

Yet these too, as has been implied, will better consult the interest of contemplation by the adoption of some keen and absorbing interest, practical or speculative, which will preserve them from spiritual lopsidedness and will, as it were, minister a body for their religion to govern, lest it should be as a head bereft of its subject members.

This principle underlies the ancient Carthusian conception of the Christian life as constituted by a three-fold labour—of heart, mind, and hand—a conception based upon the study of the Gospel, if not actually preserved by unbroken tradition from the earliest days of Christianity. This resolving of life into three main divisions—affection, thought, and action, is practically satisfactory. In each of these realms to have some strong central interest will secure the desired equilibrium of the soul. If religion be the central preoccupation of the heart, it will gain in strength, health, and endurance, if it be balanced by some keen discipline of the mind not directly connected with religion; and both will benefit by some outward work of art, skill, or ministration, which calls mainly upon the bodily powers and the practical intelligence, and not directly upon the intellect or the spirit.

As things are, this three-fold labour is largely put in commission among three classes of society, to the great detriment of each. We have those whose hands are so ceaselessly exercised that their minds are crippled and their souls stifled. And we have intellect divorced from religion and action, and degenerating into intellectualism. And we have religion neither intelligent nor practical, and out of all sympathy with intellect and labour. Some degree of such specialization is inevitable and even desirable; but when it becomes absolute and complete there is no passage from the mind of one class to that of the other, no common ground of sympathy and understanding between the men of prayer and the men of thought and the men of action; and therefore no possibility of mutual influence—of that give-and-take whereby each class can supply to the others of its superabundance, and receive of theirs.

2

Religion

RELIGION AS A FACTOR OF LIFE*

"Nihil aliud quam voluntates," says Augustine: "We are nothing else but wills," and it is in our relations to other wills—relations of love or aversion, agreement or disagreement—that we find each of us our deepest spiritual reality. It is truly in society, i.e. in our will-relation with others, that we live and move, and we have our being; and to this deepest life the surface life of our understanding, and of our external activity is subordinate. We may consider the relation of our will to each single will in particular, or to the whole world of wills collectively, or to that will which is over and in all other wills, the centre and bond of the will-world. This last relationship is the foundation of the religious sentiment or affection, which is inclusive and regulative of the sentiments of particular and collective love founded on the other relationships. Religion is the principal element in the life of the affections, and, therefore, in the whole organism of human life. But the head is not the body; nor should religion be the only, because the principal, interest. The head needs the ministry of every member; and religion suffers by any sort of pseudo-spirituality that would dwarf the other affections, or the life of thought, or of external activity, in its imaginary interests. It gains everything and loses nothing by the well-balanced cultivation of our non-religious interests.

*From George Tyrrell, *Religion as a Factor of Life* (1902), 2–13.

Yet the members need the head still more urgently; without it they are but a chaos, and their movement aimless and incoherent. As the life of outward activity is in no sense human, but merely mechanical, unless it be directed by intelligence; so if a man's intelligence be not governed by a religion his whole life lacks foundation and end; it is, at best, a detached system of energies, unconnected with the universal life, and with the centre of the will-world. Hence, in the very interests of our non-religious activities, as well as for its own sake, a certain explicit and separate exercise of religion is necessary. If the ethical effort, or endeavour, "moralises" our intellectual and practical life, the religious effort "religionises" our moral life. Not indeed that the higher grade of life is to be cultivated solely in the interests of the lower; or that it is not to be exercised principally for its own sake; but that the harmonious blending of all these elements into the fulness of a complete human life is even a greater good than the perfection of the highest element torn violently apart from the organism, which it was made to govern and control; and that, life is bigger than religion, and religion but an element, albeit the chiefest, of life.

There is, however, much obscurity as to what is meant by spiritual labour—by the religious effort—which must not be confounded on the one side with the study of religion (which is but a department of mental labour) or, on the other side, with the work of practical religion, which belongs to the sphere of external labour. To call it "prayer," even in the widest sense, does not deliver us from our vagueness altogether; and we are thrown back on the much discussed yet insoluble problem as to what we mean by religion, and to what department of life it belongs. A "religion" in the public external sense of the word is a school for the training of certain spiritual faculties; it aims at instructing the mind, and forming the will and affections, so as to determine our action, feeling, and practical attitude in relation, not to the things of this world directly, but to God directly, and to other things as viewed in relation to Him. We may say that whatever instruction it offers to the mind is not in the interests of intellectualism, but of life and action; that its chief aim is the shaping of the affections and sentiments. To speak of personal religion as a "sentiment" savours of Matthew Arnold's sentimentalism; and seems to imply that the use of religion is the awakening of certain aesthetic emotions akin to those evoked by music or poetry, and as fruitless of any after-result. Yet faith, hope, love, reverence—those various aspects under which personal religion may be viewed—are undoubtedly sentiments and affections; and the great doctors of the "art of prayer" agree that these sentiments are the true end of meditation and contemplation, and alone give life and reality to those further practical results, which are by no means essential in all cases. What then is religion in substance, and what is "the work of God" that we all must work?

In the wider acceptation, sentiment, or affection, is the main-spring of conscious life; it is created and modified by every kind of perception, and ever gives birth to some sort of self-adaptation in view of that perception. Life is an unbroken process whereby we pass continuously from one will-attitude into another in view of surroundings which are going through a similar transformation—each moment dissolving into the next. Feeling is equivalently the consciousness of the impeded conversion of perception into action; it is, in its most elementary form, the inclination to advance or to withdraw in response to a touch. The life, whose reaction to stimulus is determined passively, is *so far* automatic and unconscious. Where there is a feeling it means that the reaction is checked, and finds no ready-made outward passage; that there is place for true "action" which determines a passage for it. Hence, though the present "feeling" is not of our choice, but depends on our natural or acquired state at the time being, it is our choice to fix the direction in which it shall take effect, and by making, as it were, a furrow in the sensori-motor field, to modify the nature of future feelings. What has been done once, will be made easier to do the next time; the reaction to the same stimulus will not be so abruptly checked, but will tend to run off along the said furrow—to become a degree less conscious, less sentient, more automatic and habitual.

Feeling, therefore, is repressed and indetermined action, straining like pent-up waters, against a dyke which it is for us to open at this point or that; according as we choose to set the action free in this or that form. Give it a channel of relief, and it is no longer feeling but force. So far as we feel, we are free and self-directive; and to this end we need to perceive and understand the situation to which our action has to be adapted.

The part played by feeling in our life is, therefore, most central. To say that religion is a matter of feeling only means that it controls the main-spring of life. To say, however, that it is a pleasurable feeling sought for the sake of artistic satisfaction, like music or poetry, is

sentimentalism. The root-fallacy lies in taking one part of the indivisible movement of life, blended of perception, feeling, and action,
and treating it as a separate thing, because it has got a separate
name—"feeling."

As a kind of life, religion is a feeling, or group of feelings, determined by certain perceptions, and giving birth to certain actions.
And this may be said equally of those factors into which religion is
usually resolved—of faith, hope, love, reverence, penitence; each is a
kind of feeling derived from a certain kind of action. Thus, those who
speak of religion as a sentiment or affection are not more, but perhaps less, reprehensible than those who speak of it as consisting in
certain beliefs, or in certain good works.

As an element of life in general it is plain that religion means an
experience of certain feelings of attraction and repulsion, in accordance with which we freely shape our action. Yet as far as common
usage goes, religion lies rather in the internal will-attitude than in the
perceptions that precede, or in the activity that follows it; the former
may be barren; and the latter without root. And thus in substance
religion is an affair of the sentiments and affections.

What then is that element of our experience to which these affections have reference?

Not one that is abruptly separated, and set alongside of or above
the rest; but one that pervades and unites all the rest—the real
Whence and Whither of all being and movement, whereof our own
being and movement is an infinitesimal fraction. Prior to being gathered up into any distinct thought of the understanding about God or
gods, this *datum* lies, as it were, fused through our total experience,
co-perceived with other perceptions, but not perceived apart, and
similarly, can give a religious modification to our other actions without giving birth to distinct acts of religion. We might speak of it as
the sense of the Absolute; the sense of the ultimate and independent
value of truth, goodness, and beauty, apart from all other consequences and advantages. In the last analysis this means a sense of our
subordination to an universal order and interest. This sense, like
others, may be sharpened and intensified by indulgence; by seeking
the Absolute in the moral, intellectual, and aesthetic orders; or it
may be blunted by disuse or positive violation; but in the measure
that it is intensified, it will seek the aid of the understanding whose
office is to map out in small, and by aid of symbols, the wilderness of
our experience for the better guidance of our conduct, and to supple-

ment our natural foresight by a power of more or less scientific and infallible prediction of the absent and distant.

Hence our sense of the Absolute seeks to know itself through the symbols of the understanding, and the Absolute becomes an object, the chief of all objects, and is given a central and sovereign place in our artificial scheme of "things." No one pretends that our conceptions of God, as an object, are adequate or more than analogous and symbolic; yet they possess an equivalent or practical truth in the measure that they guide our conduct more or less surely in the right direction. The case is parallel with that of our schemes of physical nature; none of these schemes are adequate even in outline, but one gives us more power of correspondence with Nature than another; it co-ordinates and unifies a greater area of possible experience, and extends our range of prediction. Such is the truth of a religion; namely, its utility for eternal life, i.e., for the life of correspondence with the Absolute. It is truer in the measure that it gives a fuller, deeper, wider life to the soul. Life is the test of its truth—"To whom shall we go? Thou hast the words of eternal life!"

Does this mean that our religions are arbitrary fictions like working hypotheses, which may yield true results and yet be utterly false?

In reply, it should be noticed that a working hypothesis, so far as it is at all scientific, is not an arbitrary fiction; nor is it intended as a fiction at all. It is a guess at truth that may prove wrong. A fluid, for example, stands for a whole group of properties and consequences; and where we find a fair number of these together, it is so far probable that the rest may also be found. It may be proved that they can exist without the rest, or as part of some other plexus; but till this is proved it is more reasonable to think in accordance with our past uniform experience. Hence, though the hypothesis of an electric fluid may be wrong, it is not a fiction, and not arbitrary, but the closest available conception of the truth. But if speculatively doubtful, it may be quite true in its practical or working aspect, i.e., as a guide to action, or as a plan of the world of appearances. So too, a religion or theology may, as a theory, be incomplete or even erroneous, and yet in no wise an arbitrary fiction, while, on its working side, as a guide to the action and eternal life of the soul, it may be infallible truth, at least, relatively to the soul's condition and aptitude. "This do, and thou shalt live." "Act as though things were thus, and as though God were thus," might be said of many an imperfect religion, where it would not hold true of the Gospel. Our lot, even as a race, is cast in so small a space, and in so brief a time, that what is but part may be for us practically the whole, and what is but a passing phase, may be practically considered as an eternal order. Not while man endures, will the uniformity of day and night, summer and winter, seed-time and harvest fail; nor does it practically concern him to know that heaven and earth shall pass away.

Hence in his theorizings about the Absolute, about God and His ways, for practical purposes, it is not needful that he should know the whole method of Divine action in every possible realm of being, and for all possible differences of time; but only that portion of it which is universal and constant relatively to his own little experience and duration. Speculatively, this view of God as an agency to be dealt with, as a plexus of attributes and properties, is necessarily partial, and so far, even false; just as our schemes of Nature are speculatively false even if true practically. They are false in theory, just because they are not exhaustive, and because though they guide us safely through our little corner of experience, they would mislead a being capable of universal experience. He would, as it were, find changes of climate and soil and configuration, which would make his dependence on merely local characteristics somewhat disastrous.

But the understanding, for practical purposes, considers only the divine manifestations and effects, and cannot touch God in His reality. If he enters into its scheme of reality as the governing object, to which all other objects are related and subordinated, we must remember that, in the understanding a substance or subject is represented only under the symbol of some stable element or elements or a group of appearances, which abides, while the other elements change—as the very etymology of such words as sub-ject, sub-stance, ac-cident indicates. It is only in and through action and will that we have experience of substance and subject, as of realities that cannot be pictured in terms of sense. And so God, as distinct from His understandable effects and attributes, cannot be given to us in any image or grouping of the understanding, whose value is at best that of a practical and equivalent truth; but He belongs to the order of things with which the will is in direct contact; to what is called the world of "will-values"; to the world of history, not of science; (as Munsterberg explains matters).

It is in willing and acting that our reality is revealed to us; and we account other things real in so far as they seem to oppose their will to ours. We *are*, each of us, a single "willing," which, however we may analyse it into a sum-total of past and present "willings" from which it results, is, nevertheless, one simple act by which we adapt ourselves to the total situation in which we now find ourselves—the past, behind us; the present, around us; the future, before us. Every instant of our life this "willing" modifies itself and dissolves into something different, in response to a similar transformation of our surroundings. Through that world to which our body belongs, and of which our senses, memory, and understanding take account, we are made aware of other wills which express themselves therein, as we ourselves do, by the sensibly evident results of their action. It is in our *felt* relation to these other wills that our spiritual life and reality consists. That relation is, with regard to each several will, one of agreement and attraction, or of revolt and dislike, or rather of a complex building of likes and dislikes, according to the innumerable elements into which each total will-attitude may be virtually resolved. Like the motes in a sunbeam the whole world of wills is in ceaseless commotion; each changing its attitude with regard to all the rest, as moment by moment the shifting situation demands a new response. Wherever we find another will accordant with our own in any particular, we experience a sense of re-enforcement and expansion of our spiritual life and being; and this, in proportion to the nature and extent of the agreement, and the nature and number of wills in agreement. On the other hand, there is a sense of spiritual impoverishment and contraction wherever we recognise a will-force in opposition to our own—a sense as though we were losing hold of that community of souls whose being we share, and were dropping away into the void and nothingness of solitude. What first principles are in abstract science; what general laws are in physics; certain test cases, abstract or concrete, certain personalities, are in the will-world; that is, they are the principle of unification and classification.[1] By their will-attitude in regard to certain deeds, certain heroes, certain aims, in a word, in regard to certain governing will-attitudes, men can be spiritually classified and brought into that system of relations which constitutes the will-world. A Christian, a republican, a vivisectionist, and such terms by which men are grouped together imply always a common end, towards which their wills are set in agreement. It is the true function of History, as Munsterberg points out, to show the order and connection of these governing deeds, aims, and person-

---

1. See Munsterberg's essay, "Psychology and History."—G. T.

alities; just as it is the true function of biography to consider a personality in its relation to those controlling ends, and to classify it
accordingly, i.e., to describe the will-attitude of the individual in
regard to the will-world.

Surely, it is this will-world that is real to us beyond every other,
and it is in that our soul finds its deepest rest or unrest.

But if any sort of will-union with another is desirable in the
abstract (i.e., considered alone and apart from the infinity of other
will relations) yet in the concrete it always involves a relation of
disagreement with contrary will-attitudes, and a mingling of pain with
pleasure. "No man can serve two masters"; if he love the one, he
must hate the other. Hence, while this chaos and contrariety prevails,
and pending that process of sifting and settling-down through which
the stars of this spiritual firmament tend, perhaps eternally, towards
the equilibrium of some system of established constellations, we cannot take mere will-union as an end in itself, or as a decisive motive of
action. We may not seek rest in agreement, without asking—"Rest in
what?" "Agreement with what?" Throughout the whole universe of
will-attitudes the difference of evil and good, false and true, fair and
foul, passes like a two-edged sword; and gives a rule of choice clearly
higher than the blind and impotent rule of love, which would pull us
in every direction at once, and lead us in none. Even if we *might*
follow the impulse to be at one with all men, we could not. We may
err and falter in our judgement as to what is true, fair, or right; we
may turn away from our duty when we know it; but we can never
falter in our conviction as to the absolute and imperative character of
these will-attitudes; we can never doubt that we *ought* to be in sympathy with men of good-will and out of sympathy with the insincere,
the selfish, the low-minded. Now this imperative character of the
Absolute is simply the force of that supreme, eternal, eventually
irresistible Will, which we call God—that will to which the whole
will-world must be subordinate, and in union or agreement with
which each created will is saved and realised, even were it at variance
with all the rest. This love of God, this dynamic union with the
Infinite will, is the very substance and reality of our spiritual living
and being; other lovings and agreeings belong to the perfection, but
not to the essence of our blessedness.

Our will and affection are never directed to an abstraction, or an
idea; but always to a concrete object; in the last analysis, always to a
person, a will. Whatever else we desire it is always for the sake of

some person, ourself or another—which person is, therefore, the direct object of our love or hate. We do not care for such mental conceptions as Justice and Mercy, but for definite deeds of justice and mercy and, in the last analysis, for the person and will so manifesting itself. Hence, neither is our will moved or affected by the Absolute—by the Fair, the Good, and the True—which are all abstractions; but by the concrete will-attitudes which we recognise as ruled by that Supreme and Eternal Will; which are fair, and good, and true, because they are conformed to it. Implicitly or interpretatively our reverence and worship is directed to it.

With regard to the whole realm of our freedom—the government of our thoughts, of our tastes, of our conduct—we know that there is an absolute rule which looks to an interest beyond that of the individual or of the race—a rule which is willed by a will which we can either resist or obey. We should owe nothing to merely abstract principles and rules of right thinking, right acting, right feeling; it were only our own loss to ignore them, just as we should suffer in neglecting the rules of arithmetic. But as manifestations of the Supreme will-attitude, the right, the fair, and the true, in conduct, is not merely rule and norm, but *law* in the full moral sense of the term—the expression of the Infinite Will.

The true orientation of our will must, therefore, be towards that Supreme Will so far as it is manifested in the will-attitudes of those who live by it. We know nothing of that Will in its attitude towards extra-human affairs; we only feel it mingling and conflicting with our freedom.

In a sense, therefore, one might live religiously without any definite and separate act of religion, internal or external, in simply obeying conscience and following one's *sense* of the Absolute Will. But religion begins when this all-pervading, governing Will is conceived apart, outside and above all others; as partially revealed in the goodness of those wills and actions which it instigates, controls, and perfects.

Religion as an activity of the individual soul is simply the movement of its will-attitude in relation to the Divine Will and to all other wills so far as accordant with the Divine Will. It is measured by the extent to which that Will is understood and loved; the understanding may be great and the love small; or conversely.

But through association with others, this activity of the soul is awakened and educated. As Ethics, Logic and Aesthetics give us the

universal principles and practical rules of right conduct, right reasoning, and right feeling; so theoretical religion gives us those notions
about God, and those rules of religious practice which are the same
for all men, and sum up the gathered wisdom and experience of the
religious society in which we live. Left to themselves, men will reason
implicitly without any suspicion of the "Logic-world" with all its parts
and relations; but undoubtedly it is a mental gain when the system
and laws of correct reasoning are abstracted as it were, a skeleton
from the living body of human thought, and set before us in all their
articulation; for we can then guide and test the operation of our mind
with a certain inerrancy otherwise unattainable. And the same is to
be said of ethical or aesthetic systems which the understanding creates as instruments for dealing with the complexity of experience, or
as maps for our guidance in a pathless wilderness. But the map is not
the wilderness; but at best, a practical way of considering it, somewhat as the arbitrary forms into which we group the stars aid us to
thread our way about the heavens. So too, a religion is an attempt of
the understanding to systematise a certain element of our manifold
life, to find a theory of it, and thence to deduce practical rules for our
guidance. It is a way of taking things, that will, on the whole, lead to
successful results. It deals with the relation of our will-movement to
the Divine Will-movement; with that effort of ours to steer the course
of our will parallel to that of the Supreme and Universal Will. Hence
like the other regulative sciences which control the free action of our
spiritual life—Ethics, Logic, Aesthetics—Religion has a double
truth—speculative and practical; the former in so far as, unlike stellar
geography and like terrestrial geography, it pretends and strives to
represent its object as it is independently of its relation to the practical needs of life; the latter, in so far as it furnishes a successful guide
to that department of life with which it deals. As the most effectual
rules of conduct or reasoning might conceivably be deduced from
false theories of Ethics or Logic; so too a religion might conceivably
be practically true and speculatively false. Nay more, it might be
speculatively true and practically false for souls morally or mentally
unprepared for its reception; for them, what is false in theory were
often truer in practice.

Precisely as a work of the understanding, i.e., as a theology, a
religion is as purely human an effort as ethics or logic; but the world
with which it deals is given to it, not all at once, but progressively, by
what may be called "revelation"; and from such revelation springs by

natural consequence a desire of and effort at new utterance, that may be called "inspiration."

The prophet or revealer is one in sensitive and comprehensive sympathy with the general mind and feeling; who gathers into his own soul as to a focus the converging rays of light and warmth that stream from the souls around him; who, under that influence, wins a fuller and deeper apprehension of the will-world than were possible for any separate individual; and whose vision seeks inspired utterance in some new expression or setting of the public religion, proportionate to this increase of its content or signified reality.

Such modifications are rightly called "inspired," proceeding as they do from the workings of the Divine Will and Spirit in the prophetic soul; the words and mental forms are human, but the force that weaves them into a more spiritual expression is of God. Even the rudest fabrications of early religion do not lack their inspiration, though the myth or legend or scientific theory used as a vehicle of Divine utterance be wholly human and puerile. On such rough canvas God paints His own image from age to age, touching and re-touching, correcting, refining, spiritualising. It is just this illuminating touch that constitutes the inspired element of every prophetic utterance, and reveals the Divine to us. What other key or criterion can we have wherewith to discern the one element from the other, than the end and aim of all religion—i.e. the more perfect harmonising of the created will with the uncreated?

3

Revelation and Theology

REVELATION*

The distinction between Theology and Revelation, the determination of their respective rights and limits, and of their relation of mutual dependence, are matters of ever growing importance. It is now generally felt that their entanglement is fatal to both interests; that Revelation is thereby subjected to all the vicissitudes, uncertainties, and contradictions of theological speculation; that Theology is fettered in its free growth and development by the finality and divine authority which consecrate oracular and prophetic utterances. To some extent the cause in question, the principle at stake, is closely akin to that involved in the problem of the relations of Church and State. In both cases, the divorce is desired by each party in its own interest, and is assumed to be a far more simple and satisfactory solution than it really is. It is too readily supposed that wedded organisms which have grown together for centuries and lived a common life can be abruptly cleft asunder without any danger of bleeding to death. Because we have arrived at a more or less satisfactory distinction in the abstract, where formerly all was blurred and confused, we hasten to effect a separation in the concrete, as though thought were exhaustive of reality.

*From George Tyrrell, *Through Scylla and Charybdis* (1907), 264–71, 278–300.

It is, however, rather from the side of religion than from that of philosophy that the divorce of Revelation from Theology is apt to be too eagerly precipitated. It is a case of lightening an endangered vessel by throwing cargo overboard. Panic is not content with a measured and discriminating rejection, but recklessly wholesale in its sacrifices to safety, and may easily part with the necessary minimum of ballast. It may be that when we have sifted revelation of its theological implications we shall find our sieve empty of all residue. If it is true that theology but translates revelation from its imaginative into conceptual or intellectual language, it may be also urged that revelation translates theology into terms of sense and imagination, that religion is but popularised theology, that the substance and reality and truth are to be sought in the intellectual concepts, not in their imaginative expression. May it not be that theology just gets under the popular form of revelation to its solid core of intellectual truth, that it cracks the shell and picks out the kernel? That e.g. behind the more or less human mask of Fatherhood it detects Ultimate Causality, Plenitude of Being, and so forth? In that case, to sift out the implicit theology were to sift out the whole content of revelation—of what were, then, merely a symbolised theology. Above all, is not this wholesale severance of Church and State, of Revelation and Theology, perfectly chimerical? Can it ever be that a Christian should be so indifferent to theology as to profess Materialism, or Atheism, or Pantheism while holding the Faith in all its integrity? And if not, how can we deny that Revelation, directly or indirectly, fetters his theological liberty, and requires him to take account of Divine oracles in his search after philosophical truth? Or how can we blame or limit the world-old interference of priests with the liberties of philosophical speculation?

Yet, on the other hand, a certain spiritual equalising or levelling of all men in the matter of Faith and Religion, is an essential and distinctive feature of Christianity, whose truth is hid from the wise and prudent and revealed to little ones, not by flesh and blood, but by the common Father who is in Heaven. That the gifts of Faith and Grace should be conditioned by anything so uncertain, so variable, so monopolised by an intellectual aristocracy as philosophical orthodoxy, is hardly consistent with the spirit and desire of its Founder. It may be that His desire held an inherent though unobserved contradiction; yet at least His sympathies were seemingly in favour of a divorce between Theology and Revelation. Nor is it accordant with the Gospel-spirit to allow that the philosopher as such should possess a spiritual advantage over the peasant; or a cultured over a barbarous age of people. "Look at your elect," writes Paul, "how there are not many wise according to the flesh, not many great, not many noble, but the foolish things of this world hath God chosen that He may confound the wise." This is essentially the keynote of Christianity, and would seem to make its frequent lapses into "intellectualism" as manifestly discordant with its spirit as its no less frequent lapses into worldliness and moral corruption. Can we then say that philosophical orthodoxy is a necessary condition of Faith? That we must convert a man to Aristotle or to Plato, or from Kant, or from Spencer, before we can convert him to Christ?

What then? Shall we say that Christianity labours under an inherent contradiction; that the divorce of Theology from Revelation is at once essential to it and yet impossible; that its lapses into intellectualism are the inevitable fruit of the contradictory and utopian idea of a free Revelation and a free Theology, side by side in the same mind? Here, then, it would seem we have another case of the old fallacy of abstraction; another attempt to split up the organic unity of human life with a hatchet into fragments that are expected to survive the operation, and to live all the more fruitfully for it.

I have elsewhere considered the problem more from the side of Theology; I purpose now to approach it more from the side of Revelation; to ask myself what I mean by Revelation; what are its rights and its limits with respect to Theology.

First, I notice that the word is used primarily to denote an experience, and derivatively to denote the record or expression by which that experience is retained and communicated to others. For us the Revelation of St. John is but the record of an experience; for him it was an experience. St. Stephen saw the Heavens opened; we are but told that he saw them opened. To him they were revealed, to us it is only revealed that they were revealed. Here at once is an important distinction strangely slurred over, which raises the question, Can Revelation be communicated? Can I believe on the strength of God's word to another? Can such belief be (in defiance of logic) stronger than my purely human faith in the veracity of that other? Must not Conscience—God's Vicar—make the message its own, and command the homage of my Faith?

Putting aside this question, and taking Revelation in its primary sense, as an experience, I first notice that as far as etymology and even common usage are concerned, it seems to imply the sudden dropping of a veil, or lifting of a mist, or the lightening-flash glimpse of a landscape at night. "It came to me as a revelation," we say; but hardly, "It dawned upon me as a revelation." Abruptness, discontinuity with the ordinary process of knowledge is its usual (perhaps not essential) characteristic.

Again, we discover or find out by seeking, by voluntary use of our natural faculties. Revelation comes to us unsought; it is given to us, or happens to us. Sometimes its object is altogether new; sometimes it is old, familiar, use-worn but struck with a sudden sunbeam, lit up with a new light. "Startling," "Strange," "Sensational," are the terms by which our news-sheets qualify revelations. If there was no preceding mystery or problem, there was at least a tranquil unsuspicion which has been rudely disturbed.

Revelation is not merely of what is hidden, but of what is improbable or even incredible. Too often, however, we speak of "revealed mysteries" as though revelation as such proposed riddles instead of solving them. It may do so incidentally, but not formally as revelation. A revealed mystery ceases to be a secret, so far as it is revealed. The answers to one question may of course raise another, and the revelation of one mystery may create another; but the end and purpose of revelation is to kill, not to create, mystery; to enable us at least to see through a glass darkly, not to hinder us from seeing face to face.

When the subject-matter is religious, when it relates to the other world, revelation means knowledge conveyed in a miraculous or at least supernatural or extraordinary manner. It is used in contradistinction to that knowledge of divine things which is acquired through reflection on the phenomena of nature, or on the laws and uniformities of movement and life and thought; from all that is sometimes called "Natural Theology." Proficiency in this latter depends on breadth of experience coupled with philosophical acumen; whereas the simplest and most ignorant may be the recipient of Revelation. If we speak of Science or of Nature as a Divine Revelation we use the word in a derived and improper sense.

So much may suffice for the verbal definition. It enables us at once to distinguish Revelation from "Natural Theology," from that knowledge of divine things which the mind, by its own labour and reflection, derives from the observed uniformities of man and of nature. But it also enables us to distinguish it from that "super-

natural" or "dogmatic" theology,—so called, not because it is any
less the work of natural reason than any other branch of philosophy,
but because Revelation and the data of Revelation constitute the
subject-matter of its reflection. Dogmatic Theology supposes Revelation; but the converse is not true. As a rule, religions begin with
revelation and end with doctrine or theology; just as art-theory and
criticism are the reflection of an uncreative period on the creations
of the Past. "Religion," says Stade, "is the sense (*Empfindung*) of,
and the converse with, superhuman beings. Only so far as this gives
birth to a social organisation and a constructive view of life does it
result in Doctrine. Even in those religions where this result obtains,
usages and institutions play a larger part in the religious life than
doctrine does." This sense of the superhuman world issuing in, or
inspiring, an imaginative construction of the same is something given
to man. His power of creation is as little self-earned as his power of
generation. His causal action in both cases is instrumental rather
than principal, and implies a maximum of passivity, a minimum of
deliberation and design. Theology, on the other hand, as the science
or systematic knowledge of the divine, i.e. of ultimate metaphysical
realities, is essentially a human elaboration of the most artificial
description, uncertain in proportion to its abstractness, and apprehensible only by a small minority of philosophical specialists. . . .

This religious faculty, then, is capable of a twofold instruction,
natural and supernatural, or acquired and revealed; and, in fact, the
lights from these two sources are always inextricably blended. It is
only by an effort of difficult abstraction that we can conjecture what
man's religious mind would be under only one or other of these
guidances. Analogous to the first rude efforts at physical science
there are, among the earliest types of humanity, childish strivings
after some sort of religious philosophy which are simply a product of
natural reason, of reflection on observation, and are in no sense
spontaneous creations of the religious spirit. On the other hand, there
are revelations in the true sense; picturings of the other world given
by, in, and along with religious experience, though expressed with all
the crudeness of those uncultured minds from which they spontaneously spring, and to whose compeers they are addressed. At this
stage, before "theology" has attained its proper abstract and conceptual form, and while it is yet largely imaginative and pictoral, it is
most difficult to distinguish it from revelation to which such con-
creteness is normal and perpetual. There is little or nothing in their

form to distinguish one of these systems of religious knowledge from the other. Yet the one is given to man without his labour; the other is deliberately wrought out by the exercise of his reason; the one is dependent only on moral action and disposition, the other only on mental ability.

With the development of theological abstraction comes another source of confusion of forms. For Revelation spontaneously clothes itself in whatever language it finds to its hand; and where the mind of the prophet is already largely instructed with theological categories and conceptions, these will largely mingle with and govern the images in which his vision seeks to embody itself. Thus, without being theology, revelation may be couched in theological terms, which it uses not for their proper and theological values, but for their illustrative and symbolic values.

It seems to me that a very analogous duality of knowledge obtains in other departments of life; that prior to any deliberate explanatory efforts, certain spontaneously suggested picturings or imaginings accompany all instinctive action. The child who neither understands nor yet wants to understand himself and his world does, nevertheless, possess an imaginative synthesis of the same, formed in and by the very process of living and moving and acting. Incoherent though it be, yet as the direct fruit of experience, of which it is the very shadow, the mental reaction, it serves the purpose of practical guidance even more successfully than do subsequent self-sought explanation and theory, which only too often impede the easy spontaneity of instinct. Similarly, it may be that a great deal of the earliest mythology is not the fruit of an after-effort to understand Life and Nature as presented immediately to experience, but is the very form in which that direct experience has written itself in the imagination. In the latter case it is a knowledge *given* to man in and along with the experience of which it is a part; and so far is analogous to Revelation and not to Theology, which is a self-acquired or self-wrought knowledge.

The same point might be illustrated by the difference between the spontaneous and the philosophical statements of the phenomenon of Moral Conscience. Prior to any intention of explaining that experience, men speak of Conscience as a voice, as something locally inside them, in their breast, their heart, their brain,—something that whispers to them, and says Stop! or as the voice of God or of the Holy Spirit, or of some Guardian Angel, or *daimonion,* or of the indwelling Christ, or of their own Better Self. They deal with Conscience so pictured, obeying it or disobeying it. And this dramatic symbolism possesses a most evident "working-truth," which is therefore guarantee for its possessing some kind of quite indefinable metaphysical and representative truth. It may be safely said that without this imaginative apprehension men could not deal with Conscience at all; that it is given to them in and along with the experience, and is a necessary instrument for the further control of that experience. Yet a moment's reflection tells us we are here not dealing with concepts but with images and figures; that we have something quite different from a psychological and metaphysical explanation of Conscience; that we are dealing with a passive impression, not with an active expression of truth.

If, however, Revelation belongs rather to the category of impressions than to that of expression, we should do ill to consider all religious truth of the former sort deserving of the name of Revelation. For that, it is not enough that the truth be *given* us, but it must be given in an extraordinary degree, and be of a "supernatural" kind. Else it might be most reasonably contended that revelation were a perfectly normal and universal phenomenon; which would be to use the word in a very reasonable, but yet an unusual and misleading sense. The art-faculty exists in some degree in all men, but in its creative degree it is the privilege of a very few; and the same holds true for the gift of revelation. When we say that the truth revealed is "supernatural," we mean that it is not of a kind simply postulated as necessary for the ordinary course of spiritual and religious development. The normal and universal experiences of the moral and mystical life embody themselves in images which constitute a revelation of God and the other world distinct from the theories of religious philosophy, yet which do not merit the name of "Supernatural Revelation," of Revelation in the usual sense. But it must be maintained that *natural* Revelation is presupposed to *supernatural,* just as every faculty is presupposed to its perfect formation or transformation. No heightening or exaltation of our understanding or free mental activity, however miraculous, could make it an organ of Revelation. For, there it is *always* and *necessarily* we ourselves who speak to ourselves; who (aided no doubt by the immanent God) work out truth for ourselves. Nothing could ever come from the understanding but theology or philosophy or science or systematic thought. Revelation, on the other hand, is a transforming and heightening, not of the active, but of that receptive part of our mind which evades our free control; and which we may compare to the sense of hearing. We listen, we do not speak; we receive, we do not give; we are shown something, we do not show.

Classifying Revelation and Theology as alike forms of religious knowledge, we are liable to fall into many fallacies by not attending carefully to their differences. For the word "knowledge" nearly always implies a representation resulting from reflection on the thing known—a predication about a subject—a judgment. The subject *as such* (though it may itself be a product of previous judgment) is there before us; it is something given. We reflect upon it, and compare it with certain possible representations of it, whose agreement with it we affirm or deny by the act of judgment. A whale might be represented by a fish. On reflection we judge it is not a fish. The subject *as such* is something presented, something impressed upon us, something of which we are aware or conscious. But till it is actively represented and expressed in the predicate we do not "know" it properly; we have not fitted it into that scheme of things which our understanding is ever elaborating, as an instrument by which we can control experience. We possess the material, but we have not yet built it into the fabric of our systematised thought. It is given to us, but we have not yet received and appropriated it.

"Knowledge," then, is used in a very different sense of experience and of reflection on experience, of presentation and of representation. It is used in an equally different sense of Revelation and of Theology. For Revelation is not so much a representation of something experienced, as one of the elements of a complex spiritual experience—an experience made up of feelings and impulses and imaginings; which reverberates in every corner of the soul and leaves its impress everywhere; in the mind no less than in the heart and will—just as the impulse and sentiment of Conscience entail a complementary impression on the mind which is part and parcel of the same experience. It would be misleading to regard that impression as a "representation" of the impulse and feelings, and to regard these latter as the exclusive substance and reality of experience, or as the "content" or significance of that so-called "representation." It is as much a part of the experience as they are; it is as directly "given" or "presented"; and in no wise the result of reflection upon them, or of an attempt to understand and classify them. On the contrary, it is, together with them, the subject matter of a subsequent act of reflection which strives to understand the whole complex experience in the interests of theology or philosophy.

From this it follows that we must not regard Revelation and Theology as two sorts of "representative" knowledge dealing with the same theme or subject-matter, the one treating it poetically and imaginatively, the other conceptually and scientifically. We must not regard it as the function of the latter to translate poetry into prose; to substitute exact concepts for loose metaphors. Revelation is itself a part of that concrete "presented" reality which is the subject-matter of theological reflection; it is an element of the "experience" to be explained and digested.

The contrary supposition is accounted for by the fact that whereas the affective and volitional elements of the religious experience are evanescent, the mental or imaginative element abides in memory and survives as the representation of the total experience. I cannot repeat the whole experience at will, but I can voluntarily recall the impression which it made on my imagination. This remembered impression very naturally arrogates to itself the name of Revelation which strictly should stand for the total original experience, and not for the memory of a part of it. Whence it comes that we easily regard this memory of its mental element as "representative" of the remaining elements. Yet this memory only "represents" the past mental impression, which impression was as much part of the direct experience as the other elements. It did not represent those elements, but they, with it, correspond to and so far "represent" the hidden causes of the total experience. For effects are in some sense "representative" of their causes, though not by way of similitude or likeness, or as a predicate "represents" its subject.

The theologian therefore looks, or should look, upon revelation as a part of religious experience, by means of which he can, to some extent, reconstruct the whole of that experience (as an object may be reconstructed from its shadow, or an extinct species of animal from its vestiges). Viewing that total experience as an effect, he then endeavours to divine the nature of its causes and to draw certain theological and metaphysical conclusions.

Thus revelation is simply his subject-matter, the experience on which his science is founded, and which it endeavours to understand and explain. It is not a co-ordinate system of knowledge related to the same subject matter, and treating it merely in another way (i.e. imaginatively rather than conceptually; less rather than more accurately).

Against the possibility of a justifiable collision between Revelation and theological or scientific thought it is usually alleged that God, who is the Author of every sort of truth, cannot contradict Himself. This is commonly understood as though God spoke the same truths, made the same statements, with two different voices, or in two different languages—supernaturally through revelation, naturally through the instrumentality of man's reason. Plainly there is something at first sight redundant and superfluous in this notion, something discordant with Divine methods of harmonious and orderly dispensation. But this impression vanishes when we recognise that Revelation is not statement but experience. "Truth" is used differently of experience and of judgment about experience; and therefore the principle in question is that which all admit, namely, that no theory is true which contradicts experience.

It is very important to remember that, strictly speaking, Revelation consists in the total religious experience and not simply in the mental element of that experience; which is to the rest as those strange images of the nature and cause of a pain are to the pain which they so often accompany and which are so unlike its rational explanation. . . . When, therefore, God reveals Himself to the spirit in an extraordinary way and degree, it is in the total experience that we are to look for the revelation and not merely in the mental element. In this total experience He is revealed, not as a fact is revealed by a statement, but as a cause is revealed in its effect. He suddenly draws near to the soul and fills her with Himself to overflowing, flooding each spiritual faculty with His own Spirit, and thereby working at times strange transformations even in the very senses and the bodily organism. Revelation is not a statement, but a "showing." God speaks by deeds, not by words. The same shock which gives fire to the heart and impulse to the will, fills the mind with some interpretative image of the agency at work—much as the sound of a footfall evokes the image of a pedestrian; or as any sound suggests an idea of its source and meaning.

The nature of the mental element of Revelation may be illustrated roughly by the immediate effect of a thunderstorm on the mind. Whether for savage or savant the external sense-impressions are appropriately the same—blinding flashes, awe-inspiring peals of

thunder, darkness, torrential rain, and so forth. But the impression
on the imagination differs considerably according to their several
mental habits. In the savage there rises at once the image of the
angry storm-god; in the savant nothing is evoked but the idea of a
thunderstorm. In neither case is the mental reaction the result of
deliberate explanatory reflection. It is as immediate an automatic
response to the external stimuli as is that of the eye or ear. Only,
whereas eye and ear are about equally developed in both, the mind is
unequally developed and therefore reacts differently. But this automatic mental reaction is as much part of the experience as is the
sense of light and sound; it is part of the subject-matter of subsequent reflection. The savage has heard his god thundering; the savant
has witnessed a thunderstorm—not merely lightning and thunder-
peals, but all that he automatically infers or co-apprehends as connected therewith. Now though one would not accept the savage's
account of what had happened as possessing the slightest scientific or
explanatory value, one could gather from it what had really happened
just as well as from the savant's soberer and less pictorial statement.
It is valuable as a record, not as an explanation, of experience. From
the impression made on that simple mind we can divine what really
happened; as we so often do from the accounts that children give us
of what has befallen them. If they have seen an animal with a tail at
each end, we know it was an elephant.

Equally abundant illustration might be drawn from the various
mental images and categories in which the passion of love embodies
and records itself in differently cultured minds. In all cases the non-
mental element of the experience is practically the same, but the
inspired mental expressions are different. From these latter one
would not seek a philosophy of love, but one might take them as part
and parcel of the experience, which would constitute the subject-
matter of such a philosophy. Amongst the phenomena of love, almost
the chief would be the various forms of its spontaneous mental self-
expression.

It is plain, then, that there is a generic difference between Revelational and Theological truth, and that they cannot be compared as
two statements—poetic and scientific—of the same fact. "Prophetic"
truth cannot be used, as statements can be used from which we may
deduce other statements. Revelation is a showing on the part of God,
a seeing on the part of the receiver. Prophecy is but the communication of this vision to others. Theology must take prophecy not as a

statement, but as experience; must try to understand it as a religious
phenomenon, and use it as factual not as verbal evidence for its
conceptual constructions of the supernatural order.

If, then, we say there is a theology implicit in Revelation, it is not
as one statement is implicit in another, but as theory is implicit in
experience, and as a conclusion is implied in the evidential facts that
support it.

Thus, certain religious experiences have filled the prophetic imagination with images of the power, majesty, and transcendence of God;
others have evoked images of His tenderness, His mercy, His nearness, His Fatherhood. To St. Peter Christ is suddenly brought home
with a realisation embodied in the idea of "the Messias, the Son of
the living God." To the author of the Fourth Gospel He appears as
the Eternal Logos. To St. Paul He is the Second or Heavenly and
Spiritual Adam. In each case the mental reaction to the same shock
of religious experience is somewhat different. These conceptions, as
revealed, have no direct theological value; they are but part of the
experience whose character they help to determine. It is that experience, taken as concrete fact and reality, which forms the subject-
matter of theological explanation. In each case the theologian will
observe that Christ arrogates to Himself the highest categories with
which the mind happens to be equipped for the glorification of a
human being—Messias, Son of God, Archetypal Humanity, Eternal
Word. To still later Christian experience He becomes co-equal, consubstantial with the Father, thanks to a current theology which finds
such exaltation conceivable and consistent with His perfect manhood.
But from first to last the experience dealt with, the truth revealed, is
practically the same. It is because men have felt and experienced
Christ to be their God, their Saviour, their Spiritual Bread, their Life,
their Way, their Truth, that they have apprehended Him under these
forms and images, of which some are more apt than others to satisfy
the soul's need of giving utterance to its fulness.

If there is a certain contingency about the forms and images which
make part of these supernatural religious experiences, it is none the
less true that for the recipient they possess a divine authority as given
along with the other parts of the same experience and proceeding
from the same source. In this they differ from all subsequent and
voluntary representations of the event. Speaking of divine illumination in general, Ignatius Loyola bids us carefully discriminate between
just what was given to us and what our subsequent reflection has

added, and to beware of giving to the latter the authority of the former. Plainly it is of the utmost importance, for the future practical and theological use of the experience, that its natural self-expression should be retained pure and intact as something sacred. What Charles Lamb says of the creative artist's revelation has its place here. The prophet, like the artist, feels no liberty to tamper with or improve upon what has been shown him. He must be as true to it as the historian is to his facts. Dante did not *make* his visions; he *saw* them, and could no more see otherwise than had they been the common objects of bodily sense. . . .

Some sense of this tyrannical necessity of fact lies at the bottom of the sacredness with which Christianity had guarded the apostolic revelation from any sort of modification or development, and has made novelty synonymous with heresy. Instinctively the Church has felt that its truth is not the truth of theological statement, but that of fact and experience. It is the vestige, the imaginative impress which Christ made on the mentality of an age that had known and seen and touched Him; that had, through Him, been brought face to face with God, and had been filled to overflowing with the Divine Spirit. In that impression we still hold one element of that great collective religious experience. From it we can judge of the nature of the other elements, aided, moreover, by some measure of like experience within ourselves—much as a man in love will to some extent rightly interpret the self-utterances of some heroic and classical lover, even though his own passion falls short of that standard in strength and purity. Having the spirit of Christ in ourselves, we so far understand its classical self-utterance as given us in the apostolic revelation.

It is then a patent fallacy to speak of a "development" of rev-elation as though it were a body of statements or theological propositions.

We must, however, hold that a revelation is a perennial phenome-non which obtains in every soul that is religiously alive and active. As the Spirit did not cease with the apostles, so neither did revelation and prophecy. But a peculiar character rightly attaches to that which was the effect of immediate contact with Christ, and of the Spirit as it was breathed forth from his very lips. This has rightly been regarded as alone classical and normative, as the test by which all spirits and revelations in the Church are to be tried. As a fountain cannot rise above its source, so neither can the waves that circle out from that central and original disturbance excel or even equal it in intensity.

The revelations of later ages are to those of the apostolic age as the studies of followers to the works of a Great Master. With it they do not build up a logical system or whole; they may integrate it as different, though lesser, manifestations of the same spirit; they may resolve it as light is resolved by a prism into its multiple virtualities, but they do not complete it organically or develop it.

Whatever advance there may be, and undoubtedly is, in theological reflection and analysis, there is no advance in revelation. That supernatural Light shone as brightly (in some ways more brightly) in the apostolic age as in any after age, even as charity burned as warmly then as ever. For the two are correlative and proportional. If we allow that Life was lived in its fulness and purity in the earliest age, we cannot maintain that to a later was reserved the privilege of a clearer and wider illumination. Theological advance may be a gain for the understanding, but it is not directly a gain for the heart. At best it adds to the protection and preservation of Revelation in its original form and purity. Even the dogmatic decisions of the Church add nothing to, but only reassert the apostolic revelation. Their sole "faith-content" is that part of it of which they are protective. The Church but declares what the Apostles declared, and that was not theology. Dogmatic decisions are neither theological nor revelational in value, but merely protective of revelation. They no more form a dialectically developed system than do the patches and props and buttresses by which some ancient fortress has been repaired from time to time according as it had been assailed and battered from one side or another in this way or in that. The logical unity of creeds is the more or less forced result of after-arrangement. Heresies do not arise according to any logical plan of succession.

The notion of some sort of development of Revelation is possible only so long as we really confound theology and revelation. Undoubtedly these two utterly heterogeneous kinds of religious knowledge have been tangled together into one hybrid system by taking the language of revelation according to its theological values, and making it a divinely authorised basis for deduction. Theology has not taken that inspired utterance as but part of a revealing experience, which in its totality demands a philosophical explanation, and is but the subject-matter of theological reflection. It has rather treated this utterance as an inchoate theology, metaphorically and loosely expressed, which must be translated into precise terminology and then dialectically expanded. It has not recognised that the theo-

logical terms in which revelation incidentally expresses itself are not
the expression of theological effort and thought, but of a massive
spiritual experience; that they are used for their illustrative, not for
their theological value; that their theological value is in no wise
divinely authorised by such illustrative use. . . .

From its very nature Revelation admits of development as little as
does poetry or art, and for much the same reason. For in man it is,
after all, only the mind and the intellect that develop in any apprecia-
ble sense by the steady accumulation of experience and information
and by the continual effort to understand and systematise that experience for the guidance of life, thought, speech and action. But the
great driving-forces of life—the passions, affections, emotions—are
as constant as the structure of man's bodily frame and as his organs
of sensation or locomotion—constant at least in the variety and irregularity of their distribution. Here we find no sort of systematic
progress and development. Faith, Hope, Desire, Fear, Love—human
and divine—these are to be found sporadically in their highest intensity at any time in history, at any stage of mental development. It is
not in these driving-forces but in the direction which the mind gives
to them, that we are to look for development. There is no progress in
goodness, i.e. in the *love* of what is right; but only in ethics, i.e. in the
understanding of what is right. There is no progress in religion, i.e. in
the spirit of Faith, Hope and Charity; but only in theology, i.e. in the
understanding of things divine. Can it be maintained that for all our
clearer understanding, religious feeling has ever risen higher than in
some of the Psalms or in Deutero-Isaiah? or that for all the ethical
refinement that separates us from savagery and barbarism, there has
been a proportional advance on the moral heroism of the past? Has
poetry developed since Homer, or Dante, or Shakespeare? Has passion grown in depth and purity with the succession of centuries? All
we can say is that the mysticism, the heroism, the inspiration of those
creative spirits would have found in our time a fuller, more flexible,
more intelligent medium of self-expression; that the forces would
have been more skilfully, less wastefully, directed. Revelation stands
in this respect on the same level as those great creations of art and
poetry which are but the natural self-expression of that passionate
experience which they embody imaginatively—as natural as a cry, or
a sob, or a groan, which signify but do not state; whose truth is not
that of statement. Such creations would be of no greater artistic truth
had they been embodied in the terms and images of a more delicate

and highly developed culture. Nay, the ruder and less pliant the medium, the stronger and greater does the inspiration seem which could mould it like wax to its purpose. Revelation, the natural self-expression of a divine afflatus, is as the record of itself made by a passing hurricane in the wrack and ruin which it leaves in its wake. The nature of that record varies according to what lies in the track of the tempest; but whether it be written in the heaped and furrowed sands of the desert, or in the uprooted trunks, torn limbs and scattered foliage of the forest, or in the bared roof-trees, levelled walls and fallen towers of the wind-swept city, its lesson is equally legible as a revelation of the strength and direction of a mighty spirit that has passed by. Had Christ come in another age to another people, the Gospel, written in different words and deeds, had been still the same Gospel, the record of the same Power and Spirit, albeit in conflict with another class of oppositions and obstructions.

Hence, though it is preposterous for a science and, therefore, for Theology to be under the bondage of the past, and to look to its first crude essays as normative and canonical, there is no such unreasonableness in requiring art or literature to look to the great creations of former times for their inspiration and guidance; and for the same reason there is no obscurantism in holding that a revelation two thousand years old may be a standard and test for all future time. When it is a question of Christian theology or ecclesiastical institutions, which are the work of human reflection and ingenuity, the appeal to the criterion of primitive times is treason against the laws of progress. Not so when it is a question of the Christian spirit and of the Revelation in which it is embodied; for these lie outside the realm of progress and admit of no quasi-organic development. . . .

In the hagiography, in the mystical and ascetical writers of the Church, we have a vast store of materials for a scientific religious psychology, which is as yet only in its infancy. The form in which it is perpetuated for us is utterly unscientific. We have a tangle of contradictory maxims and apothegms—contradictory only because the same facts have clothed themselves in irreconcilably different figures and metaphors in different minds—have evoked different reactions. To accept these artless utterances as reflex statements, to try to reconcile them, to argue a system from them, is to forget that their whole evidential value is that of natural effects. The psychologist has to ask himself first, What were the experiences that presented themselves in this guise to unscientific simple minds? And then, What do these

experiences signify for science? Similarly, the theologian should ask,
What are the experiences expressed in revealed utterances, and what
do those experiences signify for theology?

Were it merely a question of translating metaphorical into exact
language, the result would be to void theology of all but relative
value. For when a truth is known only through a metaphor, when we
have no means of comparing the metaphor with the reality or of
defining the limits of likeness and unlikeness, every attempt to get at
the hinted truth is mere guesswork. Viewed, however, as spiritual
phenomenon, revelation, however difficult to explain, does admit of
theological explanation. Theology, like every other science, is in quest
of a truth involved in facts, a truth that is one and one only. As the
guardian of all religious interests, the Church is also the natural
guardian of theology—of the religious interests of the intellect. And
this all the more because, owing to the common confusion of theology with revelation, the statements of the former may easily seem
hostile to the supposed "statements" of the latter. Here her protective instinct rouses her to hurl defiance at even the most cogent
theological reasoning as long as it seems to endanger the supernatural truth of revelation. Still, her guardianship of theology is of a
wholly different character to that which she exercises over revelation, and is dependent on and conditioned by it. She has no gift of
scientific or theological inerrancy. She is inerrant, as instinct is inerrant, in her sense and affirmation of what is revealed and of what
imperils revelation, but by no means in her theological assertions
regarded as theological. She knows and feels the impression they
make, it is this impression which she approves or disapproves. What
is perfectly true may create a false impression; what is perfectly false
may create a true impression. Relatively to a certain mentality the
greater truth may be the greater lie. The denial of geocentrism may
for a certain age mean the denial of religion. In this way she has
interfered, and will always interfere, with theological liberty; just as
she interferes with external and profane interests for like motives. In
both cases she may err, and has erred in theology, in science, in
practical prudence, but not in her instinct of self-preservation. She
has been at once right and wrong—right in her own department,
wrong in her neighbours'. To expect anything else would be to expect
a dispensation of continual miracles. All interests in life elbow and
jostle one another in a struggle that makes for an ideal of harmony
ever approached, never attained. In the long run injustices and

violences are requited, and those who sin eventually suffer—be the sinner Church or State, Theology or Science.

It is naturally to doctors as a class that we look for the development of medical science, though there is no monopoly that would exclude others from the same pursuit; and similarly it is mainly, but by no means exclusively, to the clergy that we look for the development of theology, i.e. of the science of their profession. But we cannot regard this as part of the Church's divine mission, which is simply prophetic and practical. The Apostles were sent not to teach theology, but to preach the Gospel. It were, however, a monstrous interference to conclude that the Church should sit by indifferent as to whether her children were taught pantheism or deism or atheism.

4

Faith, Development,
and Theology

If in earlier times each generation witnessed some sort of quarrel between theology and speculation; to-day, owing to the rate of scientific and historical advance, we have a more wholesale problem to cope with; we witness more change in a decade than many a century has seen in the past. Reflection, once underfed by experience, is now surfeited beyond its powers of healthy digestion.

Nothing has more contributed to this surfeiting in our own day than the application, by way of analogy, of the theory of biological evolution to the spiritual or rational life of a man. The science of evolution has suggested the evolution of science, of language, of art, of religion, of theology, of social and political institutions. All are now viewed dynamically, as processes. It is the law of their growth that matters, not the analysis or definition of their present stage of expansion. A "scientific" knowledge no longer means a mere understanding of connected origins and developments; it means tracing all life back to the first perceptible microscopic germ in which it becomes visible out of the darkness of the unknowable.

The notion that religions, creeds, and beliefs, like everything else, are growths, conflicts rudely with their all but universal claim to a

*From George Tyrrell, *Through Scylla and Charybdis* (1907), 108–18, 120–21, 135–37, 153–54.

miraculously supernatural origin through divine revelation; it conflicts with "the old supposition as to the fixity of theology"—"a fixed theology viewed as final, with no thought either of its sources or of its possible future modifications."[1]

Between the claims of such a theology to dictate to science, and those of science to dictate theology, Mr. Ward, a true disciple of Newman, hopes to find some *via media.*

"To believe then in the Christian revelation," he writes,[2] "and to believe that it is a salutary check on the anti-theological extravagances of the men of science, and yet to believe in the methods of modern science and criticism and to see in them a salutary check to the excursions of theologians beyond their province—is not this a tenable *via media?*"

We are to believe in the fact of a divine revelation, an abrupt extra-natural intervention analogous to those which presumably bridge over the gulfs dividing dead matter from living; senseless from sentient life; and this, from human life. This fact of revelation, duly proved of course, the scientist must accept as one of the data of his problem, not to be ignored on account of *a priori* difficulty.

But with the scientists, we are able to believe that theology is a growth governed by the usual laws of mental development—a development of the formless theology of the first followers of Christ; that it is *semper eadem* only in substance, not in form; and that the function of the sane, as opposed to the extravagant theologian who would paint St. Peter with a tiara, is to criticize these developments by the original rule of faith, to reject such as are spurious; to approve, foster, and elaborate such as are legitimate. The result would be a theology encumbered by no greater scientific difficulty than is involved in the admission of the initial miraculous intervention by which Christianity was created.

Now Mr. Ward contends "that there is abundant room already provided by acknowledged theological principles" for such developments in Scholastic theology as an assimilation or at least a toleration of the results and methods of modern science would demand. "The fault in the more conservative theologians has been (if my contention is true) that they have not seen the full capabilities of their own principles, but have identified their utmost reach with the very lim-

1. Wilfrid Ward, *Problems and Persons* (1903), xi.—J. L.
2. Ibid., 102.—J. L.

ited application of them which past circumstances have demanded."3
He recurs several times to the Church's assimilation of the once
dreaded Aristotelianism as a crucial instance among many proving
that practically or by implication the Church has admitted the principle of development before it ever reached distinct formulation. He
can even find such a formulation of it as might reasonably be looked
for in that age, in the *Commonitorium* of Vincent of Lerins, side by
side with and qualifying the *quod semper, quod ubique, quod ab
omnibus.*

The prominence and growing credit which Newman's great name
has of late years given to the principle of doctrinal development
makes it important in the interests of truth to subject to a searching
and perfectly detached criticism this suggested possibility of finding
in it a *via media* between two extremes (or extravagances) of theological intransigence and scientific absolutism—between the Scylla of
the old theology and the Charybdis of the new. Should any one, in
consequence, see reason to suspend his judgment for the present, he
will not thereby commit himself to either extreme in hesitating to
trust himself to the path indicated. He may believe that there is a *via
media,* yet question whether he has really found it, or defined its
exact course.

The test of a middle position, which takes something from both
extremes, is whether these elements naturally attract and integrate
one another, blending in some higher combination; whether they are
not as oil and water violently shaken together to separate instantly as
soon as the vessel is at rest. Can it be shown that there is any *via
media* to be looked for through the doctrine of development (common to science and theology), which shall not be a syncretion of
incompatible principles in virtue of one of which we should, in all
consistence, go to the extreme right; and in virtue of the other, to the
extreme left; which shall give us rest otherwise than on a rack, that at
one and the same time drags us with equal stress in opposite
direction?

We must see, then, whether what seems an excess of conservatism
on the part of scholastic theology, be really separable from that measure of conservatism which we must justify; and similarly whether the
excesses of liberal or purely critical theology can be pruned away
without fatal results to its governing principles and methods.

3. Ibid., xviii.—J. L.

Let us then briefly compare or contrast the two systems, and see whether they can in any way be reconciled and "come to terms"; whether by way of amalgamation, or by the absorption of one by the other, or by some amicable *modus vivendi*.

Scholastic theology occupies itself about the "deposit of faith" as its principal object. By this it understands a certain body of divine knowledge revealed supernaturally to the Apostles and delivered to them under the form of certain categories, ideas, and images, to their immediate successors. This formulated revelation is the *depositum fidei*. It was not as though the tabernacle doors of the heavens, thrown open to the Apostles, were to remain so forever. What the Apostles saw they recorded and formulated. To their followers they transmitted the record; not the privilege of direct vision. Although many of the truths of the Christian faith are coincident with those of "Natural Religion," or even sacred History, yet both on account of their organic connection with those principal mysteries (the Trinity and the Incarnation) which lie altogether beyond reason, and on account of the manner in which they are communicated to us, they may be considered as organic parts of one and the same supernatural revelation. Here, on the very threshold of our inquiry, we encounter a radical and I think irreconcilable difference between scholastic and liberal theology—between the old and the new. For the realities dealt with are, in the case of the former confessedly *beyond,* and in that of the latter *within* the experience of all men. The teachings of the latter can, those of the former cannot, be brought directly to the test of experience, of comparison between ideas and things. If the heavens, once opened to the Apostles, remained open for every baptized Christian; if the same revelation, and not merely the record of that revelation, were given to each of us as to them, then we should need no *depositum fidei,* no divinely authorized standard of expression; we should be comparatively indifferent to the efforts of past ages to formulate that vision; they would be to us as men's first savage attempts to formulate Nature—the earlier the worse. But it is rather as though centuries ago men had been struck blind and partially paralyzed, and as if our knowledge of nature depended on what was handed down to us from the date of that calamity. How carefully we should have to treasure up the mental forms of that precious tradition and see that the fluctuations of language did not lead us to misinterpret the experience-values of its original terms! That which is *semper idem,* constantly the same under all developments and accretions, is in the case of scholastic theology a doctrine, a record of an experience gone, never to be repeated, preserved for us only in and through that doctrine. Just because that experience cannot be repeated, it is all important to preserve, if not the exact words, yet the exact sense and meaning which the record had for the minds of those to whom it was first delivered by the Apostles; to represent to ourselves just what it represented to them. Thus the ideas, categories, and symbols which constitute this representation are of the very substance of the *depositum fidei;* if there is a contingent and accidental element it must be looked for merely in the language, in the verbal signs that stand for these ideas.

The "constant," the *semper idem* of liberal theology, on the other hand, is the reality dealt with, and not any doctrine, or representation of that reality. It deals with those ever-present evidences of God in Nature and in the universal religious experiences of mankind which are accessible to all, at all times, and by which all theories and doctrines as to the origin, nature, and end of these experiences can be experimentally tested. Taking "Nature" in the most comprehensive sense, liberal theology is a branch of the science of Nature. It is the old "Natural Theology" enriched and improved by an application of the inductive historical and experimental method to the religions of mankind. Nature is always there to be studied and formulated, and is not given us only by tradition from a privileged past generation. Tradition and co-operation are indeed requisite for the development of a science of Nature, but not for the preservation of its object. Our interest in the crude science of the remote past is not reverential but historical; we test present results not by their agreement with that primitive science, but by their agreement with Nature.

From this radical difference in the ultimate objects of their study— in the one case a certain class of natural experiences; in the other, a record of past supernatural experiences—flows another affecting the manner of growth and development in liberal and in scholastic theology severally.

In the study of Nature (or of any particular department of natural experience, like that of natural religion), so far as that study is one and continuous through long tradition and wide co-operation (so far, namely, as it is virtually the work of a permanent society and represents the growth of its collective mind), we expect to find and do find a true development of doctrine, following analogously and *mutatis mutandis* the laws of biological development. The first conceptions and generalisations are childlike, and naively anthropomorphic; and between these and the latest scientific advances there is a certain thread of continuity—not merely that of historic succession; nor that of reference to the same object of reality, but that of a growing truthfulness, a diminishing inadequacy. The earliest is to the latest as is the germ to the more or less developed organism; this has grown out of that; that has grown into this. Now, though stages of the same process, the germ and the organism are not the same thing: a hen is not an egg; is not even the chicken that was, except so far as we recognise there some absolute unchanged, undeveloped identity of soul or consciousness. What is there thus identical in the sapling of a century ago and the oak of to-day? Neither stuff or fashion. Each stage of development dies into the next; ceases in favour of the next. Our science is "the same" as that of our ancestors only by descent and as part of the same growth of the collective mind. Thus in the department of natural religion it is not hard to trace the roads by which religious reason has often passed, in its conceptions of divinity, from grossly anthropomorphic polytheism, to the purest monotheism. Yet these doctrines are in no plain sense "the same"; they are doctrines about the same thing, but they are not the same doctrine; the latter does not contain the former as a constant nucleus amid explanatory or decorative accretions, but simply supplants and discards it. The former persists as little as the caterpillar does in the butterfly—which is not merely a winged caterpillar.

When liberal theology speaks of doctrinal or scientific development it is always in this sense. As Judaism had to die into the Gospel and be abolished, so, it conceives, the theology of one age must always be supplanted by that of the next. It looks back on its own past as a man does on his childhood—not with contempt or severity, but as on something that had to be gone through and left behind for the sake of the present, much as Chemistry, Physiology or Biology look back with a sort of dilettante curiosity to their conjectural origins in the darkness of the past.

But this comparative indifference to the doctrinal forms and categories of the past is out of the question in the case of Scholastic theology, whose principal subject-matter is the record of an ancient and never-to-be-repeated revelation of supernatural and inaccessible realities—realities, therefore, which cannot be consulted in order to determine the precise sense of that record, the precise degree of its inadequacies; for they are known to us only representatively; only in and through that record. To speak of the hidden realities as the "substance," and of the record as the "form" of revelation, is misleading if it is meant to imply that we can in some degree be indifferent to the latter, if only we hold the former. This is true for liberal theology, which can get at its object directly; not for Scholastic theology, which can only get at the representation or record of its object.

It follows at once that it is a matter of life and death for Scholastic theology, *custodire depositum,* to hold fast to its primitive record, if not to the very words, at least to the very ideas, symbols, and categories, in which the Christian revelation has been given to it. Inadequate though the representation of eternity in the language of time must necessarily be, yet we have no means of comparing it with its original, of defining the limits of inadequacy, of sundering substantials from accidentals.

As experience is the criterion to which the liberal theologian brings all developments, so this original deposit of faith is necessarily the supreme criterion of Scholastic theology. Its fruitfulness for knowledge depends, not on its dying and being changed into something else; but on its being preserved fixed and unchangeable. Round it, and concerning it, a vast body of doctrine has gathered through the prolonged collective labour of Catholic thought. But in virtue of this unchanged nucleus, Catholic doctrine may be rightly considered *semper eadem,* just as in virtue of a persistently identical soul or self-consciousness, the man and the babe (as St. Vincent of Lerins says) are "the same," notwithstanding the gradual supplanting of the infant by the adult organism. There is something there that does not develop. We might roughly compare it to the growth of archaeological lore about some such monument as the Moabite Stone: a growth partly in the interpretation of the sense of the inscription, and partly in the adjustment of history to such data as it can be considered to establish. So, too, Catholic doctrine grows in the measure that Catholic thought busies itself about the meaning of the deposit of faith and its bearing on other departments of knowledge; about its "explication" and its "application." By its "explication" is to be understood that process of analysis by which what is from the first actually, albeit confusedly, contained within the limits of the deposit of faith, becomes more distinctly and explicitly recognised, through inferences drawn from revealed data, or owing to a growth in perspicacity on the part of the reflecting mind whose, as it were, microscopic power is increased by general cultivation. And by "applications" scholastics mean inferences drawn from the combination of revealed with unrevealed premises; and other adjustments of secular to sacred knowledge. . . .

If we then speak of this body of doctrine, of explications and applications, which has gathered round the unchanging deposit of faith as a "development," it is not in the quasi-biological sense in which liberal theology uses the term; for it is only the protective husk, the clothing of the deposit which has grown; the kernel, that which is protected and clothed, remained unaltered. The contrast is like that between the simple breadbreaking at table in the bald surroundings of some early-Christian home and the solemnities of High Mass at St. Peter's. The nucleus remains, untransformed and undeveloped, in the changeless words of consecration. Nor are all the tomes of eucharistic theology and controversy otherwise related to the simple primitive sense of those words.

But though the logical development of this accumulating body of deductions is largely the work of theological inquiry and reflection applied to the deposit of faith in its relation to the rest of knowledge, yet the justice of such developments is ultimately determined, not as in the case of liberal theology by the fallible rule of theological reasoning or of the consensus of experts; but by the infallible criterion of the Church's authority—a criterion as manifestly supernatural as is the deposit of faith itself. On no other condition indeed could the benefit of a revealed theology, final and universally valid, be secured to all generations to the end of the world against the obliterating influences of time and change.

Hence the old theology consistently teaches that the value of such infallible decisions is not causally dependent on the theological reasonings on which they are based, and by which they are occasioned; that they are in some sense prophetic, "oracular," from above. The accumulation of such decisions means necessarily a narrowing of liberty of thought by a further determination of truth, just as any growth of legislation means a narrowing of liberty of action by a further determination of right. It means bringing an increasing number of philosophical and historical positions, with all their implications, under the rule of sacred doctrine; it means an ever-increasing tension between conservative theology and free thought. . . .

I [have] ventured to suggest that the attempt to find a solution of the dilemma in the principle of development of ideas was in many ways unsatisfactory; that the principle was all-dominating in the case of liberal theology; that it was dominated and brought under that of authority in the case of Catholic theology. There it was a wild horse in the prairies; here a tram-horse in harness moving up and down within fixed limits along fixed lines; there it was mistress; here it was but a handmaid; an *ancilla theologia.* And the root of this difference I assigned to the fact that liberal theology, like natural science, has for its subject matter a certain ever-present department of human experience which it endeavours progressively to formulate and understand, and which is ever at hand to furnish a criterion of the success of such endeavours; whereas our school-divinity finds its subject-matter in the record or register of certain past experiences that cannot be repeated and are known to us only through such a record. In the former case our knowledge progresses not merely (as in the latter) in virtue of mental labour and reflection brought to bear on an unchanging *datum,* but in virtue of an ever new supply of experience, presenting us with ever new aspects and parts of the subject matter. Our first naive formulations and categories soon prove too tight and narrow for our accumulating experience, and after a certain amount of stretching and adaptation they burst altogether, and more comprehensive conceptions take their place. These we criticise not by their correspondence to the abandoned forms, whose interest is henceforth merely historical, but by their adequacy to the newly revealed matter. We do not ask if Copernican be true to Ptolemaic astronomy, but if it be true to experience. Nor does the liberal theologian ask or care that his theology be substantially identical with that of the past, but only that it be truer to experience than that which it supersedes. The new contains the old, not as an unchanged nucleus with additions, not as three contains two; but only as Copernicus contains Ptolemy; as a new hypothesis is said loosely and inaccurately to contain the old, because it explains the same facts and experiences, albeit in a totally different synthesis. . . .

Ultimately the question resolves itself into this: Does thought grow architecturally or biologically? If the former, then the problem arises: Does the "deposit of faith" and do the infallible definitions of the Church, bind us absolutely to the proper values of the categories and thought-forms of the age in which they were framed? That they do, would seem to be indicated by the ceaseless polemic aforesaid between theology and profane philosophy, science, and history consequent on the indirect jurisdiction which the Church claims over the whole realm of man's thought—a claim which would be unnecessary did she hold these categories to be of but a relative and symbolic value which they could retain irrespective of the fluctuations of thought, and did she not treat them as finally assured, not as amendable results. If, as it seems, we are bound to them as of absolute value, as finally true for philosophy, science, and history, then we have a new brood of problems, for we must show that those of different ages are consistent with one another, and that those of all the ages together are still valid and furnish collectively a rule by which modern thought should be corrected. That is the difficulty on one side. On the other, if we deny that past forms are to be the criterion of present, and if we stand by all the implications of that denial, we not only contradict tradition in substantial point, but we shall find it hard in many ways to erect a secure barrier against liberal theology. . . .

These articles do not pretend to contribute directly towards a solution of the problem in question; but only indirectly, that is, by endeavouring to clear the issue as much as possible, to indicate the precise lie of Scylla on one side and Charybdis on the other.

LETTER TO WILFRID WARD*

December 11th, 1903

My Dear Ward,

A last word as to Newmanism. You say his "principles" will never die; I say his "spirit." I fancy these are but two aspects of the same thing; that "spirit" lays a little more emphasis on the moral tone and temper; whereas "principle" emphasises the corresponding mentality. If we differ substantially, it is that, while I agree with you that Newman's prophetic insight foresaw *in the vague* the intellectual revolution which is now upon us and with which e.g. Loisy is, I think vainly, trying to cope; he did not and could not have anticipated and prepared for the precise problem which is now presented to us, and which I try to state as definitely as possible in my coming article.

· Apart from the purely *ad hominem* and *anti-Anglican* values of the "Essay on Development," it was a great service to show clearly, as he did, that the Church had practically and implicitly (and to some

*From M. D. Petre, *Autobiography and Life of George Tyrrell* (1912), 2: 215–18.

extent explicitly) acknowledged that same principle of development which is the dominating category of modern science and philosophy; and that she had in the same measure repudiated the rigid *semper eadem* conservatism of the Eastern Churches and of the high Anglicans; and was, so far, more liberal, more progressive than they.

But then (and this takes me to my article)[1] the Church, as J. H. N. would be the first to acknowledge, has no intention of being dominated by this development category; she adopts it only as an *ancilla theologiae;* it is like a wild horse caught in the prairies and put to work on tram-lines, in blinkers, up and down, down and up. In the present instance the tram-lines, the blinkers are the presupposed facts of a miraculous revelation and of a no less miraculous magisterium, by which the workings of development are limited and infallibly corrected.

The Church has "adopted" development, just as she adopted Aristotelianism, i.e. she has enslaved it. The alternative would be for her to be enslaved by it; to submit her presuppositions to be criticised by it, i.e. to be accounted for and explained away as by Harnack and Co.

Development is common to the Church and to modern thought, as wood is common to a table and a tree; or rather, as growth is common to wall fruit and wild fruit-trees. Neither (the Church or Modern Thought) can absorb without destroying the other; neither can yield to the other without suicide. I do not speak of graver conclusions and details, but of the vital principles of the two systems.

Hence in my article I have laid them side by side like two snakes eyeing one another. Amalgamation in some larger synthesis that is neither, is difficult to believe in. All that I dare suggest in the *Month* is the pacific *modus vivendi* at which you hint once or twice, *sc.* diversity need not mean hostility. Let them move each in its own plane, by its own laws; let us all acknowledge the professedly *ex hypothesi* and abstract character of a philosophy which but works out the necessary consequences of certain questionable presuppositions and exclusions; and let us not fear to see how far Christianity fits into such an artificial synthesis and how much of it stands after the miraculous has been excluded (as in "Lex Orandi"). This is all I have committed you to, though I know you mean more and at least hope for, if you do not see your way to, a synthesis.

What is my own hope?

1. "Lex Orandi, Lex Credendi."—J. L.

Throughout the article I speak advisedly *not* of Catholicism, but of Catholic theology, which is related to the former as man's theory about his own nature and character is related to what he really *is* before God. It is ultimately and in the last resort to this theology that we owe what is intractable and harsh in the Christian revelation and the ecclesiastical magisterium. Proximately we quote decrees and decisions; but it is theology that determines the value of these decrees, and gives us our theory of the *Ecclesia Docens,* and to which the *Ecclesia Docens* must appeal for defence of its claims. What to us seems preposterous in Father Coupe's[2] recent letters to the *Tablet* about the *sub gravi* obligation of interior assent to the expediency of the Temporal Power theologoumenon (which the Bishop of Liverpool has just made the text of a Pastoral) or in the notorious Joint-Pastoral of 1900, is, I am convinced, the necessary and legitimate development of the two presuppositions of Catholic theology, which is always and essentially "logical" if nothing else.

But, with you, I believe that in one or two of its admissions it contains (because of its very logicality) the seeds of its ultimate dissolution; even were there not thousands working out its *reductio ad absurdum* as fast as they can. First of all the "Deposit" is professedly a presentment of strictly supernatural facts and experiences (seen once for all and then withdrawn from view) in the terms of things natural. All we hold is this *deposited expression* of doctrine; not the facts and experiences: in other words, all we hold is an analogue or metaphor of those experiences. Now there is no valid inference from analogues; the conclusion is vitiated with all the inexactness of the premise. Hence all those explications and applications of the "Deposit" which constitute the edifice of theology, are affected with the quality of their principle, i.e. the truth value of the whole system is that of analogy.

Secondly, there is the distinction *definita propter se* and *propter alia.* The whole end of the latter is the protection of the former, i.e. the preservation of the original sense of the "Deposit" of faith, as it was understood by those to whom the Apostles committed it and who had no direct touch with the supernatural experiences expressed by it. Definitions fall, not on the *realities revealed,* but on the form in and under which they were deposited; they are directed to the guarding of the "Deposit." Hence the Ptolemaic astronomy might really be

2. An English Jesuit and well-known preacher.—M.D.P.

inseparably part and parcel of the mental language of the *Depositum fidei;* might be necessary for securing the preservation of the impression produced by Christ's revelation on the sub-apostolic mind; might be ecclesiastically true, as part of a symbolism through which alone certain truths are known to us.

Thirdly, it is certain that nothing is *de fide divina* but what is *actually* (however confusedly) contained in the sub-apostolic mind; nothing but what a theological microscope could have detected there in all its form and fashion. It is also admitted that (e.g. the form and matter of the sacrament of Orders, in the decree of Eugenius IV. *ad Armenos*) mistakes may, and have been made as to what is accretion, and what primitive nucleus. Now pin theologians to these admissions and then apply the history of development of dogma to point after point, and I predict a considerable and liberating contraction of the area of *de fide divina* doctrines, and a transfer of much that now passes as such into the category of *definita propter alia.* Theologians will say, as Bellarmine said: If the earth moves that must be what the Scripture meant; if facts won't fit theology, theology must be made to fit facts.

For all their inadequacy we owe a good deal to the intransigent presuppositions of theology. For if there had been no canonised immutable doctrine, no canonised interpretations, what would have happened to Christianity? It was the fiction of an unchanged and unchangeable nucleus of sacred tradition that saved the Christianity of the Apostles from being quickly transformed out of all recognition. As it is, it is possible for us, with our improved historical methods, to reach back across the centuries to the historical Christ, to understand Him better and not worse in the impress He has made on generation after generation; to sever the wheat from the tares; to distinguish the life-giving imperishable principles from their contingent and defective applications. All this we owe to theological intransigence; to the desperate efforts to keep up the *semper eadem* fiction; to the struggle of conservatism against the irresistible laws of change and growth. Amid all the protective theological accretions the nucleus of Christianity has been preserved like a fly in amber, or like a mammoth in ice; while outside theology, the spirit of Christ has lived and developed in the life of the faithful collectively.

I cannot but think that, if the Church is to live, it will be through the very converse of what occurred as to Aristotelianism i.e. through the absorption of our theology into the contemporary philosophical synthesis. For then, the Church stood for civilisation and culture; but to-day she stands to culture as she did in the first centuries—an outsider, an apologist, asking to be heard. As then, so now, she must stoop to conquer, and die to live. That she would live and survive such a transformation may seem questionable to most; but to me it is a matter of more than hope and nearly of faith.

If you don't want to keep this letter will you let me have it back as I have no time to copy it, but might wish to refer to it later.

Ever yours faithfully,
G. Tyrrell

P.S. On re-reading, I only wish to reiterate that I am not speaking, as in "Lex Orandi," of the *lived* Christianity of the faithful or of the beliefs implied in that life, but only of the intellectual life of the theological schools—of the rationalised presentment of Christianity elaborated by the purely speculative interest of theologians.

5

The Relation of Theology
to Devotion

LEX ORANDI, LEX CREDENDI*

This essay appeared in *The Month* (Nov., 1899), and later in *The Faith of the Millions* (Series I) under the title "The Relation of Theology to Devotion." I reprint it here under a new title,† because it is fundamental to all the essays that follow, and to the whole point of view developed in the volumes, *Lex Orandi* and *Lex Credendi.* On re-reading it carefully I am amazed to see how little I have really advanced since I wrote it; how I have simply eddied round and round the same point. It is all here—all that follows—not in germ but in explicit statement—as it were in a brief compendium or analytical index.

Again: it marks a turning-point in my own theological experience. Previously, I had uncritically accepted the more rigid scholastic view of the "Deposit of Faith" as being "Chapter the First" of Catholic theology written by an inspired pen; and in the earlier essays, reprinted in *Faith of the Millions,* had sought to evade the obvious difficulties of that supposition by a liberal use of the theory of doctrinal development. Later, the insufficiencies of such apologetic became so pressing that one was forced to consider whether the

---

*From George Tyrrell, *Through Scylla and Charybdis* (1907), 85–105.
†"Lex Orandi, Lex Credendi."—J. L.

"Deposit of Faith" should be viewed as essentially a "form of sound words" and not rather as a Spirit, or a Principle, or an Idea—a view which would liberate theology and all the sciences with which it is necessarily entangled from bondage to the categories of a past age consecrated by Divine Authority.

Finally it seemed, and still seems to me, that we can reconcile the traditional notion of the "Deposit" as being a "form of sound words" with all the exigencies of mental freedom, by carefully distinguishing Revelation and Theology as generically different orders of Truth and Knowledge; by denying strenuously any sort of development of Revelation or Dogma, such as obtains only in Science and Theology.

Theology may be used in a wider or a more restricted sense. Here we employ the term to signify what is known as scholastic theology, that is, the essay to translate the teachings of Catholic revelation into the terms and forms of Aristotelian philosophy; and thereby to give them a scientific unity.

Roughly speaking the difference between the philosophical and the vulgar way of conceiving and speaking about things, is that the former is abstract, orderly, and artificial; the latter, concrete, disorderly, and natural. The exigencies of our feeble and limited memory make it necessary for us to classify our experiences into some sort of unity. A library is no use to us unless we can introduce some kind of system or order into its arrangement, and make an intelligible catalogue of its contents. We can consider the order of size, or of subject, or of authors and titles taken alphabetically, or of date of publication; or taking any of these as the first classnote, we can employ the others for subdivision. We do not invent these orders, but we find them; and so when we map out the world into categories, we do not invent but recognise one or other of these arrangements that things admit of. We can, however, classify the books, not only in our mind or in a catalogue, but also in our library; we can even classify Nature in our museums; but the world at large refuses to be harnessed to our categories, and goes its own rude unscientific way. Now who will deny that a natural-history museum does truly represent Nature? that under a certain aspect one who has studied Nature there, knows more about her than he who has lived all his life in the woods? But only under a certain aspect is this true. For such a presentation of Nature is abstract and negatively unreal. Beetles do not march the fields in such logically ordered phalanxes; nor do they wear pins

thrust through their middles; nor are birds' eyes made of glass, or
their viscera of sawdust, or their muscles of wire. A visitor from some
other creation who knew no more of our world than that, would
think it a very simple affair; very easy to remember and to retail. Still
how little would he know of its reality compared with a denizen of
the backwoods! Yet if our backwoods-man could be educated scientifically in such a museum, he would receive almost a new power of
vision, a power of observing and recognising and remembering order
where before he had only seen chaos. And in this lies the great
advantage of abstract and scientific consideration; of precisions that
are unreal; of suppositions that are impossible. Only by these devices
can we digest our experience piecemeal, which else would remain in
confused unsorted masses. But the more abstract, general, and simple our classification is, and the further removed it is from the infinite
complexity of concrete reality, the more we need continually to
remind ourselves that its truth is merely hypothetical, and holds only
in the abstract. This is what the earlier political economists (for
example) forgot, when they drew many conclusions that were perfectly irrefutable, on the purely abstract supposition that man's sole
motive is the desire to make money; but that were altogether false in
the concrete real world where thousands of other motives complicate
the problem.

It must further be noticed that on the whole the backwoods-man
has a truer knowledge of Nature than a mere acquaintance with a
science-manual could ever impart. Both kinds of knowledge are in
their own way lamentably imperfect; the one through indistinctness
and confusion; the other through unreality and poverty of content.
Yet it is less misleading to take a confused, general view of an object,
than to view one of its parts or elements violently divorced from the
rest. The rudest clown knows better what man is, than would some
being who should know nothing but the articulation of the human
skeleton—true as this latter knowledge would be as far as it went.

It is clear then that, as far as the natural world is concerned, what
is scientifically true in the abstract, may be practically false in the
concrete. But when we are dealing with the spiritual and supernatural world, we are under a further disadvantage; for we can think and
speak of it only in analogous terms borrowed from this world of our
sensuous experience, and with no more exactitude than when we
would express music in terms of colour, or colour in terms of music.

So far as the most abstract and ultimate ideas of our philosophy prescind from all sensible determinations of being, and deal with the merest outline and empty framework of thought, they may have some literal value in the supersensible world. We can say: This, that, or the other follows necessarily from the principles of metaphysics, and is therefore as true as those principles are. But it is not the whole truth; and indeed the more abstract and general are the terms under which a thing is known, the less do we know about it. A comparatively concrete idea like Man or King gives us a mine of information about the subject of which it is predicated; whereas Being, Substance, Cause, give us the very minimum of information. Now the terms that are in any sense common to the world of our experience and to the world beyond it, are, from the nature of the case, the most barren and shadowy of all. If, e.g., we look at Porphyry's tree where "substance" bifurcates into "material substance" and "spiritual substance," the former branch develops and subdivides down to the real and particular, but the latter breaks off abruptly and leaves us in the dark as to all its concrete determinations. For all reason tells us, we know nothing of angels except what can be deduced *a priori* from the general idea of non-material substance. To our imagination they are utterly characterless and uninteresting beings; quite different from the Saints, of whom we can sometimes feel the individuality in spite of their biographers.

Granted then all that the most exacting metaphysician might claim, any non-analogous ideas we can form in the other world are necessarily of the thinnest and most uninstructive description, and it is only by liberal recourse to analogy that we can put any flesh on their bare ribs. Whatever shred of truth they convey to us may, or rather must, like all half-evidence, get an entirely different complexion from the additional mass of truth that is hid from us. When, however, we begin to supplement by use of analogy, and (e.g.) to cover the bare notion of a First Cause by clothing it with all the excellences of creation, multiplied to infinity, purified of their limitations, and fused into one simple perfection, then we must frankly own that we are trying to comprehend the incomprehensible, to equal a sphere to a plane. In saying this, we do not deny for a moment, that the infinite can to some extent be expressed in terms of the finite; but are only insisting on the purely analogous character of such expression. Nor again are we denying the utility, or even the necessity, of such an endeavour; for we should be forced equally to deny the use of all scientific, as opposed to vulgar, modes of conception; whereas these two modes check and supplement one another.

It is a received principle of scholasticism that the "connatural" object of the human mind is this material world which is presented to our sense; and that we are forced to think of everything else, even of our own soul, in the terms of that world. Hence all our "explanations" of spiritual activity are, however disguisedly, mechanical at root; thought is a kind of photography or portraiture; free-will a sort of weighing process; the soul itself, so far as it is not described negatively, is described in terms of body. Having a direct intuitive knowledge of these spiritual operations we can be, and should be, conscious that our explanations of them are inadequate and analogous. Still more when we try to explain that world inferred from, but beyond, experience, internal or external, ought we to be on our guard lest we forget the merely analogous character of our thought. The error called "anthropomorphism" does not lie so much in thinking and speaking of God humanwise—for that we are constrained to do by the structure of our minds—as in forgetting that such a mode of conception is analogous. The chief use of metaphysic or natural theology lies in the fact—not that it gives us any more comprehensible idea of God—but that it impresses upon us the necessary inadequacy of our human way of regarding Him. Neither the metaphysical nor the vulgar idea is adequate, though taken together they correct one another; but taken apart, it may be said that the vulgar idea is the less unreal of the two. To illustrate this from nearer and simpler cases: The peasant thinks of his soul as a filmy replica of self interfused with his body; as co-extended with it, part answering to part; but the philosopher will tell him that the soul is present "wholly in the whole body, and wholly in each several part." But this latter statement has no real value, save so far as it insists that the peasant's view is only equivalent and not literal truth—that is, so far as it is a repudiation of anthropomorphism. What does it tell us as to the real mode of presence? That the truth lies unassignably between two erroneous extremes; first, that the soul is, as the peasant conceives it, interfused co-extensively with the body; secondly, that it is concentrated in every point of the body. There are certain advantages attached to either mode of presence; but these two modes, though incompatible for extended substances, are in some way combined in a spiritual substance, not literally, but as far as the practical advantage of them is concerned. The vulgar notion would deprive the spirit of some of its excellence, and would create many difficulties if not recognised as inadequate and anthropomorphic. Similarly, if the philosopher forgets that he has only determined the *locus* of truth, the extremes between which it lies inaccessibly; if he thinks that he has got to more than its practical equivalent, or has got any proper non-analogous notion of spiritual substance and presence, he may wake to find that, in combining two incompatible ideas, he has got zero for his result.

The same is to be said of our conception of the Divine omnipresence:

> Out beyond the shining of the furthest star
> Thou Thyself art stretching infinitely far,
> Nature cannot hold Thee, earth is all too strait
> For Thy endless glory and Thy royal state.

This is the common, human way of viewing the matter; but the philosopher sees at once that it "negates" a certain perfection or advantage to be found in concentrated, "punctual" presence; and that all such advantages, however incompatible with any mode of being familiar to us, must be realised in God. Hence he insists on this latter as well; saying, at the same time, that God is not referable to space as an extension or a point might be, but in some way quite inconceivable in itself, though conceivable as to its advantages. The effect of such an explanation on the common mind will often be that God is not everywhere, as hitherto supposed, but nowhere; not far, indeed, yet not near; not distant, yet not present. Again, eternity, to the peasant, means time without end, century upon century, *per omnia saecula saeculorum:* the divine life, like our own, drags on, part after part, experience upon experience. God is the "Ancient of Days," lined and wrinkled with aeonian cares. But to remove the limitations involved in such a conception, the philosopher tells us that God's life is *tota simul,* all gathered up into an indivisible *now,* into the imaginary crack that divides one second of time from another. As before, he tells us to take these two extreme errors together; and without attempting to fuse them, to hold them side by side in the mind, confident that the truth lies indefinably between them. And so far he does well. But if he thinks that these two assertions can be combined into a direct expression of the truth, he will come to the conclusion that God is in no way referable to time; and so miss that half-truth which the peasant apprehends.

Thus the use of philosophy lies in its insisting on the inadequacy of the vulgar statement; its abuse, in forgetting the inadequacy of its own, and thereby falling into a more grievous error than that which it would correct.[1]

It is a fact that the Judaeo-Christian revelation has been communicated in vulgar and not in philosophical terms and modes of thought. The Old Testament seems frankly anthropomorphic from the first; God lives, thinks, feels, acts under limitations, differing only in degree from our own; and it would almost seem as if the Incarnation were timed to counteract the weakening of religion, incident to the most abstract and philosophic theology of later ages. Men are influenced directly through their imagination and their emotions; and only remotely through their abstract ideas. In the measure that God is dehumanised by philosophy, He becomes unreal and ineffectual in regard to our life and conduct. God has revealed Himself, not to the wise and prudent, not to the theologian or the philosopher, but to babes, to fishermen, to peasants, to the *profanum vulgus,* and there-

1. It is curious to find the same lesson inculcated in a very different school, but in a parallel connection. Speaking of the attempts of metaphysics to describe the Absolute in negations, Professor Andrew Seth (*Man's Place in the Cosmos,* p. 218) asks: "What is the inevitable effect upon the mind of this cluster of negations? Surely it will be this: Either the Absolute will be regarded as a mere unknowable with which we have no concern; or the denial of will, intellect, morality, personality, beauty, and truth" [i.e., the denial of these attributes in their experienced forms and with their finite limitations and distinctness] "will be taken to mean that the Absolute is an unity indifferent to these higher aspects of experience. It will be regarded as non-personal and impersonal in the sense of being below these distinctions; and our Absolute will then remarkably resemble the soulless substance of the materialist. Nothing is more certain than that extremes meet in this fashion; and that the attempt to reach the superhuman falls back into the infra-human. Now Mr. Bradley, of course, intends his unity to be a higher, not a lower unity. 'The Absolute is not personal, because it is personal and more. It is, in a word, super-personal.' But he is not blind to the dangers that lurk in his denials. 'It is better,' he even warns us, if there is risk of falling back upon the lower unity, 'to affirm personality than to call the Absolute impersonal.' But there is more than a risk, I maintain; there is a certainty that this will be the result. . . . Our statements about the Absolute . . . are actually nearer the truth when they give up the pretence of literal exactitude, and speak in terms (say) of morality and religion, applying to it the characteristics of our own highest experience. Such language recognizes itself in general (or at least, it certainly should recognize itself) as possessing only symbolical truth—as being, in fact, 'thrown out,' as Matthew Arnold used to say, at a vast reality. But both religion and the higher poetry—just because they give up the pretence of an impossible exactitude—carry us, I cannot doubt, nearer to the meaning of the world, than the formulae of an abstract metaphysics."—G. T.

fore He has spoken their language, leaving it to the others to translate it (at their own risk) into forms more acceptable to their taste.
The Church's guardianship in the matter is to preserve, not to
develop, the exact ideas which that simple language conveyed to its
first hearers, knowing well that those human ideas and thought-forms
are indefinitely inadequate to the eternal realities which they shadow
forth. "This is My Body"—what did these words mean for Peter and
Andrew and the rest; that is all she inquires about. What does she
care about the metaphysics of transubstantiation, except so far as
metaphysicians have to be answered in their own language, and on
their own assumptions? If she says the soul is the "form" of the body,
it is not that she has a revelation of philosophy to communicate, but
because the question is asked by a hylomorphist; and it is the nearest
way the truth can be put to him.

This "deposit" of faith, this concrete, coloured, imaginative
expression of Divine mysteries, as it lay in the mind of the first
recipients, is both the *lex orandi* and the *lex credendi;* it is the rule and
corrective, both of popular devotion and of rational theology. Devotion tends to become more and more anthropomorphic and forgetful
of the inadequacy of revelation, and thus to run into puerilities and
superstitions. Philosophical theology tends to the other extreme of
excessive abstraction and vague unreality. The Church, by ever
recalling them to the original rule of tradition, preserves the balance
between them and makes them help one another. Just as experience
is the test and check of those scientific hypotheses, by which we try
to classify, unite, and explain experience; so revelation is the test and
check of all philosophical attempts to unify and elucidate its contents. We do not, of course, mean that popular devotions are to
dictate to theology, but that theology together with them, must be
brought to the test of primitive revelation as interpreted by the
Church. Any rationalist explanation that would make prayer non-
sensical, or would encourage laxity, or would make havoc of the
ordinary sane and sensible religious notions of the faithful, is *eo ipso*
condemned as not squaring with facts. So far, for example, as the
philosophical conception of God's independence tends to create an
impression that He is not pleased with our love, or grieved by our
sin, it is opposed to revelation, which says: "Grieve not the Holy
Spirit"; or "My Spirit will not always strive with man"; and which
everywhere speaks of God, and therefore wants us to think of God, as
subject to passions like our own. And in so thinking of God, we think

inadequately no doubt, but we are far less inadequate than were we
to think of Him as passionless and indifferent. The one conception
paralyses as the other stimulates devotion. Again, if the philosophical
explanation of God's working in our will creates an impression fatal
to the sense of liberty and responsibility, it is so far counter to revelation; and no less so is any explanation of our liberty which would
take the reins out of God's hands, or make Divine foreknowledge
impossible. Here obviously is a case where philosophy shoots aslant
the truth, first on one side and then on the other; and can never
strike it fair, but commends to us the paradox: "Watch, as though all
depended on watching; and pray, as though all depended on praying."
Again, predestination and foreknowledge are doctrines destructive
of religious energy, as soon as we forget their abstract and merely
scientific character; but revelation plainly intends us to go on as
though God knew as little of the future as we do, and were waiting
for events to develop, before fixing our doom. "Oh, did I but know
that I should persevere," cried à Kempis, puzzled with the theology
of predestination and trying to look at things as God sees them. "Do
now, what thou wouldst do if thou didst know, and thou shalt be very
safe," was the answer. Rational theology is in some sense an attempt
to look at things back-before, in a non-human, non-natural way; and
it is justified in this endeavour only so far as it tends to cure us of our
terrestrial "provincialism"; but it is not wonderful that to us things so
viewed should seem distorted and unreal, the moment we forget that
its use is mainly corrective—that it is medicine and not food.

To come to more distinctively Christian beliefs, we have examples
in the Trinity and Incarnation, of the inability of the human mind to
strike a truth fair in the centre, and of its need of seemingly contrary
and complementary expressions of inaccessible ideas. The simple
believer can successively affirm that in God there are three Persons,
and that in God there is one Nature. He can even know that what is
not simultaneously verifiable of creatures, may be verifiable of the
Creator in some higher sense as yet unsuspected; that the truth lies
midway between what he means by one person and what he means
by three persons. But let the theologian begin to explain "nature,"
and "person," and to insist on his mentally putting together, in one
whole, assertions hitherto held as true but irreconcilable parts; and
the chances are that one or other of these parts will be sacrificed in
the vain effort to secure a forced harmony.

But more particularly it is in relation to the Incarnation and its attendant mysteries, that it is important to remember the abstract character of certain theological conclusions, and the superiority of the concrete language of revelation as a guide to truth. The whole doctrine of Christ's *kenosis* or self-emptying, can be explained in a minimising way almost fatal to devotion, and calculated to rob the Incarnation of all its helpfulness by leaving the ordinary mind with something perilously near the phantasmal Christ of the Docetans. Christ, we are truly taught to believe, laid aside by a free act all those prerogatives which were His birthright as the God-Man, that He might not be better off than we who have to win our share in that glory through humiliation and suffering; that He might be a High Priest touched with a feeling for our infirmities, tempted as we in all points, sin only excepted. Yet when the theologian has finished his treatise: *De Scientia Christi;* when he has impressed upon us that Christ was exempt from the two internal sources of all temptations, *sc.,* the darkness of our mind and the rebellion of our body; that in His case, temptations from without met with no more response from within, than when we offer food to a corpse; we cannot help feeling that under whatever abstraction this may be true, yet it cannot be the whole truth, unless all who have turned to Christ in their temptations and sorrows have been woefully deluded—unless the *lex orandi* and the *lex credendi* are strangely at strife. Also when we are told that Christ's Sacramental Body is not referred to space *ratione sui,* but only *ratione accidentis;* that it is not moved when the species are carried in procession; that we are not nearer to it at the altar than at the North Pole; we can only say that his *ratione sui* consideration does not concern us, nor is it any part of God's revelation. It does well to remind us that our Lord's Body is not to be thought of carnally and grossly; that our natural imagination of this mystery is necessarily childish and inadequate. But it does not give us a more, but if anything, a less adequate conception of it. "This is My Body" is nearer the mark than metaphysics can ever hope to come; and of the two superstitions, that of the peasant who is too literally anthropomorphic, is less than that of the philosopher who should imagine his part of the truth to be the whole.

Again, what is called the Hidden Life of our Lord in the Sacrament, is a thought upon which the faith and devotion of many saints and holy persons has fed itself for centuries; yet it is one with which a narrow metaphysics plays havoc very disastrously. The notion of the loneliness, the sorrows, and disappointments of the neglected Prisoner of Love in the tabernacle may be crude and simple; but it is assuredly nearer the truth than the notion of a now passionless and apathetic Christ, who suffered these things by foresight two thousand years ago, and whose irrevocable pains cannot possibly be increased or lessened by any conduct of ours. I have more than once known all the joy and reality taken out of a life that fed on devotion to the Sacramental Presence, by such a flash of theological illumination; and have seen Magdalens left weeping at empty tombs and crying: "They have taken away my Lord, and I know not where they have laid Him."

There is perhaps a tendency on the part of schoolmen to delight in disconcerting the minds of others by a display of rare and esoteric knowledge, especially of such knowledge as owes its rarity to its abstraction and its remoteness from the wholesome concrete reality of things, and which offers to minds more acute than deep a quicker road to distinction than the laborious and humbling path of general education. But after all, destructive work does not demand much genius, nor does it need more than the merest smattering of bad logic and worse metaphysics, to be able to represent the beliefs of simple devotion in a ridiculous light, and to pull down in a moment what the labour of years cannot build up again. Even if vanity be not the motive, yet a well-meant but ill-judged desire to pluck up tares whose root-fibres are tangled with those of the wheat, will often issue in the same disaster.

This, of course, is not the use, but the abuse of theology; it is the result of a "little learning," which, in unskilful hands, is the most dangerous of all weapons.

The first effect produced upon the believing mind by departing from the childlike concrete presentment of Divine truth as put before us in revelation, is undoubtedly disconcerting and uncomfortable, like every other process of transition from one resting-place to another; and those who have not strength to carry the process through, are often injured spiritually by their inability either to go back to the older forms, or to go forward far enough to find anything as satisfying; and these are just the people who, in the spirit of the tailless fox, delight in communicating their unrest to others.

But a deeper and more comprehensive theology seems in most cases to bring us back to our original point of departure, albeit on a

higher plane; to restore to us the stimulus of our childlike conceptions, not only fully, but superabundantly; and to convince us almost
experimentally, that God's way of putting the truth was, after all, the
better and the wiser.

What, for example, is the purport of the Incarnation, but to reveal
to us the Father, so far as the Divine goodness can be expressed in
the terms of a human life? to bring home to our imagination and
emotion those truths about God's fatherhood and love, which are so
unreal to us in their philosophic or theological garb? To say that love
and sorrow, joy and anger, exist in God *eminenter,* purified from their
imperfections, identified with one another, is for us, and as far as any
effectual idea is concerned, the same as telling us that they do not
really exist in God at all. There is in Him we are told, something that
equals their perfection; but then, what that something is we do not
and cannot know. But the Incarnation assures us that whatever con-
soles and helps us in our simpler anthropomorphic conception of
God, is not more, but far less than the truth. As soon as the Divine
love becomes capable of a human exhibition, as soon as it translates
itself into a mortal language, it is seen to be, *at least,* a suffering,
grieving, passionate, pitiful love; we are shown that practically to
deny these characteristics to the Eternal is a far greater error than
practically to attribute them.

Even if, in some non-natural metaphysical sense, the Sacred
Humanity suffers nothing in the sacramental state, yet what would
such suffering avail except to reveal to us the transcendental suffering of the Divinity, and its yearning for men's souls? If the thirst of
Calvary is over and gone, was not its chief end to assure us of the
reality of the eternal thirst and passion of God which there found but
a finite and halting utterance? "For the same thirst," says Juliana[2] of

2. Elsewhere, explaining that all contrition and holy sorrow in our soul is *from*
God, and therefore must be more excellently *in* God, whose Spirit it is in us which
postulat pro nobis gemitibus inenarrabilibus (Romans viii.26), she writes: "He abideth
us moaning and mourning. Which meaneth, that all the true feeling that we have in
ourself in contrition and in compassion; and all moaning and mourning for that we are
not united with our Lord, and such as is profitable—it is Christ, in us. And though
some of us feel it seldom, it passeth never from Christ till what time He have brought
us out of all our woe. For Love suffereth Him never to be without pity. And what time
we fall into sin and leave the mind of Him and the keeping of our own soul, then
beareth Christ alone all the charge of us. And thus standeth He moaning and mourning. . . . And that time I be strange to Him by sin, despair, or sloth, then I let my Lord
stand alone, inasmuch as He is in me." (Rev. xvi.) All this is no mere concession to
devout fancy, but a far nearer, though still defective, approach to the truth than the
metaphysics of theology can pretend to.—G. T.

Norwich, "that He had upon the rood-tree (which desire and longing and thirst, as to my sight, was in Him from without beginning), the same hath He yet, and shall have unto the time that the last soul that shall be saved is come up to His bliss. For as truly as there is a property in God of ruth and pity; as verily there is in God a property of thirst and longing." What does the revelation of Christ's human heart import except so far as it brings home, as it were, to our very senses, the truth that Love is the core, the very central attribute of the Divinity round which all the other attributes cluster, from which they spring, on which they depend; that blood and water, guilt and remission, death and life, evil and good, darkness and light, both, stream from and return to the same fountain; both manifest one and the same goodness, and owe their seeming difference and colouring to the narrowness and imperfection of our weak faithless vision? And even if the Eucharist were no more than the bare remembrance of Calvary, it should speak to us principally not of that past human passion, but of the present Divine passion whereof Calvary was but the symbol. But in truth, a better conception of the unreality of time before the Divine mind, will convince us that the simple devotion which regards God's passion as continually present, as augmented by our sins, as alleviated by our love, is less inadequate and more philosophically true than the shallowly rationalistic view. For it is only the merciful fading of our memory that prevents our whole past being co-present to us. To God it is (and was from eternity) as though the nails were at this moment being driven through His hands.

Similarly with regard to all other pseudo-philosophic difficulties we have alluded to, we may say: *Lex orandi est lex credendi.* The saints have always prayed to a God, conceived human-wise, albeit with the consciousness of the imperfection of even God's own self-chosen mode of revelation, and it is this consciousness that has saved them from superstition and anthropomorphism. We say "the saints," because purity of heart is the safeguard against superstition. It is the desire to "exploit" religion, to bribe the Almighty, to climb up by some other way, rather than go through the one door of self-denial, that is the source of all corruption.

The "deposit" of faith is not merely a symbol or creed, but is a concrete religion left by Christ to His Church; it is perhaps in some sense more directly a *lex orandi* than a *lex credendi;* the creed is involved in the prayer, and has to be disentangled from it; and formularies are ever to be tested and explained by the concrete religion which they formulate. Not every devotion of Catholics is a Catholic devotion, and the Church needs to exercise her authority continually in checking the tendency to extravagate, and in applying and enforcing the original *lex orandi*. In this work she is helped by a wise and temperate theology. But theology is not always wise and temperate; and has itself often to be brought to the *lex orandi* test. It has to be reminded that, like science, its hypotheses, theories, and explanations, must square with facts—the facts here being the Christian religion as lived by its consistent professors. If certain forms of prayer and devotion are undoubtedly Catholic, no theology that proves them unreal or ridiculous can be sound. If any analysis of the act of faith or of charity or of contrition, would make such acts seem exceedingly difficult to realise, we know at once the analysis must be faulty, since the simplest and most ignorant Catholics make such acts easily and abundantly. If any theology of grace or predestination or of the sacraments would make men pray less, or watch less, or struggle less; then we may be perfectly sure that such theology is wrong. Devotion and religion existed before theology, in the way that art existed before art-criticism; reasoning, before logic; speech, before grammar. Art-criticism, as far as it formulates and justifies the best work of the best artist, may dictate to and correct inferior workmen; and theology, as far as it formulates and justifies the devotion of the best Catholics, and as far as it is true to the life of faith and charity as actually lived, so far is it a law and corrective for all. But when it begins to contradict the facts of that spiritual life, it loses its reality and its authority; and needs itself to be corrected by the *lex orandi*.

6

Science, History, and
the Truth of
Beliefs

In its external expression a religion consists of a body of theological and ethical propositions, as well as of sundry rites, ceremonies, institutions, and disciplinary observances. As the rite or sacrament has its visible and spiritual side, its value as a fact in the world of appearances and its value as a fact in the will-world; so, I have implied, each ethical or theological statement is sacramental and belongs at once to the world of the natural understanding, and to the world of faith and spiritual reality. It is as to faith and morals (i.e., as to spiritual and religious valuations) that the scriptures and traditions of the Christian Church claim to be divinely guided into all truth, as it were, by an unerring spirit or sentiment, which selects or casts aside such materials as are offered by the thought and language of each age and people for its embodiment—a spirit which, itself unchanged, changes the fashion of its outer garb to suit every variety of custom and tradition. That texture of philosophical, scientific, and historical beliefs, which the religious sentiment of Christianity has inspired and in which it has embodied itself, claims to be in harmony with the rest of human knowledge, of which it is but a part, and so far, to be true with the truth of the understanding; but its religious truth lies in "the spirit that quickeneth," in its fidelity to the facts of the will-world compared with which "the flesh," the merely mental value, "prof-

*From George Tyrrell, *Lex Orandi* (1907), 53–58, 164–71.

78

iteth nothing." From every new ingathering of knowledge the same spirit can weave itself a living garment of flesh, not less, but more pliant to its purpose of self-manifestation than all previous garments.

The world of appearance, as we have said, is simply subordinate and instrumental to the real world of our will and affections in which we live the life of love and hate, and pass from one will-attitude to another in relation to other wills than our own. This will-life becomes religious as soon as we rise to a distinct knowledge of a Divine Will as the head and centre of the will-world. In this region truth has a practical and teleological sense—it is the trueness of a means to its end, of an instrument to its purpose; and like these truths it is to some extent conditioned by what we know and believe about its object. But this will-adjustment is the end of all such knowledge and belief, and constitutes its religious value. Hence the religiously important criticism to be applied to points of Christian belief, whether historical, philosophic, or scientific, is not that which interests the historian, philosopher, or scientist; but that which is supplied by the spirit of Christ, the *spiritus qui vivificat*: Is the belief in accord with, is it a development of, the spirit of the Gospel? What is its religious value? Does it make for the Love of God and man? Does it show us the Father and reveal to us our sonship?

Such religiously true beliefs have been either created or shaped or selected under the influence of religious inspiration, that is, of the sacred enthusiasm kindled by some piercing intuition, some vivid perception of the realities of the will-world to which they correspond.

We may usefully distinguish a threefold truth or correspondence to reality in that organic body of beliefs known as the Christian creed. First, they may be viewed externally as woven into the tissue of our natural understanding, and as forming elements of our whole history and philosophy of the world—of our attempt to put things together coherently and to connect religion with the rest of our knowledge. Thus the existence and nature of God, the immortality of the soul, the freedom of the will, may be viewed as constitutive elements of our philosophy; the birth, death and resurrection of Christ, as links in the chain of history.

Secondly, as a man's spirit and character may be revealed and known by his reading of history and by his view of the world and life, by the colour they derive from the glass through which he sees them, by the shape to which his receptivity moulds them, so the spirit of Christianity is revealed and known in the Creed. This truth of the Creed's correspondence to the spirit of Christianity is only another aspect of its practical or "regulative" truth. It is by living in the light of these beliefs, by regulating our conduct according to them that we can reproduce and foster the spirit of Christ within ourselves. They furnish us with an effectual guide to eternal life.

Thirdly, a mere fiction may be practically serviceable in art or industry; and even the natural life of soul and body may be aided for a time and in particular cases by useful illusions. But no mere fiction, no pure illusion, no lie can be practically serviceable to life on an universal scale. For life depends on agreement with Nature; that is, on truth. Rogues and liars prosper just so long as there is a majority of honest men to lie to; but a community of rogues could not hold together; their theory of conduct is untrue to the nature of human society. Beliefs that have been found by continuous and invariable experience to foster and promote the spiritual life of the soul must so far be in accord with the nature and the laws of that will-world with which it is the aim of religion to bring us into harmony; their practical value results from, and is founded in, their representative value. Not indeed that the spirit-world can be properly represented in terms of the natural world. But as we can speak of thought in terms of extension, or of will in terms of mass and motion, on account of certain analogies between the two; so we can be sure that between the Christian understanding, or formulation of religion as embodied in the Creed, and the external realities of the spirit-world there exists a certain analogy whose precise nature is hidden just because we cannot compare its terms as we can those of thought and extension. And the reason of this assurance is found in the universally proved value of the Creed as a practical guide to the eternal life of the soul—a proof which is based on the experience not of this man or that, however wise or holy, but of the whole Christian people and of the Church of the Saints in all ages and nations, on the consensus of the ethical and religious *orbis terrarum*.

BELIEF IN FACTS OF
RELIGIOUS HISTORY

Christianity is an historical religion; that is to say, it proposes certain historical facts, no less than theoretical statements, for our belief; and as these latter have to be reconciled with the philosophy of our understanding—with our world-theory, so the former have to be reconciled with our reading of history. Jesus Christ is not a purely ideal creation like King Arthur, but an historical personage; He has a place, not only in the world of thought, but also in the world of fact. Our construction of either world must find room for Him. In and through Him the ideal has been realised, the Word has been made flesh and has dwelt among us.

As a mere dream of the religious sense the Gospel might have been a divinely inspired work of great spiritual fruitfulness, like the *Divina Commedia* or the *Pilgrim's Progress*; it might have conveyed a true God-given revelation of the absolute order in the clothing of analogy; it might have possessed a regulative and practical truth as a guide to life, as a way of taking things. Many who hold it to be no more than a dream, freely admit that it has been thus beneficent; but they must allow that it has been beneficent to a great extent just because it was held to be solid fact and not simple dream-stuff.

Between the inward and the outward, between the world of reality and the world of appearances, the relation is not merely one of symbolic correspondence. The distinction does not exclude, but implies and presupposes, a causal and dynamic unity of the two. Our view of the value of the outward world should be "sacramental" rather than "sacramentarian," that is, we should look upon it as being an effectual symbol of the inward, in consequence of its natural and causal connection therewith; and not merely as signifying truths to our intelligence, which can become effectual only through the subsequent action of our will.

If certain beliefs are universally fruitful of spiritual progress it is, as we have said, because they are rooted in fact, and possess at least an analogous representative value; it is because through them we are put into relation with reality. And this relation is one of action and reaction; of giving and taking, taking and giving. The beliefs are not arbitrary, like algebraic symbols, but are, like our sense-perceptions, the natural response of our mind to the influence of its surroundings. We are passive before we are active; we receive impressions before we attempt to imagine their causes and laws; or to govern our action in the light of such imaginings. Thus by experience we feel our way to more and more adequate conceptions of the world we live in. It is because God's influence in us or upon us is from the first that of a father, that we at last come to believe in His fatherhood; but the belief makes Him more effectually a father than ever; just as every truer hypothesis about Nature multiplies our communication with Nature and leads to fuller knowledge and power.

Hence the belief is sacramental; it not merely signifies the relation of which it is the natural issue or evidence, but it also effects and deepens that relation. There can therefore be no ultimate conflict between what is true for the religious life and what is true for the understanding—philosophical or historical. In the measure that a creed has regulative and practical truth, it is also representative, however mysteriously, of the same world which our understanding strives to reconstruct from the data and in terms of outward experience. That the two reconstructions, using different and partial data and proceeding by such diverse methods, should often disagree both negatively and positively, is only natural. The criterion of faith (taken widely) is simply the practical one of proved universal religious value, "Quod semper," &c. The believer is justified in showing that philosophical and historical reasoning tallies with, or does not contradict his belief, but in this he plays the role not of believer but of philosopher or historian. Further, in case of conflict, he is justified in preferring to hold on to an otherwise rationally indefensible belief until its religious value is accounted for and saved in some higher truth.

Thus a Unitarian might deny the Trinity until he were persuaded that the Unity of God was saved and transcended in that doctrine; or the Incarnation, until he were convinced that it was compatible with the Divine immutability. Faith will never allow him to deny a belief of proved religious value.

As our philosophy is a putting-together of all experience, past as well as present, with a view to understanding this world as it is, and dealing with it rightly, so too our creed is based largely on the data of history, on what has happened to us personally, and to our race from the beginning, in regard to our spiritual life and our dealings with God. There more especially, though also in every other section of experience, the Ideal has been slowly realizing itself, the Word has been embodying itself. Religion is not a dream, but an enacted, self-expression of the spiritual world—a parable uttered, however haltingly, in the language of fact. It is not an arbitrary working hypothesis shaped at one stroke by some comprehensive genius, but a construction that has been forced upon us and verified by our experiences, step by step, and part by part. Hence it is, that certain concrete historical facts enter into our creed as matters of faith. Precisely as historical facts they concern the historian and must be criticised by his methods. But as matters of faith they must be determined by the criterion of faith, i.e. by their proved religious values as universally effectual of spiritual progress; as implications of the spirit of Christian charity and sanctity; as selected by the exigencies of the development of the inner life of the soul. The unity of all experience

forbids any ultimate contradiction between the results of these separate criteria; but it does not exclude the possibility of superficial and
temporary contradictions. The believer will desire and endeavour to
play the part of historian and to harmonise every seeming discord,
often with more zeal than discretion or ingenuousness. But he will
always be justified in holding to the faith-taught facts until he is
convinced that their religious value is in no way imperilled by the
results of historical criticism.

Our reading of history is in some sort a "perception"; that is to
say, from certain points, hints and suggestions which are all that is
really given us, we construct what we call an "object," but what is
more truly a "pro-ject," inasmuch as nine-tenths of what we imagine
ourselves to see is thrown out into the object by our own fancies,
memories, expectations, inferences, associations—just as in a dim
light we shape every shadow according to our fears. Taken as a whole,
the Christian reading of history, the religious interpretation of the
aforesaid points, hints and suggestions will frequently differ from the
readings inspired by other and counter interests. In many matters it
has had to yield to historical criticism and may yet have to yield; but
of its substantial justness faith can have no doubt; nor can it have any
doubt even as to details which are essentially bound up with any
indispensable religious value. Such facts however faith holds by their
religious, not by their historical, side. To believe that Christ was
crucified under Pontius Pilot, or even that He rose from the dead
and ascended into Heaven, may need as little faith as to believe that
Wellington won the battle of Waterloo. Faith holds to these facts as
fruitful of eternal life, and on purely conscientious and religious
grounds; *Lex orandi, lex credendi*—the rule of prayer is the rule of
belief.

LETTERS TO ABBÉ VENARD*

Richmond, Yorkshire
Jan. 15, 1905

My dear Abbé Venard,

I am immensely obliged to you for your excellent piece of criticism which, it is no paradox to say, has enabled me to understand

---

*From Nicholas Sagovsky, *Between Two Worlds: George Tyrrell's Relationship to
the Thought of Matthew Arnold,* 149–53.

myself better and to see my relationship to those other three from
whom I have learned so much, and with whom I deem it a great
honour to be thus associated by you. As regards my own book *Lex
Orandi* it was a great satisfaction to me to see how exactly you have
comprehended my less obvious implications; and amongst these, my
designed ambiguity in regard to the point which divides M. Loisy
from Père L.[1] and from M. Blondel, namely the determination of
history (and, *mutatis mutandis*, science or philosophy) by dogma. At
that time my mind was groping after a sort of *via media* in the matter; but I had not as yet been able to formulate my thought. Since
then, I have hinted at this *via media* here and there in my publica-
tions, but have not ventured to develop it. I might provisionally put
my conclusion thus: we cannot argue from any *single* historical
implication of dogma to the historical truth of that implication; but,
taking the total historical implication of Catholic dogma *in globo* (i.e.
the religious or ecclesiastical reading of history, etc.) we may infer
that facts were approximately and equivalently thus; that this "religious reading" of history is related to the truth, as a dramatist's
reading of history might be; that in the interests of religion (as of
drama), thro' the instinctive, unconscious, *justifiable* bias of the religious (as of the dramatic) spirit and purpose, facts are warped and
distorted in such a way as to render inference *from particulars* unsafe
and yet to leave the religious (or dramatic) reading true *fundamentaliter, cum fundamento in re*. I would defend this conclusion by a
somewhat difficult and yet, I think, very necessary and defensible
distinction between "prophetic" truth and "historic" (or scientific, or
philosophical) truth. "Prophetic" truth is analogous with poetic,
artistic, dramatic truth in that the religious and moral values of its
utterances, like the aesthetic values of artistic utterances, are to a
certain extent independent of the fact-values or historical values. It
can, for certain purposes, utter itself equally well in the language of
facts or of fiction, or of a mixture of fact and fiction i.e. in more or
less idealised facts. Though Shakespeare's "King John" is founded
on fact we should not use it as a historical authority; yet its dramatic
truth may be greater, just because its historical truth is less; and I
would say the same of the Christian "dramatisation" of history that
is implied in our dogmatic system. To go to the root of the matter:
Prophetic truth (and artistic truth in some way) is reached, not by

1. Père Laberthonnière.—J. L.

reason working on sensible experience, but by the sympathy of man's spirit with the Divine spirit immanent in man's spirit; it is a divination guided by a spiritual sentiment. As God is the root and immanent cause of all that is and is going to be, or is in process of becoming, this sympathetic divination of prophecy reached the truth of what *is* in the divine or eternal order of reality; and the truth of what *ought to be* but *is* not, or is only in process of becoming, in the order of finite reality. In other words its concern is with the *ideal* rather than with the actual.[2] According to the greater or less imperfection of its historical information, and according [*sic*] the precise degree of its sympathy with the Divine Spirit, the prophetic spirit will be more or less successful in determining how the course of history must (a priori) have shaped itself in the past and must shape itself in the future, or how, in the present, the unknown may be interpreted by the known. We do see daily how the pious and devout (somewhat recklessly and unscrupulously) interpret history (e.g. the life of our Lady) a priori in accordance with the exigencies of their devotion; the interpretation has little value; but it may sometimes be right. There is a conceivable non-historical divination of historical facts—just as animal instinct can exercise a chemical discrimination between poisonous and wholesome food. The collective prophetic or religious spirit of the Christian Church has, no doubt, a claim to be listened to with respect to its general reading of history in accordance with the exigencies of the spiritual life. The dramatist will not, or may not, deliberately infer that *because*, in the dramatic interest, things *ought* to have happened more sensationally than they did happen, *therefore* they *must* have so happened—for he knows that the world is not ruled by God in the interest of drama; but the religious man knows that the world is ruled in the interests of religion; and hence he rightly infers that things *did* happen as (a priori) they *ought* to have happened. His "ought-judgement" is probably wrong or inadequate owing to his ignorance of facts and conditions, and perhaps to his imperfect sympathy with the Divine. But even if historically wrong it may be *truer* than history; truer to the inward reality, to the ultimate meaning of things, to what is in process of becoming. Because the world is ruled in the interest of religion, religious truth cannot be indifferent to history, as can poetic truth; there *must be* a prophetic or

2. Tyrrell added in the margin: "The 'ideal' itself being, however, the revelation of a higher order of activity."—Nicholas Sagovsky.

religious reading of history; and this is part and parcel, though it is not the whole, of Catholic dogma. But plainly this prophetic reading of history is subject to the correction of historical methods—which correction, nevertheless, affects, not the religious truth-value, but only the fact-value; it merely shows that in this particular point the ideal construction of history is discordant with the real, that what *ought-to-be* is not, yet; or that its conditions were mistakingly assumed to exist—a mistake of no *religious* importance, in many cases. We have no right to expect anything like a perfect accord between the religious and the scientific readings of history; but only *in globo* similitude—as between the dramatic and the historic pre-sentment of the same episode; or between the artistic and the photo-graphic presentment of the same landscape. On the contrary, the religious spirit desires to see God's will *already* done upon earth as it is in heaven; and this very ardent desire of the prophetic spirit inclines it to a premature completion and narrowing-up of God's designs; and thus acts as a principle of historic falsification. Thus there is a sort of opposition or tension between prophetic and historic truth; each is corrective of the other, the prophetic reading being truer to the deeper reality of things; the historical, to the actual course and nexus of phenomena. . . .

Needless to say that *Lex Orandi* is a very guarded utterance of my full opinion. I have here given you the substance of the supplemen-tary chapter that I would have written had I any hope of making myself intelligible to my censors. Once more thanking you for the keen pleasure and real help that I have derived from your admirable criticism, believe me with all respect and esteem,

Yours very faithfully,
George Tyrrell

Richmond, Yorkshire
29 III 1905

My dear Abbé Venard,

I hasten to thank you at once for your very valuable and interest-ing letter, as it is often hard to bring my attention back to a point if I procrastinate. As you say; the difficulty lies in the *application* of my theory of these two great facts of Catholic and Christian tradition.

My immediate object was to repudiate what Batiffol has since called my "radical symbolism" and to show not merely that I regarded Christianity as a religion incarnate in fact, but even that one could and *should* pass from dogma to history as far as the "substantial" facts of Christianity were concerned. To resume my illustration: There is a "substance" of fact common to the dramatist and the historian, though, in some respects, and on most occasions the historian will be better able to determine the limits between substance and treatment (or form). Yet one can well conceive that the substance of a fact should be enshrined for us in a poetic legend and yet lost altogether to history. That Christ *existed* is obviously a fact given to us by faith; it is the core of the substance of Christianity. Equally obviously, as Blondel admits, the "Visit of the Magi" lies outside the substance of Christian fact. It *may* be fact, or it may be "dramatisation." Hitherto it has been accepted that the Virgin Birth and the *physical* Resurrection are as substantial, if not as central, as the very existence of Christ. It is hard to think otherwise, even though we are shown that they did not enter into the Christianity of St. Paul as given us in the N.T. To me it seems that the question: "What is the *substance* of Christianity? What is the precise basis of fact idealised by faith?" is a question of theology in a broad sense. However, if the Church has not spoken clearly on these points of the Birth and Resurrection, when has she ever spoken clearly? If she is wrong there, when can she ever be trusted?—that is I suppose what most of us feel.

Your criticism of P. de Grandmaison is exactly after my mind. No error could be *universally* and *steadily* fruitful of life. As to Bouddhism and other religions, the most conservative theologians allow them some rays of the "Lux Vera" and their experience renders testimony to many truths common to all. Again, I state explicitly in the Preface to *Lex Orandi* that this criterion is supplementary, and not exclusive nor sufficient. It is a method of confirmation and verification, rather than of discovery. I do not mean that an individual or even a council should sit down *tout a coup* and sift the Creed by applying the *Lex Orandi;* but I only point out the process by which the Creed shapes itself and critices [*sic*] itself in the slow process of centuries.

Ever, Dear Abbé Venard
Yours faithfully,
G. Tyrrell

P.S. I am not quite sure that Abbé Loisy would agree with me when I say that to argue from the totality of Christian dogma to the existence of an historical kernel of the tradition *(quoad substantiam)* is to argue *historically.* However weak and vague, it is none the less a reason of which the historian *as such* should take account. The very existence of the Bouddha has been questioned by critics; but the existence of a religion which centres round him and is professedly built upon him is surely an *historical* argument or presumption in favour of his historical reality. And so, of the Resurrection: the dogma speaks to science as well as to Faith, albeit obscurely.

LETTER TO BARON F. VON HÜGEL*

February 10, 1907

My Dear Friend,

I had rather write what I feel about Z.'s letter, and then we can talk over it. He is instinctively right in regarding the Virgin Birth as a far other kind of crux than the physical resurrection. For centuries of developing mariology and devotion to Mary are stultified by its denial—to all seeming; nor do I see how the "plain man" (that is, ninety nine per cent of the Church) will ever be made to see that she has not blundered in a way to forfeit all credit as a doctrinal guide and as a director of worship and devotion. In other words, its denial as historic fact involves that complete revolution in our conception of what dogma is for which Loisy and Le Roy are preparing the way— a "kill-or-cure" remedy to which, however, we are simply forced by the results of the historico-critical method. In explaining how a belief could naturally have arisen without being true, we do not prove it false, but we have no reason to say it is true; and when the alleged fact is miraculous or violently improbable we have so much reason for saying it is false. I have no reason to assert or deny that you had mutton for dinner yesterday, but I am sure that you had not roast bear. To take away the affirmative reasons for the Virgin Birth is to prove it false—as historic fact; as false as any alleged violation of the laws of Nature.

Hence I am driven to a revolutionary view of dogma. As you know, I distinguish sharply between the Christian revelation and the

*From *George Tyrrell's Letters,* ed. Maude D. Petre, 56–61.

theology that rationalises and explains it. The former was the work of the inspired era of origins. It is prophetic in form and sense; it involves an idealised reading of history past and to come. It is, so to say, an inspired construction of things in the interests of religion; a work of inspired imagination, not of reflection and reasoning. It does not develop or change like theology; but is the subject-matter of theology. Of that symbolic and imaginative construction the Virgin Birth is an integral part. It is an element of a complete expression. But it must not be broken off and interpreted alone. All the elements conspire to express one thing—the Kingdom of God. The Old Testament prophets laboured at this construction, and we know, looking back, that their construction was an idealisation of a certain core of historic fact; and how time only has shown its meaning part by part and distinguished between the literal and the purely symbolic parts of the expression and the mere "cement" or frame-stuff, i.e. all the part of a parable which is merely for the sake of cohesion and is not symbolic of anything. I take the fuller construction of the Christian revelation in just the same sense. The whole has a spiritual value as a construction of Time in relation to Eternity. It gives us the *world* of our religious life. But I do not feel bound to find an independent meaning in each element; or to determine prematurely what elements are of literal, and what of purely symbolic value—which is the core of historic fact and which is idealisation. My faith is in the truth, shadowed by the whole creed; and in the direction it gives to spiritual life—in the Way, the Life, and the Truth.

The "Holy Child of Prague" stands before me in crown and sceptre and royal cope. Is this, as a child would suppose, a literal portrait of the boy of Nazareth? or is it mere symbolism? Neither wholly. There is a core of fact idealised, or artistically completed, to bring out the true inward significance of Christ's Kingship concealed by the mere historic aspect of the boy of Nazareth. I say the same of all the legendary idealisation of the historical Jesus. It is born of the same impulse which makes his love *visible* by putting his heart outside his body and setting fire to it. It is the inward truth of history, but it is not historic truth. That He was born of a Virgin and ascended into heaven may be but a "visibilising" of the truth of His transcendence as divine: "No man hath ascended but Him who hath descended and who is in heaven." The Virgin Birth may but teach the same truth as "He who does the will of My Father, is My mother," i.e. the soul which, impregnated by the Holy Spirit, reproduces Christ in its own bosom. But I do not feel bound to find *how* each bit of the creed helps to the one truth symbolised by the whole. I will not tinker or tamper with that work of primitive inspiration, with the image which truth made of itself in the mind of a prophetic era. I should as soon think of touching up the *Cenacle* of da Vinci, or correcting the *Divina Commedia* in the light of critical knowledge of history and science.

When it comes to what Dilthey calls "dogmas in the secondary sense," i.e. to authoritative uninspired statements as to the sense of revealed, or primary, dogmas, I am rather at a loss what to say. Theology, so far as adopted and imposed by ecumenical decrees, is the Church's *understanding* and translation into common language of the truths which she feels and believes and has had revealed to her in prophetic imagery. When we say "Consubstantial with the Father" is a *revealed* truth, we certainly do not mean that the expression is inspired or revealed, as is "Thou art the Son of God." We can only mean that it is the rational or philosophical equivalent of a revealed prophetic truth. Our *faith* is in the revealed truth, not in its translation. Else we are driven to suppose that Aristotelian categories and exploded science and history are matters of faith. I see no way out of this dilemma, which I first felt in my first *Semper Eadem* article. What value, then, do I attach to ecclesiastical definitions? I hint at my revolutionary answer in *Lex Credendi*, where I defend the condemnation of Galileo. More distinctly: I believe the Church is precisely and only the guardian of the deposit of revelation and that she cannot add to it in any way; and that her definitions are simply safeguards and protections of revealed truths. *What* she says is often absolutely wrong, but the truth in whose defence she says it is revealed, and to that truth alone we owe adhesion. She condemns heliocentrism because it implies a denial of the inspiration of Scripture. Therefore, scholastically speaking, the *formal object* of her condemnation is this latter denial; heliocentrism is only condemned as seeming to involve that denial. So, too, in affirming the philosophical concepts of transubstantiation or of the hypostatic union, she but protects the simple truths of revelation on which her affirmation *formally* falls. Who can doubt that the Zwinglian rationalism has *as a fact* weakened and impoverished devotion and spiritual life? In all controversies the Church must instinctively take the side that best protects the spiritual life. Her criterion is purely opportunist. In all her utterances she only repeats the truth revealed—their meaning is just the revealed truth which they protect. That a lie should be sometimes protective of truth is a consequence of the view of truth as *relative* to the mentality of a person or people. Hence, no definition of the *historicity* of the Virgin Birth could *mean* more than that the Virgin Birth was part of revelation. Because and so long as the denial of its historicity seems to destroy its religious value, she will and must affirm its historicity in order to affirm those values. In the implicit affirmation she is right of necessity; in the explicit protective affirmation she may be quite wrong. Revolutionary as all this sounds, I think it is the only position quite consistent with the distinction between *assistance* and *inspiration*; and with the Patristic *Semper Eadem* view of the Church as simply guardian of an unchanging deposit. Theology of course develops like any other science. But the Church is no more infallible in it than is any other science. About all of them alike, as also about history, she makes quite fallible affirmations protective of those implicitly affirmed revealed truths which are her sole charge and interest. Thus when I say "the sun goes round the earth" I mean "the Scriptures are the Word of God"—for that is all the Church cares about and has any business to care about.

And now as to Z.: First of all, it is true that certain religious values depend not merely on ideas and symbols of truth, but on their realisation in history. The fiction of heroism can never stir or help me as can the fact. The value of the Gospel is not that it gives us an ideal life, but that that life was actually lived. The historicity of His passion is all-important, the factualness of His resurrection equally so. But the mode, not equally so. What imports is the triumph of the Gospel through His death.

The fact of Mary's virginity seems to add little to its spiritual value. "What honours the Mother honours the Son" is the source of all Mary's glorification—down to the Immaculate Conception. In all cases the implicit assertion is the glory and divinity of Christ. This is equally expressed whether by the language of fact or by that idea and image. These glories of Mary may be but as the crown, sceptre, and cope of the Infant of Prague—the Church's prophetic symbolism of what Jesus really signified. The irregularity of His physical conception might symbolise, but could it possibly constitute the dignity of His person? The *fact* of the miracle would be perhaps a divine attestation; but is not the Church's attestation just as divine? If, however, it be asked, Can this symbolism square with currently approved ideas of what dogma is? the answer is an emphatic No. The question is whether criticism is not forcing us to criticise our notion of dogma, and making a quiet revolution inevitable.

7

The Church and Authority

FROM HEAVEN OR OF MEN?*

For all who believe in institutional Christianity in any form, the problem of Church-authority, its nature, its extent, its limits, is one that presses more acutely every day, and does not seem to be nearing its solution. It has been rudely solved in the past, sometimes to the utter destruction of individual liberty, sometimes to the practical annihilation of law and order, occasionally by compromises which offered up consistency on the altar of expediency.

There is great mischief in "precipitating things" and leaping forward to syntheses for which the times are not ready, and of which perhaps some of the essential elements are yet lacking. But it is only by ceaselessly dragging our nets through the waste waters that we may hope at least to enclose what we have sought patiently through so many dark hours of failure. For this reason I am not ashamed to make another grasp at an elusive truth that has so often slipped through my fingers before, and will no doubt do so again. We often get more instruction and edification from the mistakes than from the successes of our neighbours; and my vain endeavours to struggle out of the labyrinth of my difficulties may possibly suggest the right path to some quieter spectator of my struggles. . . .

*From George Tyrrell, *Through Scylla and Charybdis* (1907), 360–74, 378–85.

For the occasion I will use the word "priesthood" widely as the equivalent of all ecclesiastical authority. It is this conception of "priesthood" in its widest sense which I wish to examine, and more particularly that perversion of it known as "sacerdotalism."

The priest is an official who has received power and authority to teach and govern the religious community, and to administer its sacred rites. From whence has he received this power, from Heaven or of men? In one sense, from Heaven and not of men; in another, of men and not from Heaven. And for whom has he received it? Plainly not for himself, not for his own profit or aggrandisement, but for the community. He is the "servant of the servants of God."

"Sacerdotalism" corrupts and perverts this conception of priesthood in two respects. First of all, in the more vulgar and obvious way of regarding the sheep as purely ministerial to the ease and dignity of the shepherd. In this form the perversion is easily detected and universally reprehended. But it lurks more subtly and perniciously in the notion that the whole ecclesiastical apparatus and system is something which exists for its own sake and not merely and purely as an instrument for the spiritual service of those who support it. We do not escape egotism by ministering, however selflessly, to the egotism of the corporation of caste or trade union to which we ourselves belong. There is "sacerdotalism" in forgetting that the Sabbath and the whole Law is made for man, and not man for the Sabbath or for the Law; that the sacraments are for man, and not man for the sacraments; that the priest is for the layman and not the layman for the priest. The "son of man" (i.e. *man*) is lord even of the Sabbath. He who put all things else under his feet and at his service, last of all ordained even the Sabbath for man's rest and refreshment, to be his servant, not his tyrant. Man is therefore master and lord of the Sabbath, the Law, the Church, the Sacraments, the Priesthood. The sacerdotalism which forgets this has, of course, its direct counterpart in the abusive conception of civil and political offices and institutions as being ends in themselves. The human mind is so easily and so absorbingly interested in the mechanism of government that it rarely criticises the machine itself by the supreme criticism of utility and productiveness. Now and then it wakes from its wondering ecstasy to the world of plain fact, and asks: What, after all said and done, after all this clanking and grinding and spinning of cumbrous wheels, what has become of "the man in the street," of some millions of neglected units for which all this Stately or Churchly apparatus is supposed to exist? In this sense Sacerdotalism is Bureaucracy in the Church; Bureaucracy is Sacerdotalism in the State.

But in the second place, the legitimate idea of priesthood may be perverted by a false conception of the source from which, the channel through which, the priest derives an authority to teach, rule, and minister, which in a true sense is divine and supernatural. However immoral in many of its consequences, this error is not necessarily the fruit of immorality, or the egotism of individuals or corporations, but derives from that more or less pictorial and imaginative way of representing truth which is proper to religion as distinct from philosophy. The immanental aspect of God can never be that of popular religion, which necessarily addresses itself to the imagination, and speaks of things divine in terms of things human and easily visualised. For such a religion, God, the source of all power and authority, stands entirely outside of, and above, the creature. He guides and governs the race and the unit only from without, not also from within. Heaven is His throne, Earth is His footstool. From His dwelling on high He looks down upon the wide world outspread at His feet, and through the ministry of ascending and descending angels He rules as a king over His subjects, a shepherd over his flock, being in no sense identified with that which He rules.

We know how authority is imagined in this scheme, and how easily the symbol or parable is mistaken for the truth which it symbolises. To the priest or the ruler, as to his delegate or viceregent on earth, this external God imparts a measure of His own spirit—a spirit of wisdom, a spirit of power, a spirit in all cases conceived somewhat materialistically and even impersonally. And in virtue of this gift the priest or ruler is raised in spiritual character and quality above his fellows. He is raised to a higher order of being, his official words and actions are spoken and done by God Himself, whose passive instrument he is. As God, so also God's viceregent stands outside and above the community over which he is set. Officially he is no constituent part of its organisation. It does not act through him, but God through him acts upon it. In a word, he is the delegate of a purely transcendent, not of an also immanent God. The power and authority is, of course, given him not for himself, but for the service of men. Yet, since he derives it not from men, but from Heaven, he is responsible to Heaven and not to men.

As mere symbolism, as a pictorial and imaginative explanation of the source and meaning of authority, all this may be quite harmless,

useful, and even necessary. Our sacred scriptures are full of this language and imagery. They show us the heavens opened and the Spirit
descending and resting on God's delegates in the form of a dove, or
of fiery tongues, or transmitted from soul to soul through bodily
contact. Nor has Christian tradition ever departed from these figures
and metaphors by which alone the highest truth can enter into the
lowliest doors. But squeeze any metaphor hard enough and it will
yield poison; in this case the poison of absolutism and irresponsible
government, the poison which constitutes the second objectionable
element of "sacerdotalism."

It is possible for the priest to use his power and authority disinter-
estedly, and solely in the service of the community, and yet to hold
himself in no wise responsible to that community for the use of his
power; to consider himself the superior of all collectively, and not
merely of each singly; to account himself answerable only to an
"absentee" transcendent God to whom appeal is impossible; or to an
assize for whose sentence we must wait till the dawn of eternity. The
existence of men or classes of men who so conceive their authority
has been and must always be fraught with mischief and danger for
societies whether civil or ecclesiastical. To trace the growth of this
conception of religious authority back to its first beginnings almost in
apostolic times would be to discover the ultimate fibres of a malig-
nant cancer which has steadily undermined the strength and vigour
of Christianity, century after century. That it has not slain Christianity altogether is only because the wheat of truth is more deep-rooted
than the tares of error. It is because of that instinctive, unconscious
(or sub-conscious) spirit of sane democracy which breathes through
the Gospel from beginning to end; which underlies those same
inspired figures and images to which absolutism perversely appeals—
a spirit which, in the eyes of absolutists, makes the Bible one of the
most dangerous books not yet put on the *Index.* . . .

It is no longer difficult for us to believe that "no man has seen
God at any time"; seen Him, that is, as something external and apart
from the world and humanity; or that no man has heard God at any
time calling out from the clouds, or from the burning bush, or from
the summit of Sinai. We have long since not merely resigned ourselves to a silent and hidden God, but have come to recognise our
seeming loss as a priceless gain. For now we have learnt to seek Him
where alone He is to be found, and seen, and heard; near and not far;
within and not without; in the very heart of His creation, in the
centre of man's spirit; in the life of each; still more, in the life of all. It

is from the Sinai of Conscience (individual and collective) that He thunders forth His commandments and judgments; it is from the heights of His holiness that he looks down in pity upon our earthliness and sinfulness; it is in His Christ, in His Saints and Prophets, that He becomes incarnate and manifest, and that He tabernacles with the children of men.

Along with this sense of the Divine Immanence has grown that of the authority of the general over the individual mind and conscience, as being a relatively more adequate organ and expression of God's truth and God's will; as furnishing a standard from which the individual may not fall short, and which he must first attain before his is competent to criticise and develop it. The fragmentary revelations of Himself which God makes to every mind and heart coalesce in the mind and heart of the community, and form a steadily developing body of traditional beliefs, laws, and customs, through contact with which the individual spirit is wakened, guided, and stimulated. If individual judgments and impulses are liable to the warp and bias of private aims and interests, there is a strong presumption that the consentient mind and will of the community are free from such limitations, and are determined by an end that is more approximately universal and divine, more truly representative of the normal developments of the human spirit.

Yet we must not confound this general spirit, this authoritative mind and will of the community, with its provisional embodiment in certain formulated beliefs, laws, and customs. To give to this latter the honour that belongs to the former would be to imprison the spirit in the letter, and to make progress impossible. The formulation of a living and growing spirit can never be of more than approximate and relative value. It is, at best, a compromise for purposes of social intercourse and co-operation. Growth and progress demand that under certain conditions the individual may and even must depart from established forms of belief, law, and custom, in obedience to the higher and more ultimate law of the spirit itself. It is a false explanation which makes a certain lawlessness of private will and judgment a condition of advance, as though it were only through disobedience and rebellion that new paths of progress could be discovered. Disobedience is never lawful, but fidelity to the letter may be infidelity to the spirit; obedience to a lower may be disobedience to a higher authority; loyalty to our rulers may be disloyalty to our Church or to our country, in whose interest they rule and for whose sake alone they are to be obeyed. To disregard law, custom, or command solely from self-interested motives is plainly disobedience; it is a sin against society, against the Spirit of God as revealed in the general mind. To disregard it simply for the negative reason that we do not understand its social utility—which is so often proved by a far wider and longer range of experience than lies within the field of individual vision—is an exercise of private judgment in the most objectionable sense. Here a certain "blindness" of obedience is surely to be desired; but when we see, or sincerely think, that such a law or custom is generally hurtful, that its abolition or modification is clearly for the common good, we not only may, but we ought to depart from it in obedience to that highest social law from which all lower laws depend. Thus, among the first women who claimed certain liberties unknown to former generations, but now universally admitted to be just and beneficial, some may have been merely forward and shameless, but others clearly saw the public mischievousness of the rules and conventions which they were transgressing. It is not to the blamable transgression of the former, but to the blameless and courageous transgression of the latter, that the merit is due.

Analogously, those who depart from current and well-established traditional beliefs solely on the strength of some personal view— which, in such matters can never be quite self-evident—are following private judgments in its bad sense. But when it is clear that a counter-belief is gaining ground in such a way that it represents the "consensus" of the future; when the same conclusion is reached simultaneously and independently by different thinkers, one may, and at times one ought, to follow the belief that lives in the spirit (however small the number of its supporters) rather than that which stagnates in the formula (however vast the multitude of its passive adherents); for in so doing one departs from the dead letter only to conform oneself to a truer, higher, and more authoritative expression of the living spirit.

Thus, it is in the widest, the most enduring, the most independent consensus that we possess the fullest available manifestation of that Divine Spirit, partially and imperfectly manifested in our own individual mind and conscience—the spirit of Truth and Righteousness, the source of all moral power and authority—God revealed in man. Authority, then, is not an external influence streaming down from heaven like a sunbeam through a cleft in the clouds and with a finger of light singling out God's arbitrarily chosen delegates from the multitude, over and apart from which they are to stand as His vice-regents. Authority is something inherent in, and inalienable from, that multitude itself; it is the moral coerciveness of the Divine Spirit of Truth and Righteousness immanent in the whole, dominant over its several parts and members; it is the imperativeness of the collective conscience.

For us, once freed from our imaginative representation of an external God, who works upon humanity from outside; for us who recognise that the Divine Spirit is to be sought in the human spirit where alone it speaks to us and reveals itself, the question as to whether authority (civil or religious) is from Heaven or of men assumes a new complexion, and needs a new formulation. We should rather ask, whether it is from what is Heavenly in man, or from what is earthly; from the Spirit or from the Flesh; from what (according to the idea of Gamaliel) is true to the law of his spiritual development and therefore permanent; or false to that law and therefore evanescent. This is the philosophy that underlies such religious and imaginative expressions as, "If this counsel or work be of men it will come to naught; but if it be of God you cannot overthrow it" (Acts v. 37); or, "Every plant that My Father hath not planted shall be uprooted."

If then the community to be governed is a higher organ, a fuller manifestation of the immanent Deity, than any of the laws, councils or rulers, by which it is governed; if God is never to be found by man so truly outside as inside humanity—in conscience, both individual and collective—there is no such thing as an authority for whose use or abuse its bearer is accountable solely to an absentee external God, and to an indefinitely distant assize. He is accountable, perhaps, to no higher officer or council; he is accountable, in a sense, to God alone; but it is to God immanent in the collective mind and conscience of the community, and to a tribunal whose throne is always set in judgment, whose will, revealed not in words but in events, is always eventually ascertainable.

To say that all spiritual and moral power is inherent in the people and derives from the people, in no wise contradicts the truth that it derives from God and is divine. It is only to insist that, for us, God's highest and fullest manifestation is given, not in the clouds, nor in the stars, but in the spirit of man, and therefore most completely in that completest expression of man's spirit which is obtained in the widest available consensus, and is the fruit of the widest collective experience, of the deepest collective reflection. With the clear recognition of this truth, which gains ground rapidly on all sides, the second element of "sacerdotalism" is robbed of all its apparent justification. The priest is not only *for* the people but *from* the people; his baptism is indeed from Heaven, but it is also from men. That it is *from* the Spirit, *through* the community is inevitably implied in the practice of ceremonial ordination. That it is from the spirit *in* the community is only the rational interpretation of the symbolic and pictorial account of its heavenly origin which religion gives us. It is from Him Who dwells not in temples made with human hands, but in that human temple which His own hands have made. The priest stands above the layman solely as the representative of the whole organism of the Church of which he and the layman alike are constituent members. From that organism, as from God, all his spiritual powers are derived, and to it, as to God, he is responsible for their use or abuse.

Such seems to me the inevitable results of a more adequate emphasis of the Divine Immanence. Let us now see whether in this, as in so many other matters, reason and revelation, the Gospel of Nature and the Gospel of Grace, are in harmony one with another. In other words, let us try to understand our Lord's attitude towards "sacerdotalism." It makes a great change in that understanding if we frankly accept the truth that He either believed in, or at least accommodated His language to, the current belief in the speedy consummation of the world; that Judaism was His religion; and that what He personally inaugurated was not another religion, but a reformed Judaism; that the earliest Christianity was not a substitute for, but a supplement of that religion, somewhat, within limits, as the earliest Wesleyanism was of the religion of the Church of England: that to His human mind religion implied an institution, with priesthood, hierarchy, ritual, sacrifice, theology, tradition, and all those features which history shows us to be in some form characteristic of all religions, and therefore to be postulated by something in the very nature of man. Since it was not against the reasonable use, but against the anti-spiritual, anti-social abuses of these things He set His face; since He came not to destroy, but to perfect and spiritualise, we cannot say that the subsequent transformation of the Christian movement into a religion of the same universal and catholic type was in any way counter to the mind of Christ; we cannot say that the very notion of a priesthood is antagonistic to the Gospel.

But that "sacerdotalism" is antagonistic, we can most confidently affirm. This is perfectly obvious as far as sacerdotalism implies that the priesthood, the ecclesiastical officialdom, exists for its own sake and not purely for the service of the people. Here it is notorious that

Christ but continued the burden of Ezechiel's rebuke to the shep-
herds of Israel, who fed themselves rather than their flocks; who
viewed their own corporation or caste as the more precious and
privileged part of the community, as an aristocracy worthy to be
supported by the profane laity who "knew not the Law." Against this
spirit we have the lifelong example and most explicit teaching of Him
Who came (He tells us) not to be ministered to, but to minister—the
Good Shepherd Who gave His life for the sheep, Whose "good news"
was precisely to those "poor" who were so scorned by the ecclesiastical aristocracy, Who was in the midst of His own disciples as one
Who serves, Who warned them that the greatest of them must be as
the least, and that their serviceableness was the only ground and
measure of their greatness. When he inveighs against the theologians,
canonists, casuists, and priests, the ground of His indignation is ever
the same—this inversion of the right order of means and end, this
subjection of Man to the Sabbath, the Law, the Temple—of man, for
whose service all these things had been instituted by God. It is
needless to develop so familiar a topic. Nothing could be more
antagonistic to the spirit of the Gospel than the usage by which in
certain quarters the "Church" has come to be almost a synonym for
the clergy. . . .

It is surely in accordance with this notion of authority as immanent in, and emanating from, the highest in man that Christ says:
"Where two or three are gathered together in My Name, there am I
in the midst of them"; and that He bids a dispute to be referred first
to the judgment of two or three witnesses as to a fuller manifestation
of the Divine Will; and finally to the whole community as to the
highest available manifestation.

I think, then, that though our Lord necessarily spoke about
authority in the language of His hearers, there can be little doubt
that His Spirit was governed entirely by the truth of which that language was a most inadequate and easily misleading expression; that
the real substance of His teaching demanded, and has eventually
brought about, a truer and less imperfect way of thinking and
speaking of the matter.

When we turn from Christ to Christianity it seems to me that what
we find is, at first, a very pronounced democratic sentiment still
clothing itself in the dress and unsuitable forms of scriptural thought
and expression, and then its gradual decline and extinction owing to
the persistence, conservation, and literal interpretation of those same
forms; and, finally, a revolt against the extreme logical, and pro-

foundly anti-Christian, consequences of such misinterpretation, and the explicit recognition and more adequate expression of the imma-nence of Divine Authority in the human spirit, in conscience both individual and collective.

In its first amorphous state, as a brotherhood of saints preparing for a near Advent, the Christian body was bound together by no other tie than that of one and the same indwelling Spirit of Christ, imparting gifts in various kinds and measures to each for the edifica-tion of all. Its sole hierarchy was one of charismata and graces. Office and competence went hand in hand. When any member of the organism might be filled with the indwelling spirit; when none was wholly ungifted or without office; when the individual was subject to the judgment and approval of the group, and the lesser group to that of the larger, there was no place for the sacerdotalist conception of irresponsible authority derived from a source outside and not in the community. Christ was the source; but Christ was immanent, not absent. He was with every two or three. He was with His Church always, even to the end of the world.

Later, when it was necessary for the Christian movement (one might almost say the Christian "revival") to form itself into a perma-nent religion, with all those institutional features without which it seems no religion can battle with and conquer the world to any great extent, its organised hierarchy of officials was still conceived, not only as instrumental to the general good, but as authorised by, and answerable to, the whole body of the faithful taken collectively, both lay and cleric. Its function was just to mediate between the more and the less spiritually gifted levels in the community, to secure the com-munising of those richer graces and powers which were given to the few for the help and edification of all. The Spirit, in whose name they ruled, and ministered and taught and baptised and consecrated, was still viewed as immanent in the whole body, as audible in the collec-tive voice.

The very process by which, under the influence of the imperial conception of authority, and of that current in the religions which Christianity overcame through a policy of assimilation, the demo-cratic nature of the Christian priesthood was gradually forgotten, is fairly well known. The language and imagery of sacred scripture and inspired history lent themselves readily enough to such a perversion.

As soon as the bishop came to take the shepherd metaphor quite literally; to regard himself not as representing and "recapitulating" his flock; nor as drawing his power and authority from the Holy

Ghost immanent in the flock, he could no longer consider himself as answerable to the body of whose organism he formed no part, and which he ruled as an outsider with a commission from afar.

If he subjected himself to the collective episcopate, such a council was bound in its turn to consider itself not as the organic head, in which the whole Church and the spirit pervading it became self-conscious and vocal, but as ruling the passive Church from outside, as a shepherd rules his flock (from which he differs in species), in virtue of powers, whether derived directly from an external heaven or through the mediation of a monarchic, universal bishop matters not one whit. Against the Pope, the Council of Bâle had no logical standing so far as it regarded itself as responsible not to a living, accessible tribunal, not to the Holy Ghost immanent in the Church, but only to the Holy Ghost in Heaven, to an inaccessible tribunal to whom the subject Church might appeal in vain. As to who is the repository of such irresponsible power it matters but little. The vital question is, Where is that God to Whom alone both Pope and Council claim to be responsible? Is He immanent in the whole Church where we can ultimately learn His mind and will; or is He away beyond the stars where we can know nothing of either, save what the episcopate is given to know by some mysterious intuition? By what vehicle does He speak and communicate with us? By voices from the clouds or by the gradual evolution of His Mind and Will in the collective spirit of mankind?

It may be denied that there is any institutional tribunal by which the laws and formulas of Pope or Council (whichever be held supreme) can be revised; that there is any formal appeal to the general vote of the faithful on which the validity of such decisions depends. But, above the constitutional headship, there is the preconstitutional, which is a necessary fact and not a doctrine. It cannot be denied that in the life of that formless Church which underlies the hierarchic organisation, God's Spirit exercises a silent but sovereign criticism; that His resistlessly effectual judgment is made known, not in the precise language of definition and decree, but in the slow manifestation of practical results; in the survival of what has proved itself life-giving; in the decay and oblivion of all whose value was but relative and temporary.

The path of the Church's progress is simply littered with the bleached bones of long-forgotten decisions and decrees which, in their day, were revered as immortal.

One thing, at least, is certain, that democracy has come to stay; that to the generations of the near future any other conception of authority will be simply unthinkable; that if the authority of Popes, Councils, and Bishops cannot be reinterpreted in that sense, it is as irrevocably doomed as the theologies of man's childhood. The receptivity of the general mind is a fact that priesthoods have to reckon with, and always do reckon with in the long run. They cease to say, nay, they cease to believe that to which the general ear has become permanently deaf. They would fain seem to lead, but, in fact, they follow the spirit in its developments; for it is there, and there only, that truth is worked out. To command Nature, man must obey it; to command the general mind, priesthoods must obey it. If they assail it, if they fling themselves against that rock, they, and not it, shall be bruised; if it turn against them and fall upon them, it shall grind them to powder. . . .

If a religion is to influence and leaven our civilisation and culture it must be recognised as a part of it, as organically one with it; not as a foreign body thrust down into it from above, but as having grown up with it from the same root in the spirit of humanity. Our forefathers too believed that civilisation and religion had but one source; that both came from God who taught man the use of speech, who instituted marriage and government, who dictated the laws of family and social life. Hence they knew nothing of that fatal discord which arises when religion is derived from outside and civilisation from inside. To their belief we must return in a better form, and derive both one and the other from God, but from God immanent in the spirit of man. Else we must expect to witness a steady advance of that alienation of the laity from the Church, of which there are manifest signs all round us. To retain them or to win them back we must restore them to their original active participation in the Church's life of which they have been deprived by the gradual prevalence of the absolutist over the democratic interpretation of priestly authority.

Need I waste a paragraph to explain that by democracy I do not mean the subjection of the clergy to the laity; of the few to the many; but of clergy and laity alike to the whole body which exists logically prior to any division; to that formless Church, to whose service the hierarchic institution is but instrumental, from which its authority is derived, to which it is responsible, by which it is reformable. That body of the Holy Ghost, which underlies and gives life to the superimposed ecclesiastical organisation it has evolved for itself, has ever retained its own charismatic hierarchy of gifts and graces; its royal priesthood after the order of Melchizedek to which the official priesthood is related as a sacrament to its substance, or as the material and temporal to the spiritual and eternal. To this aboriginal Church, to this Christian demos, clergy and laity alike are subject and answerable. Its voice is not heard in the streets, its will and judgment are not formulated, but sooner or later they prevail, and all that is framed against them comes to naught. Say what they will, bishops, popes, and councils await its verdict, and await it trembling.

We do not then want to laicise the Church, but only to recognise the participation of the laity in that sovereign priesthood and authority from which those of the official hierarchy are derived.

He may expect to be laughed to scorn who suggests that the spirit of democracy in the Catholic communions is not dead, but only slumbering. And he would perhaps merit ridicule who placed his hope in any cession of their claims on the part of priesthoods. It is said reforms must come from below. Let us rather say they must come from above, from God immanent in the entire community which stands above both priesthood and laity. To trust in that is to trust in God, in nature, in the spirit, in the irresistible force of truth and right. There is no need of violent revolution, but only of a quiet, steady re-reading and re-interpretation of existing institutions. For what we have to combat has come about by a like noiseless process of misinterpretation. We need not destroy or even invert the hierarchical pyramid; we need only regard it from above instead of from below. Abundant traces still remain of the primitive view of the priesthood and its powers, and these traces we must deepen and follow up and insist on. The deviation was not wilfully planned, and so the footsteps of the past were not carefully obliterated, but remain for our guidance, involuntary witnesses of the truth.

LETTER TO A UNIVERSITY PROFESSOR*

Let it be granted, for argument's sake, that things are quite as bad as you say, and that the intellectual defence of Catholicism breaks down on every side as far as you are concerned; or that at least your mental confusion is so hopeless that you dare not commit yourself to any affirmation one way or the other—does it straightway follow that

*From George Tyrrell, *A Much-Abused Letter* (1906), 51–65.

you should separate yourself from the communion of the Church? Yes, if theological "intellectualism" be right; if faith mean mental assent to a system of conceptions of the understanding; if Catholicism be primarily a theology or at most a system of practical observances regulated by that theology. No, if Catholicism be primarily a life, and the Church a spiritual organism in whose life we participate, and if theology be but an attempt of that life to formulate and understand itself—an attempt which may fail wholly or in part without affecting the value and reality of the said life.

We are familiar now with the distinction between the conscious and the subconscious in the individual; still more between a man's diagnosis of himself and what he really is, unknown to himself; between the sum-total of memories and ideas, of deliberate aims, purposes, and intentions of which he is, or can freely make himself, conscious; and that immeasurably vaster resultant of forgotten and unregistered experiences personal or ancestral, and of impulses and tendencies determined by the same experiences, which constitute his unknown, unformulated self, compared with which his freely-fashioned, conscious, formulated self is as but the emergent point of a submerged mountain whose roots broaden out till they are merged with the bulk of the entire earth.

Our active life as free, self-forming personalities, is necessarily limited by the character and capacities of this buried soul which is committed to our cultivation, as it were, an unknown wilderness. In the measure that we come to understand more truly the nature of the soil and climate we shall reap more abundant returns and shall be able to render the soil itself more fruitful. True, the husbandman works for the sake of the fruit, and not for the sake of the work; whereas our active and spiritual (as opposed to our passive and psychic) life is an end in itself, and the psychic produce is but subordinate and secondary. It is the struggle, the thought, the labour, the conflict with the stubborn soil, with the weeds and briers, with the caprices of climate, that constitute our truest personality; what we make ourselves actively, not what we are. But how often do we diagnose ourselves partly or wholly amiss! How little do we understand our deepest beliefs and feelings; of our strengths and weaknesses; of our capacities and incapacities for good or for evil! How often are we surprised and thrown out in our calculations by "up-rushes," as they are called, or passions or irresistible determinations—by "possessions" as it were of alien spirits counter to our conscious voluntary self—and forced perhaps to reconstruct our whole theory of ourselves from the foundations, to readjust the whole system of our aims and purposes—like a physician suddenly aware that he has radically misjudged the case before him!

Well, if this be hardly questionable as psychology of the individual, it is far more evident by way of analogy when we deal with states and societies and communities. There, obviously, a good representative government is supposed to gauge and formulate the mind and will and sentiments of the governed masses, and to bring them to consciousness. So far as it does so correctly, it is instrumental in the civilizing and improvement of those masses; in bringing them into spontaneous sympathy with the laws of their growth and development. But how seldom is this realized! and how often is revolution the only possible remedy of bad government based on total miscalculation of the disruptive forces—the ideas, sentiments, and tendencies—buried in the collective subconsciousness!

Can we be very wrong in applying all this to the Christian Society, to the Catholic Church? Must we not there too distinguish between the collective subconsciousness of the "People of God" and the consciously formulated mind and will of the governing section of the Church? May not our faith in the latter be at times weak or nil, and yet our faith in the former strong and invincible?

We know that the psychic subconscious self of the individual is a very wilderness of conflicting elements, good and evil, false and true; and that it is the task and very life of the free, conscious spiritual self to develop the better, to repress the worse; and that the resultant owes its individuality not wholly to the freedom of our choice, but also to the limits and character of its subject-matter (i.e. of the psychic, passive, subconscious self). It is idle to deny that some have a happier temperament, a less thorny and stubborn soil to deal with, than others; that their spontaneous uncultivated judgments and tendencies are more generally to the side of reason and right. If it is true that, in some degree, the free spiritual self succeeds in modifying and improving the psychic self, in training it, so to say, to a more willing and effectual serviceableness; it is also true that the psychic self, in its own order, by its passive resistances or its propensions, can obstruct or further the development of the free self, can present to it temptations or "graces," vicious or virtuous inclinations. There is a practical limit to what a man can make out of himself; there are good or evil propensities which he may overcome for a time, but which will assert themselves again and again as long as he lives. Hence we feel sure of some men that though they may go wrong for a time they will come right again; and of others, that though they keep right for a time yet they will fall again sooner or later. In the one case we have faith in the man; in the other we have not. Analogously, it seems to me that a man might have great faith in the Church, in the people of God, in the unformulated ideas, sentiments and tendencies at work in the great body of the faithful, and constituting the Christian and Catholic "Spirit"; and yet regard the Church's consciously formulated ideas and intentions about herself as more or less untrue to her deepest nature; that he might refuse to believe her own account of herself as against his instinctive conviction of her true character; that he might say to her: *Nescitis cujus spiritus estis*—"You know not your own essential spirit."

Hence it seems to me that unless a man identifies Catholicism with the formulated ideas and intentions of those in whom at the present moment the spirit of the whole body of the faithful strives to arrive at some degree of self-consciousness or self-understanding, his quarrel with the expression is no reason per se for quarreling with the thing expressed—any more than his dissatisfaction with the political theory and action of his country's representatives would be a reason for denying his nationality. "But who," you will ask, "is to say what Catholicism is if not the official representatives of this Society? if not her Popes, Councils, Bishops, theologians?" No one, *officially or with authority*; but when authority is dumb or stultifies itself, private conviction resumes its previous rights and liberties. It sent us to authority in the first instance not by a suicidal self-contradictory act; but in basing our trust upon reasons and sentiments it thereby assigned a limit to that trust which is reached as soon as authority would seem to violate those reasons or sentiments.

Again, it is not absolutely necessary that anybody should be able to say precisely and adequately what Catholicism is. We can live and be, without knowing how to explain and define ourselves; the greater and healthier part of mankind do so.

The truth is, that our official representatives and exponents, those in whose mind Catholicism tries to define itself, being but mortals, are dominated by a sort of corporate or class interest, and are prone to exaggerate their own importance and to identify themselves with "the Church" much as social and political theorists and agitators are prone to identify themselves with the people, with the great silent masses of the population too busied about living to think how or why they live. We are apt to be passively receptive under the self-assertion and self-advertisement of a class whose interest it is to prove its own services to the community to be as indispensable as possible, to show that there is no hope for us unless we accept their views, follow their directions, and buy their wares. Though the inert multitude cannot or will not controvert these claims, it does not take them quite seriously, but opposes a considerable common-sense passive resistance to them. We do not buy our grocer's tea because he says it is the cheapest and best in the world, but because we have tried it and found it satisfied our more moderate requirements. Let us then clear our mind of illusion and recognize that, in spite of its noisy advertisements, this self-conscious, self-formulating Catholicism of the thinking, talking, and governing minority is not the whole Church, but only an element (however important) in its constitution.

Is it not because you forget this that the prospect seems to you so hopeless? Is it not because you are looking forward to the necessary developments of the ideas and principles of formulated and organized Catholicism and taking no account of the inscrutable voiceless life which it strives feebly to formulate, of the eternal truths, the Divine instincts that work themselves out irresistibly in the heart of the whole people of God? Every "Active" is limited by the receptivity of its "Passive"; as the artist is by the capacity of his tools and his materials. To forecast the future developments of Catholicism we must look to those of lay receptivity as well as to those of theological or legislative activity; and as they are on the whole in contrary directions it may be hoped they will healthily neutralize each other's defects and excesses.

I do not then see why, from your own present point of view, your inability to understand and sympathize with theoretical Catholicism should necessarily separate you from the body of the faithful—so long as you are not required in any way to belie your inmost sentiments and beliefs. But of course I am supposing the existence of certain positive reasons, of heart, if not of head, which bind you to the Church, that is, to the body of those who are united throughout the world and across the centuries under the denomination of Catholic and Roman; I am supposing that though formulated Catholicism does violence to your intelligence and your moral sense, yet unformulated Catholicism, or rather the living multitudinous reality thus perversely formulated, draws and holds you to itself by ties of affection and of instinctive spiritual sympathy. I am only showing that the breakdown of the formula does not at once alter the nature, or peril the existence, of the reality, nor of your relations to it. You are, I perceive, as clear as ever against the psychological fallacies of individualism in religion; you see that, like the musical or any other artistic or spiritual capacity, that of religion needs the educational influence of a widespread and permanent Society for its development and progress; that it needs its schools, its teachers, its great masters, its laymen and its experts, its traditions and rules and principles and criteria. Moreover, in the measure that it takes the form of a universal and world-wide Society, a religion needs an organization whereby its parts may be brought to bear upon one another, and its ideas, desires, and energies, scattered among millions, may be focussed to a point, and determined to a common resultant.

You see also that the principle of schism or disintegration is per se a very mischievous one; that it contracts the area of that collective life and experience which it is the function of such a society to gather up from all, and to digest and distribute in the form of nutriment to each; that the schismatic body or individual is cut off the living organism and from its historical past; that schism deprives the organism of the force of certain vigorous ideas and impulses which, working within the restrictions of its periphery, would have eventually modified its permanent character throughout, and perhaps saved the said ideas and impulses from the fate, as it were, of steam that has escaped from the boiler, the pressure of whose prisoning walls was the secret of its utility. Here, at last, we are cordially at one—namely, in holding that from the nature of things schism is hurtful, Catholicism conducive, to the richest development and diffusion of Christianity.

We both see in the Catholic and Roman Church the unbroken extension of the little society gathered round Jesus of Galilee two thousand years ago; we both condemn every voluntary schism as a mistake, not on the Philistine ground that the Church was all right and the Schismatics all wrong; but, contrariwise, because there were vigorous vital elements of goodness and truth in nearly every schism, which were thus dissipated and lost to the Church.

Again, I think you agree with me, that though the one thing needful is communion with the invisible Christ (i.e. with God as presented to us in Christ and in all Christ-like men past, present, and future; with all those who, whatever their professed creed, in any way or degree suffer and forsake themselves for God's cause and God's will), yet communion with the visible Church, with those, namely, who *profess* to be Christ-like, is a great *desideratum*, is a condition of more fruitful communion with the invisible. For, besides the more obvious reasons which will occur to every one, there is a depth, height, width, and fulness added to our inward life by our conscious and sympathetic association with a great world-wide cause or work such as that of Catholicism; something analogous to the spiritual expansion produced in us by an intelligent, self-sacrificing and active participation in the life of our state or country. If God's cause on earth should be championed by each individual, it is certainly rational that, like other causes, it should be championed by a society; not merely by knights errant, but by an organized army. In the Catholic Church, God's cause on earth, the cause of Christianity, of Religion in its highest development finds its visible embodiment and instrument.

The Church is, after all, the development of what was primarily an apostolic, propagandist, or missionary body sent forth to preach and prepare the Kingdom of God, and is itself a "Kingdom of God" only in a secondary sense. What personal religion should be among the factors of our inward personal life (personal but distinct; as the head is the principal part of the organism distinct from the others), that the Catholic Church should be among the other factors or instruments of our public civilization. Plainly, I do not mean a sectarian Catholicism at war with heretics; nor a political Catholicism at war with the States; but simply a spiritual society organized purely in the interests of religion and morality. To belong to this world-wide, authentic, and original Christian society, to appropriate its universal life as far as possible, to be fired with its best enthusiasms, to devote oneself to its services and aims, is to go out of one's selfish littleness and to enter into the vast collective life—the hopes and fears, joys and sorrows, failures and successes—of all those millions who have ever borne, or bear, or shall yet bear the name of Catholic, and who have in any degree lived worthy of that name.

Reasons like these may hold a man fast to the Church by a thousand ties of affection and loyalty, of moral, religious, and Christian sentiment, which can in no way be weakened by any collapse of his intellectual formulation of Catholicism.

8

Catholicism

═══════════════════════════════════════

CATHOLICISM: NATURAL AND DIVINE*

One of the results of the comparative study of religions has been to convince us that religion is just as necessary and universal a factor of general culture and civilisation as language is; that it is "natural" to man in just the same sense. Like language or the arts of life, in all its infinite varieties and degrees of development, it is governed by one and the same end, and by certain generally uniform characteristics and methods. Gradually the genealogical tree, in which the parentage of religions each and all may be traced, is advancing towards completion, and shows us that the religious process is but an integral part of the great historical process of human civilisation and development.

This conception confirms rather than denies the Catholic tenet of the Logos, which gives light to every man coming into this world, not one of whom is left without sufficient means of salvation. And since that Light, at once transcendent and immanent, at once above and within Nature, guides all men to one and the same supernatural end, it is plain that the process is at once, and without contradiction, natural and supernatural.

As little as one civilisation is as good as another, though all civilisations aim at the utmost plenitude of life; so little is one religion as good as another, though all religions aim at the same plenitude of

*From George Tyrrell, *Through Scylla and Charybdis* (1907), 20–42, 55–58, 72–73.

truth and righteousness and of communion with the Divine. They differ infinitely in their methods and in the degree of their actual attainment. Nor is it the difference between the babe, the boy, the youth, and the man; for spiritual development is not like organic development—as has been already explained. The need they would satisfy, the end they would serve is the same; but it is understood with different degrees of truth and explicitness; and the means are determined partly by chance conditions, partly by free choice.

Yet in spite of this the religious process is one; and the unity of the need and of the end on one hand, and the unity of the human spirit on the other, secure a certain uniformity characterising all religions; rendering the definition of "a religion" possible, however difficult, and making it practically easy to recognise a religion as such when we see it.

Now Catholicism with its priesthood, its sacraments, its ritual, its dogmas, its traditions, and all their uses and abuses is plainly a "natural" religion in the same sense as Judaism, Christ's own religion, was. It as plainly takes its place as a member in the universal family of religions, and presents the unmistakable family features. It is as evidently a product of the same general process by which God is bringing man into conscious relationship with Himself.

Now one of the reasons for trusting Catholicism is because it is in this sense "natural"; because it is a growth, a part of a larger growth—*Nascitur non fit.* Its conformity to the psychological laws that govern the growth of religion everywhere proves it to be a product of those laws, which after all are God's laws. So far it is from God, and not, like thought-out systems, from man. There is a huge presumption in favour of what is "natural." Its adaptation to human nature in its entirety, to every factor of man's being, to every level of his culture, proves the Church's divinity—not as their proximity to rivers proves God's miraculous care for the needs of great cities, but as what is natural, in the adequate sense, is thereby proved to be divine. A true religion is a growth and not a manufacture. The so-called founders of new religions have one and all sprung from old religions, which they have but modified and stamped with their individuality. They have been reformers, not creators. What seems the most original and independent religious experience of the solitary mystic has invariably some historical religion behind it, of which it is the unconscious product. Our seemingly simplest ideas and words have been elaborated by generations of organised human life. Revolutions have their own place, not in organic, but in spiritual developments, and do not break continuity. As little could one man create a new religion as a new language. A Chaucer, a Shakespeare, a Dante may at most inaugurate a new philological epoch.

But the true revolution must be wholly constructive; destructive only of what is destructive. It must take up in a higher synthesis all the truth and experience of the old system. It must obey, and not defy, the natural law of its development. Else continuity is broken. For reasons that may presently appear it seems to us Catholics that the Protestant synthesis is too crude and hasty a simplification in many ways, too artificial and reflex; that it has so far broken itself off in several respects from the natural religious process and suffered grave impoverishment.

On the other hand, what is so often used as a reproach against Catholicism—its various affinities with non-Christian religions, with Judaism, and Graeco-Roman, and Egyptian paganism, and all their tributaries—seems to us one of its principal glories and commendations. We like to feel the sap of this great tree of life in our veins welling up from the hidden roots of humanity. To feel so, to possess this sense of solidarity with all the religions of the world; to acknowledge that they are all lit, however dimly, by the same Logos-light which struggles, unconquered, with even their thickest darkness— this is to be a Catholic; this is to rise above exclusiveness and sectarianism, without in any wise falling into indifferentism; this is to be His disciple Who, believing salvation to be of the Jews, found such faith in the Samaritan and the Gentile as He found not in Israel.

To have thus recognised the "natural" character of religion and of Christianity and of Catholicism is no novelty, but only an "explicitation" of the thought of the greater prophets, of Christ, of St. Paul, of Tertullian, of Origen, of Clement of Alexandria—a thought which had to struggle long with opposing tendencies, traditional opinions and sentiments that have only gradually yielded and made way for its full manifestation in these latter days.

I am not concerned to defend this conception of Catholicism as a natural and therefore a divine religion against those friends or foes of the Church who, using the term "natural" in a now unintelligible and obsolete sense, choose to stigmatise the view as rationalistic, naturalistic. I am only stating a consideration which, rightly or wrongly, weighs with certain minds in favour of Catholicism as distinguished from more artificial and reasoned-out syntheses—the products of man's freedom, rather than of God working, through the universal laws of man's nature.

Allied with and dependent on this consideration there are others. Catholicism is characterised by a certain irrationality, incoherence, and irregularity—a certain irreducibleness to exact and systematic expression—which, far from being scandalous, is another presumption in its favour. As an illustration we might point to its Breviary or its Ritual—manifestly composite works—wrought at different times by hands guided in no two cases by quite the same ideas and principles, or by an adequate grasp of the exact meaning of preceding efforts. To criticise the result as guided by one steadfast aim and rule, to ask why this and why that, is to seek for a consistency that does not and could not exist in a product of spiritual development, whose regularity must be continually broken up by the accumulation of fresh experience, to be reconstituted by a new constructive effort. Catholicism as a religion of the people must in its growth betray the same sort of irregularities as the other co-factors of civilisation, as language or social custom or traditional political institutions. It requires two principles for its development; one, a principle of wild luxuriance, of spontaneous expansion and variation in every direction; the other, a principle of order, restraint, and unification, in conflict with the former, often overwhelmed by its task, always more or less in arrears. The tangle and undergrowth of the forest is always more than the woodmen can cope with. The growth and fertility is not from them, but from God through Nature. They by taking thought can but secure the conditions of Nature's free play and fullest fruitfulness. By understanding and obeying her laws, Art and Cultivation can win her richer favours. Were they to fail wholly or in part, the forest would not forthwith disappear, but would at worst return to its primitive wildness. Thus its very wildnesses and barbarisms point to the natural character of Catholicism, and distinguish it from all planned-out philosophical religions, whose over-trimness is an indication of their poverty and exhaustion; for nothing that lives and grows can keep its shape long. Its durableness is therefore not dependent merely on the wisdom of its theologians, or the prudence of its officers, or this or that theory of its essence, or this or that form of its organisation. As long as a fibre of its roots remains anywhere, it is capable of renewing itself and spreading abroad over the face of the earth. It has the durability and indestructibleness of the natural as against the transitoriness of the artificial. Because it is a natural religion Catholicism is full of compromises. In all the opposing elements of its syncretism there is a part-truth to which the religious spirit clings in spite of logic, and wisely. For a syncretism, a more or less violent forcing together of incompatibles, is the preliminary stage of an harmonious synthesis which can never be finally and fully realised just because new elements are ever coming in. Ground one against the other the fragments lose their angles in time, and approximate to coherence and continuity. Art can compel a premature and poorer unification by throwing out this or that recalcitrant member of the various antitheses; but God in Nature works slowly and surely through the unimpeded struggle of opposites.

Now it would be paradoxical to say that the greater incoherence of Catholicism were without more ado an argument in its favour; or that the mere completeness and tidiness of other systems were fatal to their claims. Nature is orderly; chaos is incoherent and not divine. But when the order is suggested by experience and waits on experience it can never be finished and logically satisfactory; when it is complete and logical it means that irreducible tracts of experience have been artificially excluded from the synthesis.

True, the Anglican reproaches Roman Catholicism precisely because of its logical and artificial unity, and uses the above argument in his own favour. But first of all, minor controversies apart, Anglicanism is far more of the Catholic than of the Protestant type, and belongs to the same tradition more or less. Secondly, the objection identifies Roman Catholicism with its present dominant theological system, or its present ecclesiastical polity. These are but examples of the incoherence in question; parts of the whole, factors in the syncretism, elements at war with other elements; not to be thrown out but reduced and penetrated by the vital principle of Catholicism. Their persistence must be explained, their essential values must be saved, before their husks are discarded.

Again; viewing religion as a natural process, as a factor in the general process of man's rational and spiritual development, it seems to us that in Catholic Christianity that process attains, not indeed to an impossible finality, but to a crisis that begins a new epoch. For in it the mystical process and the "moral" process (understanding "moral" widely, as including the "ought" of intellect, feeling, and will) run into one and recognise their former separateness as merely the result of imperfect enlightenment. The mystical need of conscious communion and self-adjustment with the super-sensible and superhuman world, to which the sensible and human world is felt to be subordinate, seems distinct from the "moral" need until the character of the superhuman order is realised as "moral," and till the voice of Conscience—moral, intellectual, and aesthetic—is accepted as the Voice of God. Nor till then is it felt that obedience to every sort of conscience puts man in harmony with the universe of being, and is the very essence and inwardness of religious worship and sacrifice. Of the two, the religious interpretation of "morality" is a greater gain for mankind than the "moral" interpretation of religion. It is more important that the "moral" life should gain a mystical height and supernatural sanction as a life of union with the eternal and universal principle of all being than that the religious life should be, at once, levelled up and flattened down to the plane of "moral" symbolism. In Catholicism, Conscience—moral, intellectual, and aesthetic—is raised to the throne of God, and worshipped with all that religion has ever offered in honour of its divinities. The whole system, centred round the crucifix, invests such "morality" with the awe and reverence due to the mysterious all-pervading, all-sustaining Will of the Eternal.

Here, then, it seems to us that the rationalising antimystical tendencies of many other Christian bodies are impoverishing, both in their narrowed conception of morality as merely ethical, and in their reduction of religion to morality; and that they overshoot the mark in their revolt against the residues of non-ethical pagan religiousness not yet subdued in the Catholic synthesis. As for systems of independent conduct-morality they have yet to prove their ability to do what the Church has so often done on so large a scale for the masses. The ethical code she enforced was often more barbaric than Christian; yet she did enforce it, and precisely by giving a mystical and religious depth to ethical requirements, however crudely understood.

Again; it seems to us that Catholicism is, more than other systems, a religion of the whole man, body, soul, and spirit; a religion for every stage of his culture, and not for one only; for every mood of his variability, and not only for the highest; for every sort of man, and not merely for a religious, ethical, intellectual, or social aristocracy; that it enters as an organic part into the whole process of civilisation with its multitudinous interests; that it makes us sensible of our solidarity with, and dependence on, the whole of humanity, past, present, and to come; all this, of course, in virtue of principles and ideals to which it has never been wholly faithful or unfaithful, and in spite of discordant elements in the Greco-Roman paganism over which the Christian leaven can never be fully victorious.

It is a religion of the whole man. A made and thought-out religion is governed by some theoretic and abstract view of man and of the hierarchic order of his faculties and exigencies. Not so, one that is slowly being shaped by the play of man's conflicting requirements over a world-wide area. In Catholicism we find the competing claims of his intellect, his feelings, his heart, his senses asserting themselves more or less discordantly and, as it were, fighting their way towards an unattainable ideal of harmonious agreement. We find mysticism and intellectualism at war; practical and contemplative religion looking askance at one another; externality and inwardness contending for the mastery; the asceticism of John despising the humaneness of Jesus. No interest of man's complex nature has been disregarded or unrepresented in deference to a forced and premature unification.

The modern psychologist, with his deepened knowledge of the sub-conscious self, of the nature and play of habit, suggestion and automatism, must confess that instinctively and experimentally Catholicism has always acknowledged and utilised these psychological laws and principles, which thought-out syntheses were bound to ignore as long as they were unrecognised by contemporary science. Perhaps nothing is more characteristic of the difference between Catholicism and that sort of scholastic Protestantism which ripened into the cold eighteenth-century deism than the attitude of the two systems towards the sub-conscious, towards that deep and wide-spreading basis of the visible emergent peak of our clear consciousness. Both accepted the crude definition of man as "a reasoning animal," but while Protestantism applied it to the condemnation of all that was not reason, Catholic experience ignored and belied it.

Thus Catholicism has always known, not theoretically but experimentally, the use and value of suggestion and auto-suggestion in the formation of habits good or evil, religious or otherwise. It has known the need of continually building up and perfecting a complex mechanism of habit as the condition of a fuller and more fruitful exercise of free conscious action. It has learnt the utility of certain deliberately induced narrowings and concentrations of the field of vision, and of the range of interests, without which nothing great has ever been accomplished, and to which we owe the effectiveness not only of saints and prophets, but of scholars, discoverers, heroes, and conquerors. A psychologically false spirituality, in despising these almost mechanical bases and conditions of free origination, has fallen to the ground through striving to fly without wings. Suggestions, auto-suggestions, and fixed ideas are spiritually indifferent. They guarantee nothing for the truth or falsehood, goodness or badness, of what they impose upon us. But the True and the Good must be so imposed on us by ourselves or by our educators; must be worked into the mechanical and automatic basis of our rational life, if they are to fructify and not to be as seed sown by the wayside.

And in the same way, Catholicism has learnt to recognise, allow and provide for the non-religious temperament, and for the religious temperament in its non-religious moods, in its states of mere poten-tiality, in its rudimentary stages of development. It has learnt that though men ought to, men cannot, pray without ceasing; that in the best of us the spirit slumbers and sleeps through many of our waking hours; that in most of us its moments of full self-consciousness are few and far between; and that in the dull intervals we are left to the guidance of habits, formed or deepened in those better moments. Catholicism recognises a certain lower goodness. When the mind is barren and feeling is dead, mechanical prayers and reli-gious practices are not so merely and utterly mechanical but that they are also exercises and acts of conscience and freewill—earnest of "the better" we fain would offer if we could, in "the day of small things," when the flax smoulders without flame, and the bruised reed cannot lift itself upright. Catholicism refuses to despise the half because it is not the whole, or to confound little with nothing. In the bare-walled conventicles of pure reason, if the soul cannot do her best she can do nothing. In a Catholic temple she can do her second best or her third. There are altars to visit and candles to light, and beads to finger, and litanies to mutter, and the crucifix to gaze on, and a hundred little occupations not less good because others are so much better, or because abuses are easy and frequent. In short, man is psychological as well as spiritual—mostly the former; and in Catholicism he finds a lower psychological religion ministerial to the higher and spiritual; and this, not designed, or planned, or even quite acknowledged, but shaped by the necessities of humanity in the mass and on the average.

Similarly, Catholicism stands out as a religion of the whole man against the pedantry of a purely reasonable religion that would abolish the luxuriant—doubtless at times too luxuriant—wealth of symbolism in favour of a "ministry of the word" alone, taking "word" in its baldest literal sense; and that would limit the converse between God and man to what can be uttered in spoken or written language.

Yet all language is poetical in its origin. It tries to express the whole inner state—not merely the truth, but the emotions and feelings in which the truth is embedded; for the so-called "faculties"—mind, will, feeling—have not yet been marked off from one another by abstract thought. It is only later that the utility of exact ideas and corresponding verbal signs leads to prosaic precision, and turns what once were living metaphors into sober measurements. But outside this region of strict usefulness, and wherever man would utter his whole spirit or receive the whole utterance of another spirit, the language of poetry becomes indispensable; for inward feelings are not directly communicable, but only suggestible through their outward and natural signs. We know them in ourselves alone; in others we can see but their symptoms. Because religion is of the whole soul and of no single faculty, because it springs immediately from the deep root of our nature, and not from any one of the branches, therefore the converse of man with God, of the finite spirit with the infinite, must of necessity be in the symbolic language of poetry; for it is the indistinct utterance of all that man knows, feels, and wills about God, and of all that God knows, feels, and wills about man. But not only is all exact lingual expression, but all possible lingual expression, inadequate to such fulness of utterance. In Religion as in Nature, God speaks to every sense with a thousand voices, and bids us to answer Him again, as far as we can, in His own tongue. There is, then, no small pedantry of intellectualism in the notion that worship in spirit and in truth must necessarily be conducted in circumstances of sought-out plainness, and divested of all appeal to the senses, the imagination, and the emotions; of all sacraments and symbols—a worship which would suffer no more of God's message to enter the soul than can find its way through the narrow slit of common sense, and clothe itself in the stiff primness of colourless prose. Of such worship Christ and His apostles—Jews as they were and lovers of the Temple with its soul-stirring symbolism—knew nothing, nor has any religion ever thriven long on such a fallacy of puritanism strictly adhered to. If it has exercised a soul-compelling power over the masses, it is only because it has, in fact, appealed to more than the mere understanding through psalms and hymns, and through a preaching that was impassioned as well as argumentative; that addressed the eye as well as the ear; that spoke by glances, gestures, intonation, and all the symbolism of will and emotion. A strict "rationalising" of worship would, therefore, mean an infinite impoverishment of the language of religion. One need not deny the advantages of a vernacular liturgy. Yet it may be that the mere "dumb-show" of a high mass, with all its suggestions of mystery, faith, and reverence, speaks more fully and directly to the spirit of man; does more for the right attuning of his soul, than could the most exquisitely balanced theological discourse on the sacrifice of the altar.

Here, again, it seems to us that the conservative position, as the product of the slowly accumulated experience of multitudes and centuries, has probably more to say for itself than plain common sense can see at a glance or two.

Again, under the alluring semblance of simplification and a return to the spirit of a Gospel preached to the poor and unlettered, puritanism seems to us in some way to be vitiated by a false simplicity—a simplicity of impoverishment, not a simplicity of comprehensive unification. God, the theologians say, is infinitely simple, and yet he is the plenitude of every sort of being and perfection. And our evolutionists tell us that the highest type of organism is that in which the greatest multiplicity of structure and function is most perfectly unified. Given equal richness of content, the simpler unity is the better; but not if the simplification be at the expense of content. The tendency of puritanism is to reduce Christianity to its lowest terms; to cast off all that has grown out of, or on to, its primitive expression; to bring it down to the level of the lowest and most universal spiritual capacity; to make it democratic in just what seems to us the wrong and popular sense of the term. For it is to favour one section of the Church at the expense of another; to starve the higher and rarer capacity in the interests of the lower and commoner; to assume that the spiritual equality of God's sons means an equality of gifts and graces; to forget that the Christian *demos* includes and needs every grade and kind of spirituality from the lowest to the highest.

For this reason as well as for its severe rationality puritanism, in spite of its studied abstract simplicity, has always been the religion of a certain class, and a certain temperament, and a certain culture. Whereas Catholicism, in spite of, or rather because of, its vast complexity, has been, as no other, a religion both of the crowds and masses, and also of the intellectual, the cultivated, the mystical, the aesthetic minority.

Seeing the intimate psychological bond that exists between the letter and the spirit, the body and the soul, the outer expression and the inner significance of a religion, we are not fanciful, but thoroughly philosophic in concluding that as a Catholic church (say S. Etienne in Paris) is to a puritan conventicle, or as Catholic public worship is to the simplicity of prayer-meeting, so is the Catholic spirit to the puritan—both simple; one with the simplicity of an imperfectly harmonised fulness and multiplicity; the other, with that of an exclusive and rigorous parsimony. It is true that the religion of Christ is the religion of the poor and simple. But popular folk-religions have always been of the Catholic type in their untrimmed luxuriance; whereas Unitarianism, for all its abstract simplicity, has never been popular; and what commends Methodism or Salvationism to the crowd is really their departures from dryness and severity; their concessions to the experienced demands of the non-rational elements of human nature. The religion or spirit of Christ has the simplicity of a principle of life and growth; but what grows out of it is an organised multitude of beliefs, precepts, observances, and institutions in which its potential fulness and fruitfulness is progressively and endlessly revealed. The Pantheon is at once an exceedingly simple and exceedingly complex structure, the product of repeated applications of a single law. Complex as Catholicism is, it is governed by a few simple ideas. The whole church of S. Etienne, with its altars and furniture, its ritual, its music, its cycle of fasts and feasts, is subordinated to and governed by the figure of the Crucified which surmounts the Tabernacle of His mystical presence. All is but the expansion of the meaning and significance of Christ the crucified for humanity. "The Fatherhood of God, the brotherhood of man"—there is Christianity in a nutshell; the very kernel of the Gospel. Yes; but Christianity in a nutshell is not enough. If it is to cover the needs of humanity; to spread its branches more widely, century after century; to reveal its latent possibilities; the kernel must be taken out of the nutshell and planted.The inexhaustible plenitude of all truth lies wrapped up in the innocent formula: "The Fatherhood of God, the brotherhood of man." As it stands it is not simple but "mysterious" in the deepest sense. The complex doctrinal system of Catholicism is really an attempt to simplify and explain it.

Moreover, we find in such a church as S. Etienne the expression, not of an individual, but of a collective spirit, world-wide and ancient, of which it is the product. Everything there speaks of communion with a great international religious organism; with the remote past of Catholicism; and, through Catholicism, with the past of those older religions out of which it has grown. It is a visualised and sensible expression of the religious experience of the best part of humanity, by means of which the religious sense of the individual is wakened, stimulated, and informed; and his consciousness of solidarity with the general life of mankind deepened and strengthened. Every such renewed consciousness of communion with Catholicism is a sacramental reinforcement of the spiritual and "over-individual" elements of his interior life—an inward grace mediated through an outward sign. It brings the soul into a more or less dimly understood, but sensibly felt, union, not only with the religious life of past centuries, but with the secular history of France, of Europe, of the world. For Catholicism means the leavening of every human interest with the leaven of the Gospel, the christianising, not merely of the religious process, but of the whole process of civilisation—of labour, science, art, of social and political institutions. The life of the Church has not been eremitical and aloof, but tangled—often far too much tangled—in that of the world around it. In her temples we are surrounded by the memorials, not only of saints, but of heroes and warriors and statesmen and poets and philosophers and writers; for these too, contribute to the multitudinous elements unified in the spirit of Catholicism. To be a Catholic is to be historically related to them, to feel one's kinship with them as children of the same civilisation which Catholicism has fostered and impregnated, and of which it has been a constituent factor.

As a complexus of feelings, judgments, and impulses, a "spirit" necessarily tends to increase in complexity with every moment that brings new experiences to be drawn into its synthesis. Our life-task is one of unification, of building-in these accumulating experiences so skilfully as not to destroy, but rather to perfect the harmony of our multitudinous thoughts, desires, and sentiments. If our religion, our Christianity, is alive and growing, it must necessarily be ever evolving a complex system of feelings, determined by and determining an equally complex system of judgments, fructifying in a correspondingly complex system of impulses. Simple as is the law of these developments, the product is not simple in content, but inexhaustible beyond all formulation.

And what holds for the individual spirit, holds still more evidently for the collective spirit—the spirit of Catholicism—that resultant of the religious experience of whole nations and centuries, which is presented to us in the institutional Church, and which acts as an instrument of spiritual education in enabling us to feed on and appropriate, according to our several needs and capacities, the gathered riches of so vast and ancient a tradition.

While, then, condemning that superfluity and lavishness which fails to secure a good, or a truth, or a loveliness that may be attained more effectually by fewer and simpler means, we condemn no less heartily that impoverishing puritanism which values such simplicity absolutely, and not merely in proportion to the richness of the result secured. To use a thousand words in expressing what could be said better in a hundred is a sin against simplicity; but it is no less a sin to use a hundred when a thousand are necessary, and to sacrifice content and clearness to brevity. Religion aims at communicating God to man, at filling the soul with the inexhaustible riches of divine truth and goodness and loveliness. It cannot put the infinite into a nutshell; it cannot put the whole truth into three words. Though it may—and often does—sin against simplicity, both by undue compression and undue diffusiveness, all the language and symbolism at its disposal is not enough for what it has got to convey.

Life on a desert island is simplified—and starved. To find everything for oneself; to be dependent on God alone—that is, on God as outside and transcendent, not as mediated through creation and humanity—means sterility in every department of life, inward and outward. Can religion be an exception? Is it not plain that its possibilities are increased in every dimension through our connection with a close-knit, world-wide, world-old communion?

This point of antiquity, of continuity with the past, weighs with us a great deal in favour of Catholicism as one of the older surviving religions.

There are poorer and richer, thinner and fuller, moments in every life. Our best moments are those which bring the fullest light from our past and present to bear on our future; our worst, those when our past is largely obliterated, and our present narrowed just to the most immediate perceptions; when our consciousness dwindles to a point and is robbed of all breadth and depth. The ideal experience is one that would lay bare all the hidden treasures of memory. And the same holds good of the people or community whose present consciousness is richer and more fruitfully active in the measure that it is fed from the treasury of the past, and that its collective memory reaches back to remoter generations, and can produce its well-ordered stores at command. To break with the past is to cut away the roots of its life. The corporate spirit, the national sentiment, is tridimensional. It is not merely a sense of fellowship with the living; but still more a sense of fellowship with the dead. It is a sharing of a collective experience, whereof the greater part by far is memory and imagination. Hence the folly of that wild eighteenth-century revolutionism, which in its blind rage against the abuses of authority and tradition strove to obliterate the past as such. Hence too its necessary failure, and the return of dethroned authority, sobered but not cured of its excesses, to the temple from which the goddess of Reason-gone-mad had driven it. Hence many an extravagance and counter-extravagance yet to come, before Reason, clothed and in her right mind, shall finally take her seat at the feet of Christ as identical with sane Authority and purified Tradition. For Authority is as blind in its way when it refuses reverence to the present and future, forgetting that growth and progress are the ends to which conservatism and stability are but ministerial. The Past may not be imposed as a dead burden on the shoulders of the Present, but needs a criticism of its values, so as to retain what is essential and to discard what is merely accidental to the process of growth. For the meaning and drift of that process reveals itself gradually. We to-day can know better than our fathers what they are aiming at and feeling after; and each generation interprets itself less wisely than it interprets its predecessors.

Catholicism, then, means a sense of communion, not only with the present but with the past multitudes of the Church's children. It is a solid, not a surface, sentiment. Its depth is even greater than its extension. Schism impoverishes the spirit even more by breaking its sensible communion with the past, than it does by severing it from the life of the present. Doubtless the conflicting claims of past and present, of authority and reason, of tradition and progress have not yet found, and may never wholly find, their adjustments. Theorisers can do little to hasten, and much to impede, Nature's slow experimental process of solving the difficulty. It was, however, a mere accident of his times and circumstances that Christ died at the hands of authority in the cause of reason and liberty. In other conditions he would have died at the hands of liberty in the cause of authority and tradition. . . .

Again, we feel that Catholicism is, in tendency, a religion of all levels of spiritual development, and not of one only; that it has milk for babes and meat for adults; that it is a language in which the simplest and the subtlest can hold converse with Heaven on the shallowest themes and the deepest. And this range and versatility commends it to us as a product of experience, of God working through Nature; and not a device of human reflection. We should find a more exclusively aristocratic or a more exclusively popular religion hard to reconcile with the universalism of Christ's spirit. If there is much that offends my taste, or violates my reason, or shocks my moral sense, what right have I to make my subjective needs a standard for all so long as I am free? It is not enough that my religion suits *me,* it must suit mankind; it must cater for all—just as the State must look to the interests of every class, and not only to mine. I could not be satisfied with a religion which, however much it did for me, did nothing for the masses or for the classes—too academic for the former, too barbaric for the latter. The board spread for all must have every sort of fare, so that each may find something, though none can find everything, to his taste and requirement. It is no small gain to be forced into one pale and communion with spiritual sorts and conditions so unlike our own, and to be compelled to bear with, and learn from others who have to bear with and learn from us, and thus to overcome our mental insularity.

Thus there is an aesthetic intolerance that despises the day of small things, and would impose abruptly upon the worship of the rude and uncultured a severity in music, decoration, and the like for which they are educationally unprepared, which fails to detect in their woefully barbaric beginnings a partial, if inadequate, self-utterance of the beautiful, which forgets that our own higher expressions are only relatively less inadequate.

And there is an intellectual intolerance which treats truth as an exact equation of thought to thing, which knows no half-truths, but only Yea and Nay, and brands as a lie whatever deviates from mathematical precision. Of the merely approximate character of our best religious conceptions it has no suspicion, but would force, as finally true, on childish minds what even for adults is only a less inadequate approximation. It will not tolerate what it considers the falsehoods through which the unfolding mind must pass if the fuller truth is to be of its own growing, and not merely stuck in rootless from outside. To it the malice of superstition consists in mental error and igno-

rance, and not merely in the demoralising and decadent results that
sometimes attend it—not merely in the evasion of duty by external
observances—in the neglect of natural means through trust in charms
or in prayer.

It is not superstition if men turn to Mary, as a truer embodiment
of the divine, rather than to a God, whom they ignorantly suppose to
be inhuman and vindictive. But if they think her intercession and
favour will allow them to live more carelessly for having a friend in
court, that indeed is essentially superstition. Yet God Himself may be
worshipped superstitiously by the most infallible theologian who
ever lived.

And lastly, there is an ethical intolerance, both as to moral stan-
dards and to moral attainments, which seems again to make no
account of the laws of growth, to demand an impossible uniformity
of level, and to forget that the ethical, like the aesthetic and intellectual, education of persons and classes, must be graduated. Nature
does nothing in jumps. The highest cannot abruptly be fitted on to
the lowest. We must be content to lead men from where they stand
to the next stage, and not to the next but one. And this wisdom and
toleration is forced on us in a Church which is the home of all sorts
and conditions of men, of whom no class or level can say to the
other: "I have no need of thee," and where the law of Christ bids us
bear one another's burdens. . . .

To conclude, Catholicism seems to us to stand for the widest, the
oldest, the deepest stream of collective Christian experience. As such,
its mind moves more slowly than that of younger and narrower systems. It reaches the truth more tardily because its experiments are
conducted on a far larger scale; because it looks back on a longer
past, and round on a wider present; because it advances with the
grave pace of Nature and will not be rushed on by its theoricians.
Better, we feel, to be borne more quietly along on the bosom of this
broad, slow current than to be hurried along more rapidly on the
surface of some brawling stream. If our religious life is a corporate
superindividual life; if it approximates in ideal to the religious life of
humanity, we will not wish to press forward alone, but will gladly
hold back to help on the rest of our fellow-travellers.

CATHOLIC MODERNISM*

The term "Modernist" has been used in a sufficient variety of senses to cause a considerable amount of confusion. If not invented, it has, at least, been established by the Encyclical *Pascendi* as the prejudicial designation of a party in the Roman Catholic Church. But already it is accepted as the designation of liberal Christians of all sorts, and bids fair to supplant the older term "liberal," which, as standing for a political as well as a religious principle, is somewhat less exact. "Modernist" as opposed to "modern" means the insistence on modernity as a principle. It means the acknowledgment on the part of religion of the rights of modern thought; of the need of effecting a synthesis, not between the old and new indiscriminately, but between what, after due criticism, is found to be valid in the old and in the new. Its opposition is Medievalism, which, as a fact, is only the synthesis effected between the Christian faith and the culture of the late Middle Ages, but which erroneously supposes itself to be of apostolic antiquity; which denies that the work of synthesis is necessary and must endure as long as man's intellectual, moral, and social evolution endures; which therefore makes the medieval expression of Catholicism its primitive and its final expression.

Medievalism is an absolute, Modernism a relative term. The former will always stand for the same ideas and institutions; the meaning of the latter slides on with the times. If we must have a sect-name, we might have a worse than one that stands for life and movement as against stagnation and death; for the Catholicism that is of every age as against the sectarianism that is of one.

A good deal of the force of the Encyclical as an appeal to the Christian sense is due to its ambiguous use of the term Modernist.

It professes to be describing those Roman Catholics who believe in this principle of "Modernism," and who are confident that a synthesis between faith and the established results of criticism is possible without damage to either. But, in fact, it describes as Modernists those Catholics also who possess no such confidence; who consider that criticism is fatal to Catholicism and to its principal beliefs and institutions, who ridicule such syntheses as utopian, and who, in many cases, are among the most active opponents—official or unofficial— of "Modernism." In short, it describes as "Modernists" all those professed Roman Catholics who accept the results of criticism, however those results may tell upon their faith, whether disastrously or other-

*From George Tyrrell, *Medievalism: A Reply to Cardinal Mercier* (1909), 143–58.

wise. Thus it cleverly lays every "Modernist" open to the suspicion of
being an unitarian or an atheist or an agnostic; it brands them all
alike as hypocrites and pretenders. Unfortunately there are, and there
always have been, such men in the Church even on the Chair of
Peter; and that, long before the days of criticism. Scepticism is not
modern, nor is atheism, nor hypocrisy. Let us, then, keep the word
"Modernist" to designate those who believe in the Roman Catholic
Church as firmly as medievalists do; but whose deeper faith is not
frightened but stimulated by the assured results of modern criticism.
For, as it is belief in the living Christ that makes a Christian, and not
any particular Christology, so what makes a Catholic is not this or
that abstract theory of the Church, but a belief in the historical
apostolic mission. No one who has lost faith in the mission and destiny of the Roman Church and in the advantage of being identified
with it is a Roman Catholic.

To believe in the living historical Catholic community means to
believe that by its corporate life and labour it is slowly realising the
ideas and ends in whose service it was founded; that through many
fluctuations and errors and deviations and recoveries and reactions it
is gradually shaping itself into a more efficient institution for the
spiritual and moral development of individuals and societies; that by
its continuity and extension it is the collective subject of a vast experience of good and evil, of truth and fallacy, and of a slow but sure
process of reflection on the same; that if it advances laboriously and
imperceptibly it is because its evolution, like that of nature, is the
result of so vast, so costly and even so cruel an experience, and
because the contributions of individual effort are opposed tooth
and nail until their right to survive and conquer has overcome
almost every conceivable objection. One's belief in the Church as
the organ of religion is to some extent one's belief in the laws of
collective psychology, which are the laws of nature, which are the
laws of God. . . .

But the Modernist is a Catholic with a difference. What is this
difference?

The difference is that whereas the Medievalist regards the expression of Catholicism, formed by the synthesis between faith and the
general culture of the thirteenth century, as primitive and as practically final and exhaustive, the Modernist denies the possibility of
such finality and holds that the task is unending just because the
process of culture is unending.

Hence the new historico-scientific methods and their results, the new social and political ideas and institutions, being irreconcilable with the medieval synthesis, seem to the Medievalist irreconcilable with what he considers to be the primitive final and perfect expression of Catholicism. The old synthesis has been perhaps modified at the Councils of Trent and the Vatican; but only along the same lines and categories, and by way of defining more closely its opposition to post-medieval culture. The Modernist is no blind worshipper of present culture. He knows it is a medley of good and evil, and needs careful criticism and discrimination. But he believes that, on the whole, it stands for gain rather than loss; and that its new and true values must be absorbed into the Catholic organism if the latter is to live.

If he believes in the Church as a Catholic, as man he believes in humanity; he believes in the world. To regard the world outside the Church as God-forsaken; to deny that God works and reveals himself in human history, that he is in and with mankind in all its struggles against evil and ignorance and degradation, that he is the primary author of all intellectual, aesthetic, moral, social, and political progress, seems to the Modernist the most subtle and dangerous form of atheism.

Nay, of the two, his faith in the world is more fundamental than his faith in the Church—in the world of which it is written, "God so loved the world that he gave his only begotten Son." For he who sits at meat is greater than he who serves; and the Church, like her Master, is sent for the service of the world; to serve it, not to rule over it, or trample on it, or despise it. If she has something to teach it, she has much to learn from it. It is the living whole of which she is but an organic part; and the whole is greater than even its most vital organ. The Modernist loves the Church for the sake of the world and humanity; which means that he loves humanity more, as the fuller and all-inclusive revelation of God. The Manichean dualism that opposes the Church to the world, as light to darkness, is to him a compendium of many heresies. Any barrier that hinders their free interchange of benefits is impoverishing to both alike. Each must absorb the quickening forces of the other under pain of a monstrous and lop-sided development.

Again, whereas the Medievalist, with his mechanical and static idea of ecclesiastical infallibility, canonises the entire medieval synthesis indiscriminately; the Modernist, with his dynamical idea of a process that will infallibly work out right in the end; with his conception of our highest truth as ever alloyed with error, of our highest good as ever alloyed with evil, is one who discriminates and qualifies, who distrusts absolutism of every sort.

He does not view the essence of Christianity as consisting of one or two simple principles given from the first and abiding unchanged beneath a bewildering mass of meaningless and mischievous encrustations. Its essence is continually being built up by the expansion and application of these normative principles; by their combination with all that is good and true in the process of human development. It consists not merely in the leaven but in the whole mass that is leavened and christianised, and that grows in bulk from age to age. So far he agrees with the Medievalist against the Protestant. But he does not believe that the process stopped with the thirteenth century, and is, therefore, truer to the Catholic principle.

For him, however, it is a double process of good and evil; of false and true. He recognises, what the reformers could not recognise with their dim historical light, that the tares were sown almost contemporaneously with the wheat; and are always being sown; that if the wheat has grown, the tares have also grown even from the Apostolic age—from the first pious tamperings with the Gospel text; that there has been a development not only of good but of evil principles, not only of truths but of errors, not only of the leaven of the Gospel but of the leaven of hypocrisy. He sees that in every generation some tare or another ripens and betrays its true character and needs to be uprooted; that there are epochs when a perfect harvest of such tares demands a sort of revolution—a ruthless thrusting in of the sickle of criticism, a binding in bundles and burning of noxious weeds. He recognises in the recent developments of the Roman-law conception of ecclesiastical authority on the one side, and on the other in the recent results of biblical and historical criticism and of social and political developments, the signs of such a crisis in the life of the Church. His is no blind Philistinism that would raze the Church to the ground and run up a smart up-to-date structure on the old site. He holds firmly that nothing which has, on a large scale and for a long period, both lived and given life can be destroyed without irreparable loss and impoverishment. His sole effort is to separate the perishable from the imperishable elements in all such cases; to change as little, to preserve as much, as truth and truthfulness will permit.

Alive to all abuses and errors connected with dogmas and institutions, he is not less alive to the services they have rendered; to the principles they have imperfectly expressed. Christ-worship, saint-worship, miracles, sacraments, dogma, theology, uniformity, ritual, priesthood, sacrifice, papacy, infallibility, nay Medievalism itself, all stand for so many attempts to satisfy the religious requirements of human nature. Whatever is mechanical, gross, unhistorical, or decadent must be so removed as to save those values by which they have lived in spite of their evident limitations. If the marriage of Christian principles with the sane principles and elements of growing civilisation has been fruitful of true developments of the Catholic idea, their marriage with the unhealthy and evil elements of the same has produced spurious developments, in which, however, the nobler strain must be recognised and purified. Even things so utterly evil as persecution and inquisition have been not merely approved by good men, but approved as right, because they were the perverse and stupid application of the undoubted truth that the destroyer of souls is a greater danger to the public than a murderer; that temporal death is a lesser evil than spiritual. No immorality could have lived and thriven unless it had perversely appealed to conscience under some appearance of morality. We must not empty out the baby with the bath. We must save the apparent morality if we would reveal the full deformity of what is covered and what will else return in the same guise.

And so, for the Modernist, even the errors, sins, and follies of the past are valuable experiences which the Church is all the wiser and deeper and richer for having passed through and beyond. In this, the same law governs the formation of collective as of individual character. Virtues that have not been driven home by hard struggle lie light on the soul's surface; the storm that rocks the tree roots it.

It is by the experimental method that Nature gropes her way to what is more useful, more true to life's laws. Catholicism is a great experimentation in religion; a quest of the fullest and most perfect expression of Christianity. Medievalism, in the eyes of the Modernist, is a necessary experiment which must be worked out to its extremest and bitterest consequences if the Church is to realise inwardly and comprehensively a truer, deeper, richer notion of liberty and authority, of faith and orthodoxy, of revelation and theology, of growth and identity, than were possible otherwise. Thus it is that God in history is ever judging the world, gathering the wheat into his barn and burning the chaff with the fire unquenchable. For ourselves, with omnipotence and omniscience at our disposal, we should have arranged things differently; we should have saved all the waste and woe of this tedious experimental process; we should have created an immutably perfect Church by the fiat of our will. But God's ways and thoughts are not as ours, nor can we wonder if he works as slowly and wastefully in the Kingdom of Grace as in the Kingdom of Nature. The argument from what we ourselves should have done to what God must therefore have done is the principal basis of the ultramontane Church-theory; but it is somewhat shaken by the consideration of what God has actually done and does daily.

Finally, the Modernist demands, not greater freedom, but absolute freedom for science in the widest sense of the term. He will not have it fettered except by its own laws and methods and by the experience which is its subject-matter. He will not allow even theology to be tied down to any revealed and stereotyped statements, but only to the religious experiences of which certain statements are the spontaneous self-chosen, but at most symbolic, expressions. Such experiences are the substance of revelation; the inspired statements are but its classical and primitive symbols, and cannot be treated as premises for deduction.

Science for him is one general system dealing with all experience and trying to arrange it into a single synthesis of the understanding. As a theologian, he takes account of spiritual and supernatural experiences as part of the totality of experience; he considers the religions of mankind; the religion of Israel, the religion of Jesus and his apostles, the religion of the Catholic community—all, as so much experience. He considers the spiritual forces and tendencies and sentiments that have embodied themselves in the history, institutions and doctrines of the Roman Catholic Church and in the lives and actions of her children, and which are revealed in defeat as well as in victory, in false as well as in true developments. And from such consideration, he arrives progressively at a better idea of the essence and aim of Catholicism and at a truer criterion by which to shape the course of its future developments.

Modernism therefore has nothing to do with that sort of more educated and temporising ultramontanism that shrinks from an inopportune pressing of principles which the world has unfortunately outgrown; that loves to rub shoulders cautiously with science and democracy; that strives to express itself moderately and grammatically; that would make a change of circumstances and opportunities pass for a more tolerant spirit; and that is usually rewarded for its pains by finding itself between the hammer and the anvil.

Modernism does not seek to modify this or that tenet or institution. It is an all-pervading principle affecting the whole of Catholicism from end to end with its distinction between the divine and the human element; the spirit and the embodiment; the permanent and the variable. If it is a heresy at all, it is "the compendium of all heresies."

Thus, if we speak of it as a movement or tendency guided by certain principles and methods which it is prepared to follow with a certain blind faith whither-soever they may lead, it admits of a fairly clear description. But if by Modernism we mean a finished theological system like that of the scholastics with a definite and final answer to every theological problem, and if I am asked what is to be the upshot of these methods and principles, what is to be the modernist theology of Christ and the sacraments and the scriptures and so forth, I have a perfect right to answer "I do not know"—just as a socialist has a perfect right to say that he does not know what socialism is; that he cannot provide a finished theory of it; cannot see below the horizon; cannot define an idea that is slowly working itself into consciousness and is necessarily incoherent and elusive in its earlier self-utterances. He knows that the whole world is in labour; but he knows what is going, better than what is coming. As against existing social institutions and ideas, which are clearly definable because they are played out and dead, he is dumb and easily convicted of folly, just because he is feeling after something living that is coming to birth through a series of uncouth embryonic developments. But if by socialism we mean not the theory or idea but the process, tendency, or movement which binds millions of men together for a common end and for a work that is directly constructive, and indirectly destructive, socialism is quite definite and concrete.

And the same is to be said of "Modernism" so far as it stands for the living assembly of Modernists and not for the idea or end, as yet obscure but most real and active, that inspires and binds them together. In the abstract, Medievalism is definable because it is dead; Modernism is not so, because it is living and growing. A system that perforce ignores all the results of man's mental, moral, and social development since the thirteenth century is naturally more simple and definite than one that not only tries to assimilate those results, but that holds its conclusions as merely provisional in view of further and yet further results, that has abandoned the idea of finality and recognised the work of synthesis as an abiding and unending duty. . . .

The Modernist therefore denies the scholastic's right to challenge him for definitions and conclusions that are ever in the making and never made. And if it be objected that at that rate he has no message for the millions—for the poor and the simple—he replies, first, that their need of definite statements would not justify false and premature statements or a pretence of finality where none existed. Secondly, that the issue is not between popular religion and modernist theology, but between scholastic theology and modernist theology, both of which are the scientific, non-popular justification of popular Catholic belief and practice. What we preach to the poor is not theology, but revelation—the inspired and simple expression of those experiences which theology translates into the technical language of philosophical systems.

Finally, we reply that the scholastic system, for all its meretricious simplicity, is fully as unintelligible to the crowds as the immanental or the pragmatist system. For does any serious man believe that its theological expressions concerning the Trinity or the Hypostatic Union or Transubstantiation which Medievalists teach the faithful to repeat, correspond to or evoke any coherent conceptions in their understandings? Do we not know that theologians themselves when pressed close are found to be dealing with words and words only? Has Your Eminence any clearly different concepts answering to the words "generation" and "procession" in the Athanasian Creed; or to such expressions as "spiritual presence" or "wholly in the whole and wholly in each part" or "three persons in one nature" or "one person in two natures"? If you think you have, is it not only because you think that other people have? No, Your Eminence, when we preach to the people what Christ preached—the coming of God's Kingdom, the baptism of repentance and a new life—we feed them with bread; when we preach scholasticism, we feed them with words and wind: "For this cause many among you are sick and weakly, and many sleep."

But it would be wrong to suppose that because the growing ideas of modernist theology are necessarily incomplete and indefinable they are therefore worthless. For man, truth is an unending process of adequation, not a finished result. His understanding and analysis can never do more than outline the growing masses of his experience. The inadequacy of his conceptions is not merely quantitative; they are not a mathematical half or quarter or tenth of the whole. Each addition changes the quality, the truth-colour, of all that has gone before, as each new ingredient changes the quality of a chemical compound. Still, what is acquired is acquired, though it be transformed and transcended by subsequent acquisitions. The grub survives in the moth, the foetus in the adult; and so of the successive expressions which the same reality or experience creates for itself in the human mind. Each expresses the same thing; each begets its follower and is begotten by its predecessor. Furthermore, each is of permanent value in determining the direction of the whole process which cannot be rightly understood or criticised except from the study and comparison of its several phases.

When therefore it is a question of preaching Christianity to others, or of living it himself, the Modernist apprehends and presents it under the same inspired and imaginative symbols as the Medievalist. When it is a question of giving scientific intellectual expression to the experiences for which those symbols stand, when it is a question between theologians, he refuses to regard any theology as final or to predict what form it may assume in its endeavours to unify religious experience with future accumulations of general experience. It will be tied by no statements, by no graven inscriptions; only by the facts of experience for which such statements stand, and by the laws of the mind.

Hence, because a Modernist's theology, i.e. his intellectual construction of Catholicism, is living and growing, it cannot be presented with the clearness and definiteness of a theology that is finished and dead, and that is impervious to the quickening influence of contemporary culture.

Further, it is perfectly obvious that modernist theologians will not agree among themselves as do those who learn, almost by rote, a system imposed upon them in the name of authority, by an appeal to their conscience rather than to their reason; who are supported by this uniformity, this spurious semblance of unanimity, in their confident defence of the same, and who fancy that what is held so firmly and generally must be self-evident to others if not to themselves. If faith works miracles, faith in the faith of others is more mighty still. It can clothe the naked with a garment of glory, admired by all and seen by none.

9

Criticism and Christology

THE CHRIST OF LIBERAL
PROTESTANTISM*

The Jesus of the school of critics represented to-day by Harnack and Bousset, was a Divine Man because He was full of the Spirit of God; full of Righteousness. He came (it is assumed rather than proved) at a time when the Jews were full of apocalyptic expectations as to the coming of the Messiah, who was to avenge them of their enemies and establish a more or less miraculous and material Kingdom of God upon earth. He Himself seems to have shared this view in a spiritual form, translating it from material to ethical terms. As destined by a Divine vocation to inaugurate a reign of Righteousness, a Kingship of God over men's hearts and consciences, He felt Himself to be the true, because the spiritual, Messiah. With difficulty He trained a few of His followers to this conception of the Kingdom and the Christ. He went about doing good (even working cures which He supposed to be miraculous) and teaching goodness. The essence of His Gospel was the Fatherhood of God and the Brotherhood of man; or else the two great Commandments of the law—the love of God and of one's neighbour; or else the Kingdom of God that is within us. True, these were platitudes of contemporary Jewish piety, and even of pagan philosophy. But Jesus drove them home to the heart by the force of

*From George Tyrrell, *Christianity at the Crossroads* (1909), 39–45.
136

personal example and greatness of character—above all, by dying for His friends and for these ethical principles. Of course He was, to some extent, of His time. He believed in miracles, in diabolic possession; above all, He believed in the immediate end of the world; and a great deal of His ethics, coloured by that belief, was the ethics of a crisis. But these were but accidents of His central idea and interest, in regard to which we may say He was essentially modern, so far as our rediscovery of the equation Religion = Righteousness is modern, not to say Western and Teutonic.

For this almost miraculous modernity the first century was not prepared. No sooner was the Light of the World kindled than it was put under a bushel. The Pearl of Great Price fell into the dustheap of Catholicism, not without the wise permission of Providence, desirous to preserve it till the day when Germany should rediscover it and separate it from its useful but deplorable accretions. Thus between Christ and early Catholicism there is not a bridge but a chasm. Christianity did not cross the bridge; it fell into the chasm and remained there, stunned, for nineteen centuries. The explanation of this sudden fall—more sudden because they have pushed Catholicism back to the threshold of the Apostolic age—is the crux of Liberal Protestant critics. The only analogy I can think of is the sudden appearance of Irvingite Catholicism in the bosom of Presbyterianism.

The theory is curiously akin to that of the neo-Roman theologians. In both, Revelation is suddenly eclipsed with the Apostolic age, to regain its primitive brilliance only after the lapse of centuries. Here it is the Immaculate Conception that is rediscovered; there it is the Fatherhood of God and the first principles of morality.

It was to the credit of their hearts, if to the prejudice of their scientific indifference, that these critics were more or less avowedly actuated by apologetic interests. They desired to strip Jesus of His medieval regalia, and to make Him acceptable to a generation that had lost faith in the miraculous and in any conception of another life that was not merely a complement, sanction and justification of this life. They wanted to bring Jesus into the nineteenth century as the Incarnation of its ideal of Divine Righteousness, i.e. of all of the highest principles and aspirations that ensure the healthy progress of civilization. They wanted to acquit Him of that exclusive and earth-scorning otherworldliness, which had led men to look on His religion as the foe of progress and energy, and which came from confusing the accidental form with the essential substance of His Gospel. With eyes thus preoccupied they could only find the German in the Jew; a

moralist in a visionary; a professor in a prophet; the nineteenth century in the first; the natural in the supernatural. Christ was the ideal
man; the Kingdom of Heaven, the ideal humanity. As the rationalistic presupposition had strained out, as spurious, the miraculous elements of the Gospel, so the moralistic presupposition strained out
everything but modern morality. That alone was the substance, the
essence, of Christianity—*das Wesen des Christentums*. If God
remained, it was only the God of moralism and rationalism—the
correlative of the Brotherhood of man; not the God of Moses, of
Abraham, Isaac and Jacob; of David and the prophets.

Now it is clear that every scientific inquiry must be impelled by a
motive and guided by a hypothesis. A method is in itself a dead tool
without force or direction. Were truth not advantageous, the will
could not seek it. The question is whether we are thinking of some
particular, personal or party advantage or the advantage of human
life as a whole; whether our desire is individual or universalistic in its
interest—a desire of the separate or of the spiritual self. The weight
of a given planet has no immediate bearing on practical politics, but
only on the completeness of the human understanding, which is a
co-factor of human life in general. Truth for truth's sake means truth
for life's sake, it only excludes an eye to any less universal advantage.
What we call "idle curiosity" is often healthy instinct—a desire to
integrate our general view of the world in which we have to live.

True, scientific inquiry cannot be coldly disinterested, but any
other interest than the integration of knowledge distorts its vision.
Here the Liberal Protestant critics failed no less than the positively
anti-Christian critics. Their hypothesis was an article of faith, not an
instrument of inquiry. If they had been beaten off the field we need
not, perhaps, set it down to the severer detachment of their conquerors, but to the stricter application of that critical method which
they invoked.

It is by that method that Johannes Weiss and his followers have
been forced back, very unwillingly in most cases, to the eschatological and apocalyptic interpretation of the Gospel. Very unwillingly,
because it destroys the hope of smoothing away the friction between
Christianity and the present age; because, in closing the chasm
between the Gospel and early Catholicism, it makes the Christianity
of Christ, in all essentials, as unacceptable as that of Catholicism.

Of this state of things Loisy was not slow to take advantage in
L'Evangile et l'Eglise, directed against the Liberal Protestantism of

Harnack's *Wesen des Christentums*. The Christ that Harnack sees, looking back through nineteen centuries of Catholic darkness, is only the reflection of a Liberal Protestant face, seen at the bottom of a deep well. Applying Newman's notion of development to a broader and deeper problem than Newman's, Loisy contends that the "idea" of Christ, in its substance and character, is identical with that of Catholic Christianity and opposed at nearly all points to that of Liberal Protestantism.

Rome (profoundly ignorant of the critical movement, its currents and tendencies) thought that even a victory over the Protestant might be purchased at too great a cost, and repudiated a notion of development different from that of her theological dialecticians, and disastrous to their idea of orthodoxy. Her hostility to the book and its author have created a general impression that it is a defense of Liberal Protestant against Roman Catholic positions, and that "Modernism" is simply a protestantizing and rationalizing movement. This confusion is widespread within and without the Roman Church, and many who account themselves Modernists are disciples of Harnack rather than of Loisy.

THE CHRIST OF CATHOLICISM* = a development of apocalypticism of the Gospel?.

We must now try to get hold of the "idea" embodied in the apocalypticism of the Gospel and compare it with that embodied in Catholic Christianity, to see whether they are merely different embodiments of the same, and whether the latter can be considered as a development of the former.

Plainly we must distinguish between the substance or content and the form or expression of an "idea." As we use the word here, an "idea" is a concrete end, whose realization is the term of a process of action and endeavour. It is akin to that Augustinian *notio* (or *ratio*) *seminalis*, with which every living germ seems to be animated, and which works itself out to full expression through a process of growth and development. It does not change in itself, but is the cause of change in its embodiment. Transferred from the realm of organic life to that of human activity, an "idea" is still a good or end to be realized and brought to perfect expression. But it is rather a volition than a concept. Every volition, however blind and instinctive, is

*From George Tyrrell, *Christianity at the Crossroads* (1909), 62–90.

directed by the idea of an end to be reached. That idea is implied in
the volition, but it is not necessarily given to the clear consciousness
of the person who wills. Animals obey instincts without any knowledge of the ends with which they are pregnant. The meaning of many
of man's spiritual and rational instincts is revealed to him only gradually, as he follows them step by step. In most cases their full meaning
will never be clear to him. Thus civilization, education, society, liberty, justice, are spiritual instincts with man. He does not start with a
clear conception of what he wants; but his conceptions grow clearer,
more explicit, more complex, more organized, as he moves along. In
the embodiment or expression of the idea we must, then, include its
intellectual expression or form.

Thus man's religious idea is first felt as a vague need of adjusting
his action to that whole, of which all but a little part is hidden from
him; of coming to terms with an invisible and mysterious world. This
"idea" is the soul of the lowest and of the highest forms of religion.
But the conception of the invisible world and its denizens, of its
relation to man and the visible order, of the conduct by which the
adjustment is to be effected, belongs to the embodiment or expression of the idea. It is determined by the idea and its environment—
the intellectual, moral, and social conditions of man. Its only criterion and corrective is the idea itself, which is no practical corrective
since man only apprehends it in the very form that needs correction.
His measure is at fault and cannot be tested by itself. But the idea,
like Nature, eventually heals itself and asserts itself triumphantly
over all obstacles. . . .

By the "idea" of Jesus I mean, then, the religious idea in a certain
stage of development, along a particular line. I ask myself: Is Catholic Christianity on the same line or, as Liberal Protestants suppose,
on an entirely different line? Is it the outgrowth of the same branch,
or did it fork off in the first century? Is it simply a Hellenic process,
violently grafted into the Liberal Protestantism of Jesus—the latter
being interrupted at that point until the graft was broken off by
criticism?

Now so far as we find an actual identity of form and category we
are plainly justified in supposing the same idea to be at work on the
same line. No doubt the expression or form is more ample and complex in Catholicism than in the Gospel, but its main and central
features are the same.

Transcendentalism, or other-worldliness, belongs to the idea of religion as such, but in varying degrees. The whole tendency of Liberal Protestantism is to minimize the transcendence by establishing a sort of identity of form between this life and the other. So far as man's life is moral, it is an eternal life. The moral life has mystical and transcendental roots. It postulates a spiritual principle and end in Nature which we may call God. Heaven and the Kingdom of Heaven are in our midst; they are the spiritual or moral side of life.

Without this concession to transcendentalism, Liberal Protestantism would not be a religion at all. As it is, it is rather a system of religious ethics than a religion. It merely insists that morality is religion and adjusts our life and action to that spiritual and invisible side of the world which is an object of faith, a necessary postulate of morality. No doubt this is the truth of Christianity; but it is not the whole truth. Emphasis is laid on it in the Fourth Gospel; in the synoptics it is implicit rather than emphatic. Christ had not come to emphasize the religion and the revelation implied in righteousness that were within the reach of man's reason. His emphasis was on the other-worldly, supermoral life of the coming Kingdom. How could it be otherwise on the very brink of the destruction of the present order? What need of a new ethics for expiring humanity? His whole emphasis, therefore, was on the other world, and on the conditions by which men might attain it and flee from the wrath to come. Of these, repentance and true inward righteousness were the chief. But men did not so much need to be told what righteousness was, as to be called back to it or converted to it. And this Jesus did by giving the will a motive: "Repent ye, *for* the Kingdom of Heaven is at hand."

If, then, the religion of Jesus was not exclusively transcendental, its emphasis was almost entirely on the other world—the world that is least present to man's mind and most easily forgotten. And this excessive transcendentalism is the great reproach made against Catholicism by the Liberal Protestant as well as by the Positivist. It is true that the *immediacy* of the End very soon dropped out of Catholic consciousness, and so restored the depressed value and importance of the present life. But the belief in the End; in the eventual appearance of the Son of Man in the clouds; in the general Judgment and its preceding tribulations; in the destruction of the present order; in a transcendental and eternal Heaven and Hell, figures as the final and, in a sense, dominant article of her creed.

In her Advent liturgy one finds even the note of immediacy;
though naturally it evokes no response in her consciousness. The
contention that this immediacy was not essential to the idea of Jesus
is not without plausibility. The words "Of that day or that hour
knoweth no one, not even the Son," although consistent with a certainty that the End would be very soon, and within a generation, at
least disclaim any sort of revelation on the point and imply that any
prediction can be no more than a private conjecture. The fore-short-
ening of time in the prophet's mind does not affect the substance of
the situation. The supposed near approach of death will often make
a man reorder his life, as he ought to have reordered it in any case, in
view of the certainty of eventual death. The scare has not given him a
new reason but a new stimulus. It has made him attend to what he
should have always seen. The public scare at the thought of the
immediacy of the Kingdom, that all expected eventually, acted similarly. The Kingdom, not the immediacy of the Kingdom, was the
reason for repentance, detachment and righteousness; the immediacy
was but a stimulus to rouse the sluggish imagination—to change a
"notional" into a "real" assent. Hence it may be said that the conception of immediacy was no part of the idea of Jesus; it was a supposed
circumstance of the situation in which that idea was applied.

If Jesus Himself, as seems likely, experienced one or more disappointments in the matter, we cannot say that the further disappointments of His Church were for Him outside the range of possibility.
Still those who now expect the End at all no longer expect it immediately, and have given up speaking of "those last days." Only now and
then is there a recrudescence of apocalyptic panic in times of earth-
quakes, comets, wars, and pestilences.

Christianity is, perhaps, the better and not the worse for the loss
of this stimulus, to which it owes its birth. For the violent detachment, justified by such an expectancy, is hurtful to the duties and
lawful interests of social life. No man who believes he has but a day
to live will make proper provision for his future years. The scare may
be useful to make him amend his ways. But a sustained scare would
paralyse his energies. This evil was soon felt by the early Church in a
certain anarchy and neglect of plain social duties. It was not worth
while to assert the claims of justice, to establish and provide for a
family. Men pooled their wealth and lived in the clouds and in idle-
ness. "If any will not work neither let him eat" was a rebuke leveled
against this state of things.

Yet this contempt of the world preached by Jesus was not Buddhistic in its motive. It was a contempt of a lower and transitory form of existence in favour of a higher—a proximate pessimism but an ultimate optimism. That the world was thought to be in its death-agony made it doubly contemptible. But when this thought was dropped by the Church, the world still remained contemptible. It was but a preparation and purgatory; the antechamber of Heaven; the theatre of the great conflict between the forces of good and evil—a conflict that could be decided in favour of Good only by the Coming of the Son of Man. It was a world in which the Christian was but a stranger and a pilgrim, looking for a City whose builder is God. The notion that Good was to triumph by an immanent process of evolution never entered into the "idea" of Jesus or of the Church.

But the impression of the first days remained with the Church long after the immediate expectation of the End had ceased: what Christ had said, what the early Christians had done in view of that immediacy, has lingered on as a rule of life, in diminishing measure, even to the present day. It was this excessive otherworldliness, which enters largely into the monastic and ascetic idea of Catholicism, that provoked that revulsion, which began with Luther and ended with the purely ethical Christianity of the Liberal Protestant, for whom the Kingdom of Heaven is but the ideal term of the moral evolution of man on earth.

To this ethical idea of the Kingdom some colour is given by the early tendency to view the Church as the Kingdom of God upon earth in a certain anticipatory sense—a tendency that appeared when men had ceased to look on the Heavenly Kingdom as imminent. Nor was it without warrant from Christ, who considered that, in Himself and in the Baptist, and in the victory of God's Spirit over the Devil, the Kingdom had already begun to touch the earth. This conception of the Church, as the Kingdom *in fieri,* prepared the way for that of a moral humanity as the Kingdom. But the conceptions are radically distinct. Here a natural evolution is to complete the work; there, a supernatural cataclysm.

Again, the emphatic Persian dualism of Good and Evil, of the Kingdom of God and that of Satan, is common to the idea of Jesus and the idea of Catholicism. The Devil is essential to the Catholic scheme. Renunciation of the Devil and his retinue (*pompa*) is the preliminary of that Baptism which enlists a man in the service of the Kingdom. Till then he is possessed by Satan, in virtue of his natural birth. This is the teaching of Jesus no less than of St. Paul or St. Augustine. Satan is exorcised to make room for the Holy Spirit. Every priest is an ordained exorcist, and exorcism has its prescribed ritual. A host of mental, moral and physical evils, which science now deals with, not to speak of storms, plagues and other destructive phenomena of nature, have, till quite recent times, been ascribed to the Devil by the Church, and treated by prayer and exorcism. Even so modern a Pope as Leo XIII accepted the fables of Leo Taxil and his mythical Diana Vaughan, and exorcised Rome daily; and the prevailing mind of uncritical Catholics is still quick to explain all the evils of the time by the Devil and his human agents—Jews, Freemasons, Protestants and Modernists. The Devil introduced sin and mortality, with all their attendant evils, into the world.

On the other hand, with Christ came the fullness of the Holy Ghost poured out on all the baptized. Possessed by this Divine Spirit, the baptized becomes "a new creature" by an inward transformation of his nature. Ethical perfection is the congruous fruit but not the substance of that change. He is not divine because he is moral, but moral because he has become divine. So, too, the main fruit of all the sacraments of Catholicism is not the moral life of the present, but the supermoral life of the future. They as it were, store up potential glory in the soul, which shall be liberated by death. Hence the contention that a life of very average morality, with frequent sacraments, is more pleasing to God than a life of heroic morality, without sacraments. It is only the sacraments that make us sons of God. Morality can never do so. It is but the congruous natural condition of grace, and gets all its lustre and merit from grace. Thus the baptized infant, incapable as yet of moral life, is made a divine creature by the expulsion of the Devil and the introduction of the Holy Ghost. In virtue of this new nature man is made immortal by a quasi-natural necessity. If he dies before the End he will rise in a spiritualized body; if he lives to the End he will be transformed and caught up in the clouds. As the Fourth Gospel says, he *has* eternal life in him already. Like Christ on earth he is only waiting for the eventual manifestation of the glory that is in him. Grace is the germ of glory. As little as the natural world could grow into the transcendental Kingdom of God, so little could the natural man, by a process of moral development, grow into a son of God, a spiritual immortal being. In both cases the change—a veritable transubstantiation—is effected by an irruption of the transcendental into the natural order; by a triumph of the Spirit of God over Satan. It is not a work of nature, but of unmerited grace.

Uncongenial as this dualism is to our modern minds, is it possible to deny that it is common to Jesus and Catholicism? It is not between Jesus and Catholicism, but between Jesus and Liberal Protestantism that no bridge, but only a great gulf, is fixed.

It is, however, a dualism between spirit and spirit rather than between matter and spirit. This latter dualism came from the farther East and, through Hellenic philosophy, has left its traces in the Paulo-Johannine writings. But it was no part of the Jewish and synoptic tradition. Here, too, the Church has been faithful to the idea of Jesus in opposition to Gnostic and Docetan tendencies. For her, as for Him, the body is, by nature and by original destiny, the servant and not the foe of the spirit. Both were to be glorified. The new body and new world were to be made out of the old by a process of miraculous transfiguration. The mortality of the Son of David was to put on the immortality of the Son of Man. And so, throughout, the material was to be made the instrument, the sacrament or effectual symbol of the spiritual and transcendent.

For Catholicism as for Jesus baptism is no idle symbol, but an effectual cause of the new life of the spirit, and of that Divine Sonship which gives right of entrance into the transcendent world. As for the Church, so also for Jesus, the bread of blessing is the bread of eternal life, the antidote of death, the food of the angelic nature. Sacramentalism was a principle of Jewish as of all ancient religions, to which the miraculous was no scandal, since they knew nothing of a mechanically determined nature. In the absence of all proof of sacramentalism in the thought of Jesus, we should need positive and convincing proof that He did not share that idea with His religious surroundings.

And so as to externality and ritual in worship. Liberal Protestants are satisfied that He swept it away for a "worship in spirit and in truth"—as though there were an incompatibility between the two. They assure us that were Jesus to come on earth He would be quite at home at a prayer meeting, and quite at sea at a high mass. This is profoundly uncritical and unhistorical. He might say, perhaps, "This is your synagogue; now show Me your temple"; or, "This is your temple; have you no synagogues?" From first to last Jesus revered and practised the religion of His fathers. As to the Divine authority of its moral and ceremonial law, even to the last jot and title, He is at one with the Pharisees. He differed from them in emphasis; in the stress laid on the spirit as opposed to the letter, on the end as controlling the means. In this He had no consciousness of attacking but of defending the true tradition. He never hints at the idea that His followers are destined to break away from Israel: nor did they ever do so by any definite act of separation. During His life they were in the Jewish Church as the Wesleyans were once in the Church of England—a school of pietists, whose aim was to purify, not to abandon, their Church. Naturally we do not hear much in the synoptics of what is taken for granted—of His scrupulous observance of the Jewish religion; but only of the new piety and its practices. But it is preposterous to suppose that His insistence on inwardness meant a repudiation of outwardness or a puritanical sense of opposition between them. By nature and by original destiny the bodily was for the service of the spiritual, however easily sin and Satan might pervert it from its end. Even the transcendent world of the Kingdom was not purely spiritual in the Hellenic sense. It was embodied, as glorified humanity was embodied. However refined and etherealized, it was sensible and phenomenal; nor was the Messianic banquet a mere parable of moral values. He did not say that He would destroy the Temple, but that, were it destroyed, He would raise it up again. When He purged it, He did not rend the veil or throw down the altar and its ornaments, saying: "Take these things hence." He drove forth those whose traffic dishonoured the sanctity of what He recognized as a house of prayer for all nations.

When by the course of events, His followers were driven forth from the Jewish Church, it is not to be supposed that they ceased to recognize the need of a Church and of public worship, or were content with informal piety. If the Temple-worship entered into the religion of Jesus, a similar idea of worship belonged to the early Church, and was gradually realized by borrowings from Jewish and Hellenic sources. While the End was still felt to be imminent this externalism was but rudimentary and incoherent; later it became what it remains to this day. Naturally the worship at St. Peter's is not the worship of the Temple; but it is of the same type and belongs to the same idea, which was that of Jesus and His Apostles. In this respect, too, the Catholic Church is identical and continuous with the Apostolic band that Jesus gathered round Him. Its later independent organization and externalism were contained in the idea of Jesus. There is no chasm; no need for a bridge. The temporary disorganization of Apostolic Christianity, consequent on its separation from Judaism, was an abnormal state of affairs. The "idea" was bound to reassert itself as it did. Of that reassertion Liberal Protestants speak as of a deplorable relapse into the legalism from which Christ had made us free. What Christ freed us from was not externalism, but its abuse; not the letter, but its oppression of the spirit; not the priesthood, but sacerdotalism; not ritual, but ritualism; not the Altar, but the exploitation of the Altar. Here there has indeed been a relapse, but not more scandalous than the general relapse from righteousness and inward spirituality, due to the loss of belief in the immediacy of the End. When the Lord delays His coming His servants wax wanton or slumber.

Again, in the conception of Eternal Life as a supermoral life, as a state of rest after labour, of ecstatic contemplation of the face of God, Catholicism is true to the idea of Jesus and of the Apocalypse, as already stated. Liberal Protestantism is more anthropomorphic. So far as it admits another life at all, it is the strenuous life of the moral hero continued to all eternity—although in conditions that rob every known human virtue of its occasion and subject-matter. It seeks only "the glory of going on and still to be." For Jesus the moral is not the highest life but its condition. Eternal life is, undoubtedly, the reward or wages of righteousness, as Hell and Death are the wages of sin. This too, has always been the Catholic idea; though the reward is only for those who are truly righteous, i.e. who love righteousness for itself and independently of the reward. In a word, it must be an inward righteousness of the heart, not only an outward righteousness of the hand. Neither the fasting nor the almsgiving of the Pharisees were condemned, but their self-complacency and consciousness of merited reward.

To regard the Communion of Saints as an exclusively pagan importation is again gratuitous. For Jesus, Abraham, Isaac and Jacob, Moses, Elias and David, were not of the dead past but of the living present. The blood of all the just, from Abel onward, who had been martyred by Satan's emissaries in the cause of God, was ever crying aloud for that vindication which was to be effected at the coming of the Son of Man. The tribulations of the Saints were to hasten that day and take the Kingdom of Heaven by storm, and this in union with and through the merits of His own blood. And in the Kingdom it was with Abraham, Isaac and Jacob that the redeemed were to sit at meat. Whatever the extension, ramification and superstition of

Catholic saint-worship, it is idle to deny that it pertains to the "idea" of Jesus.

Nor can it be contended that, whatever explicitness it may owe to St. Paul, the sacrificial aspect of the Eucharist is alien to the thought of Jesus. If it be true that it was with the purpose of hastening the coming of the Kingdom that Jesus, after the return of the Apostles, went forth to provoke His death at Jerusalem, that death was in His mind a sacrifice for the benefit of the elect, and a ransoming of many from the thralldom of Satan. Even if the words: "This is my Body; this is my Blood" were but a Pauline amplification of His thought, suggesting a parallelism with the pagan sacrifices, they were a justified amplification. If the bread and wine were truly sacramental tokens or sealings, effectual symbols and pledges of a participation in the future banquet of the Kingdom, every repetition of the rite must have been a commemoration and pleading of that death, which was to hasten the Kingdom with all its attendant benefits for the redeemed. It must have been viewed as a hastening of the day when they were to celebrate it with Jesus in the Kingdom of God; as a showing or pleading of His death till He should come. If this be so, then the centrality of the Eucharist in Catholic worship is true to the "idea" of Jesus. It is something far more than a mere reminder to the communicants of their Teacher martyred in the past, or a pure symbol of moral fellowship with Him and His true disciples. What the Liberal Protestant calls the "magical" conception of that sacrament belongs to the "idea" of Jesus.

Finally, when we turn to the personality and nature of Jesus Himself, we find that His own idea and the Catholic idea are at least closely akin, while that of Liberal Protestantism is another idea altogether. We find two natures—that of the earthly Son of David and that of the Heavenly Son of Man—mysteriously united in one personality. We find an earthly period, in which only one nature is manifest, opposed to a period of glory in which both are to be manifest. It would be at least hard to show that, whatever Catholic theology may mean by the doctrine of a hypostatic union from the very first of these two natures, that doctrine is excluded by the notion that Jesus was *made* the Christ only by His glorification after death. For Christhood may have meant the state of manifestation; and in this sense Jesus may have considered Himself as but destined to be "made" or declared the Son of Man through death. For Jewish thought the union would be conceived as a sort of "possession" of the lower by the higher nature. The distinction of *ousia* and *hypostasis* would have had no meaning.

As the just already possessed eternal life virtually at their baptism, so Jesus may well have considered Himself in a like virtual possession of His Christhood before it was actually made manifest—to have been thus virtually the Son of Man from the very first. This the more, as predestination was no mere purpose in the Divine mind, but something stamped in the very nature of the predestined. It was a seal, a token, imprinted on the soul.

It was certainly not in a moral and adoptive sense, but in a natural and metaphysical sense that Jesus claimed to be the Son of God by the fact that He claimed to be the Heavenly Son of Man. He was conscious of differing, not only in degree but in kind, from even the greatest of prophets. If the redeemed were His brethren, it was in virtue, not of their moral, but of their supernatural life, which they derived from and through Him, who had given them power to be made the sons of God. This power was the spirit—the seed of eternal life sown in baptism and blossoming in the Kingdom. Righteousness was the condition of its reception and retention, but was not the substance of Divine Sonship.

The position of Jesus in humanity is unique in kind. Not only is He the giver of participated sonship to others. He has come as God's plenipotentiary and vice-regent, at the end of time, to bring the world to an end, to judge the living and the dead, to separate light from darkness, tares from wheat, and gather the fruits of time into the garner of eternity. In virtue of His double nature He stands mediatorial between God and man. He is the Gate, the Way, the Truth, the Life, through which alone men can have access to the Father.

If, in her endeavour to fix the relation of Christ's heavenly nature to that of the Eternal Father, the Church may seem to have exaggerated the known claims of Jesus, this cannot be said of the Johannine and Pauline Christology, in which those claims are rather amplified than heightened.

Altogether it must be owned that, between Christ's idea of Himself and the Catholic idea of Him, there is no practical or substantial difference.

On the other hand, to maintain that it was only as a righteous man that He claimed to be the Son of God in a pre-eminent degree; that the Hellenic mind misunderstood this Hebraism and leaped at a bound to a belief in His Godhead, is almost grotesquely uncritical.

Such convulsions of thought do not take place in silence or in one night. If the claim of even the best of men to be of a heavenly nature was blasphemy in the ears of the High Priest, and of the crowd that turned against Jesus when they heard of it, it would have been blasphemy in the ears of the early Church had it been an innovation. The supposition of such a chasm between the Paulo-Johannine Christology and that of the Synoptics is not credible.

Closely connected with the mediatorial nature and function of the earthly heavenly Jesus, Son of David and Son of God, is the doctrine of the Atonement wrought by His death—a doctrine which Liberal Protestantism attributes to St. Paul. Yet it is really inseparable from the apocalyptic idea of the Kingdom of God. The long battle between Satan and Heaven for the possession of the world and man was to culminate in a final and unparalleled outburst of the Powers of Evil and Death against the saints of God, through whose sufferings and perseverance God would be provoked to arise and scatter His enemies and establish His Kingdom. Jesus speaks of the blood of the just, from Abel onwards, pleading for vindication. In the Apocalypse of St. John the martyrs cry: "How long, O Master, the holy and true, dost thou not judge and avenge our blood?" But the culminating crime of Satan, the crowning merit of suffering Righteousness, was the death of the destined Son of Man. This filled up the measure of Satan's iniquity and paid the full price of God's grace and mercy. Through the blood and suffering of Jesus the blood and suffering of the just became effectual to make atonement. Satan was brought out, his rights over the world forfeited, his slaves set free. So great was the crime, so great the merit of the death of Christ, that this alone would have sufficed to bring the Kingdom of God from Heaven to earth. The sufferings of the saints became, in a way, supererogatory. The great persecution could be shortened and mitigated for the sake of the elect. Hence, in every sense, His death was an atonement, a ransom for many; His blood was shed for many for the remission of sins. Thus we find a substantial agreement between the apocalyptic doctrine of Jesus and the theological doctrine of Catholicism. When we remember that Purgatory is only a displacement of the fiery trial that was to purify the saints, the shortening of Purgatory, through the supererogatory sufferings of martyrs and confessors, is not at all out of harmony with the idea of Jesus.

As to miracles, it is fairly evident that Jesus repudiated their apologetic value: "A faithless and perverse generation seek after a sign";

"If they hear not Moses and the prophets, neither will they be persuaded if one rise from the dead"; "Blessed are they that have not seen and yet have believed." These and other texts express the early tradition as to His mind on the subject. But to suppose that he did not believe in miracles, or did not believe that His cures and exorcisms were miraculous, is to suppose a miracle, namely the existence of a nineteenth century mind in the first century. Doubtless it was not the miracle of our modern apologists and their assailants—a violation of the mechanical order of nature, of a system of rigid uniformities. No such system was dreamt of by the religious mind of those days. Miracles were not supernatural—for nature strictly did not exist—but superhuman. They were the natural works of a superhuman spirit, by which the wonder-worker was "possessed." Even such "possession" was not supernatural, but only unusual. At most miracles were evidence of "possession," but left the good or evil character of the spirit undecided. Hence a moral test had eventually to be applied to discern diabolic from divine miracles. The mere extent of the marvel was of no use. Jesus seems to have discarded the marvel as apologetically worthless, and to have appealed directly to the moral test—to the sign of preaching and prophecy. Allowing, then, for the change that modern science has gradually effected in the conception of miracle, it is plain that the tenacity with which Catholicism defends the miraculous is not out of harmony with the idea of Jesus, and is in no sense a relapse.

One prominent feature of Catholicism we miss in the Christianity of Jesus—namely, any sort of formal theology.

This marriage of revelation with Greek philosophy could only take place on Hellenic soil at a later stage. It was from visions and revelations alone that Jesus drew His knowledge of Heavenly things—from the prophetic and apocalyptic writings and from His own mystical experiences. The casuistry and rationalism of the Scribes and Doctors were profoundly repugnant to Him. What was gathered by such inferences was revealed by "flesh and blood," and not by the Father—vain traditions of men making void the word of God. In form, His revelations were not conceptual and abstract, but imaginative and imaginable. For Him spirit is not the negation but the refinement of matter. It still possesses imaginable content. Later, in her endeavour to philosophize His revelation, the Church had to translate it into conceptual form, and began to draw logical inferences from these concepts and so to build up the whole system of

Catholic theology. It is undoubtedly not more easy to recognize the doctrine of Jesus in this form than to recognize nature in the present-ments of physical science; and Liberal Protestantism seizes on this difference of form in order to deny that the Church's doctrine was that of Jesus, or that He taught more than an ethic of inward righteousness. As "dogma" usually stands for some defined point of theology, imposed by ecclesiastical authority, it is affirmed confidently that Jesus was not dogmatic. But it is vain to deny that Jesus imposed, with the authority of Divine revelation, and as a matter of life and death, that vision of the transcendental world which the Church has clothed in a theological form. If He did not impose philosophical formulas He imposed the revelation, the imaginative vision, which they formulate. Nor, in theory, does the Church impose the formula except as safeguarding the vision, which it translates into intellectual terms. The authority to which we bow in accepting the formula is not that of theology, but of Christ's revelation as thus formulated. Thus where the difference seems most great it is apparent rather than real.

All said, if the Jesus of Liberal Protestantism is not a pure myth, a shadow of the present darkening the Past, it is only that, having eliminated what was principal in the Gospel, they have retained and segregated what was but secondary and subordinate—the moral element; that which alone can have value for those who have no patience either with the miraculous or the transcendent. For such, Christianity is but the morality of Christ; the Kingdom of Heaven is but the term of moral evolution on earth. God is the law of Righteousness and Jesus the Son of that Law. His life was significant as that of a moral teacher and pattern; His death, as an example of devotion to Righteousness. He has risen in the triumph and spread of His moral teaching, and ascended to God's right hand in the estimation of mankind. His doctrine is an abiding judgment of the world. His second coming will be at the ideal and unattainable term of man's moral evolution, when all shall be saints and the Kingdom of God realized in its full development on earth. All this is true in a sense, and is ever implied in Christianity. It is an implication that was brought out by a revolt against an excessive transcendentalism under which it had been long stifled. But in vindictively stifling transcendentalism, it has stifled the Jesus of history.

Liberal Protestant Christianity may claim Jesus, if not as the founder, yet as the Great Teacher of its morality. But the morality of Jesus was not the substance of His revelation, any more than it was

the reason of Jesus. It was not new. It is given by an immanent
process to all men in the measure that they use their reason and
follow their conscience. The religious idea of Liberal Protestantism is
not especially Christian; it is not the "idea" of Jesus. The chasm that
Liberal Protestantism finds between Jesus and the earliest Catholicism is of its own creation; the work of prepossession.

In Catholicism we find, amid many accretions no doubt, but in a
scarcely altered form, all the leading ideas of Jesus as determined by
the steady progress of criticism towards impartial objectivity. Had
this criticism any sort of apologetic bias it would certainly not be in
favour of Catholicism. Such minor alterations of form as we find are
still in harmony with the governing "idea" of the Kingdom of God,
and are the result of its protracted delay. Thus the lost stimulus of
the immediacy of the End for all was replaced by an insistence on its
immediacy for each, on the uncertain certainty of death which was to
be followed at once by a private and particular judgment and an
entrance of the disembodied soul into Hell or Heaven or Purgatory.
The General Judgment was thus reduced in importance and was
viewed rather as a solemn pageant of justice already done. The bodily
resurrection ceased to be the necessary condition of other-world
existence and served only to integrate the joys of Heaven and pains
of Hell. The purifying fire of tribulation, through which the just of
the generation of Jesus were to pass into Glory, was supplied by
Purgatory—a doctrine which is still supported by texts referring to
the *Peirasmos*—the fire that is to try every man's work. But plainly
these rearrangements of the apocalyptic vision do not seriously affect
its substance—the idea of the Church is the idea of Jesus.

THE APOCALYPTIC VISION OF CHRIST*

The Transcendency of the Kingdom

How, then, must we, here and now, understand the apocalyptic and
transcendental revelation of Jesus, so as to shape our spiritual life,
feeling and action in harmony with His? How must we re-embody
the same "idea" if it is to live for us?

*From George Tyrrell, *Christianity at the Crossroads* (1909), 114–15, 117–20,
124–30, 133–34, 138–47, 149–53, 157–58, 165–69, 170–71, 177–86.

First of all we must recognize that morality is not our highest life, but only a particular manifestation of it under certain contingencies. So far as morality is the will of God, it unites man dynamically with God. But it is not conscious union until the moral experience receives a religious and transcendent interpretation—until the absolute peremptoriness of right over all personal, social or racial interests is more or less recognized as that of a Will, whose object is universal and eternal Right, and in subjection to which our wills find their true life and expansion. It is just the conscious aiming at this union with the transcendent, through the moral life, that raises morality to religion—to conscious self-adjustment to the realities of the transcendent world.

But besides the "ought" of conduct there is the "ought" of thinking and the "ought" of feeling—the duty of a complete and ever completer harmony of the whole spirit—mind, heart, will, and action—with what we necessarily conceive as a perfect Spirit without limitations. However obscure and rudimentary, the need of this harmony becomes explicit in the love and exercise of any sort of rightness—moral, intellectual, or aesthetic—for its own sake. Man's need of harmony with the Divine is as natural as his need of bread. If this harmony be an ideal or end "in process of becoming," it supposes, as its other term, the Divine, as something actual and given. The moral life, therefore, is potentially, and may become actually, religious; it may help to satisfy man's mystical need of conscious union with the transcendent; but it can never be the whole of religion, and need not be religious at all. . . .

The religion that grew out of morality is something higher and fuller than morality. "Higher and fuller" because, with it, man becomes consciously and actively the organ of an universal and eternal life, the instrument of an universal and eternal end; because, with it, his physical self-hood is transcended and subordinated to his spiritual self-hood or personality. Religion deepens and is deepened by his profound and divine discontent. With every development of his spiritual faculties his rebellion against his own relativity, finitude and evanescence increases. He feels that no mere extension of his individual life could satisfy him; nay, by experience he learns that such extensions leave him less, and not more, content. He wants to pass εἰς ἄλλο γένος; and the want implies an unsatisfied capacity for so doing. There is that in him which nothing can satisfy but some sort of union with and appropriation of the infinite and eternal. In the measure that he tries to live widely, deeply and nobly he is bound to

become a pessimist. If optimism is usually associated with the youth
and pessimism with the age of persons or peoples, it is because pessimism is the verdict of experience. Whether in himself, or in the
world, if a man has ideals for both, he is bound to find not only
failure, but an iron law of inevitable failure, of progress thwarted and
frustrated even by its multiplicity and fecundity—its waves dashed to
futile spray by their very force and volume. From such a world and
such a life he must seek refuge in an abiding City, that hath foundations whose builder and maker is God. Only so established can he
have patience, courage, and hope to join in the struggle between
Divine Will and the forces of evil in himself and in the world, not
asking to see the meaning and issue of it all, but working blindly
along with Him who sees.

Born of a felt contrast between the actual and man's wakening
spiritual ideals, combined with the gradual recognition of the schism
as inevitable and unconquerable, this pessimism is the presupposition of that optimism of blind faith by which it is overcome. They are
two stages in the same process of spiritual growth—a process that we
find arrested in Buddhism. If it be not arrested, it is strangely perverted in what may be called Modern Christianity, whose optimism is
begotten of faith in this world, not of faith in the other; whose courage and hope is maintained by the belief that the schism between the
ideal and actual will eventually be healed through an inherent *vis* *healing*
medicatrix Naturae, that the Kingdom of God is the natural term of a *power of Nature*
process of moral and social development.

Nothing is more evident than that Jesus had no such faith or hope.
The revelation of the apocalyptic Kingdom of Heaven was a Gospel
or Good News for those who despaired of the world. It supplanted
and reinterpreted, in a transcendental sense, the earlier prophetic
Gospel of the temporal triumph of Israel and the reign of moral and
legal righteousness on earth—a Gospel that experience of the law of
failure had discredited. The mere fact that he expected the Kingdom
to-morrow proves that the faith and hope of Jesus was not in progress
or evolution. What sort of Gospel had it been for the poor, the sorrowful, the persecuted, the oppressed, to know that, not they, but
their class, would be relieved in some remote age by the advance of
civilization and morality? Had it not been to satisfy their hunger with
stones and their thirst with gall and vinegar?

The verdict of the deeper spiritual intuition on this life is always
pessimistic, and it is a verdict that is only confirmed by experience
and reflection. It is evident that there are vital and progressive forces

at work everywhere, but it is equally plain that there are destructive forces, that life is strangled by its own fertility, that it is faced by the insoluble problem of finding room for its expansion in every direction, that the utmost its ingenuity can do is defer the inevitable day of defeat and to prolong its periods of uninterrupted progress. The world is the arena of a conflict between a multitude of irreconcilable ends. The belief that they are ordained to an eventual harmony, however useful as a stimulus to combat, falls to pieces on closer inspection, which reveals an inherent fault or rift in nature. All life is under the sway of sad mortality. . . .

In the tangle and contradiction of the world of our present experience goodness, beauty, truth and happiness are at discord. Against this discord our whole spiritual nature revolts. It strives, and is bound to strive, to overcome this violation of order. And yet it can do no more than mitigate an inevitable and perpetual evil. No conceivable degree of progress could ever satisfy this deepest demand of our nature. And even if it could, the vision would not be for our eyes but for those of a final, and immeasurably distant, generation. The whole idea of the subordination of past and present humanity to the interests of a remote futurity, as means to an end, belongs to the false comparison of the life of the race to that of an individual organism. We live for our own sakes and not for a posterity that never comes. We have equal rights with any generation of the future. The truth is that neither we nor they shall find goodness, happiness, truth and beauty united in this life. . . .

As far, then, as the apocalyptic Kingdom of Heaven stands for an order of transcendental experience, in which sorrow, pain, temptation and sin shall be done away; in which the moral struggle shall be explained, justified and brought to eternal rest; in which the spiritual discords of our present experience shall be harmonized; in which man shall understand the meaning of those deepest needs, to which the present order is educational and preparatory; as far as it stands for that which is the gift of God and not the result of development— so far it seems to me to express symbolically the religious idea, brought to an advanced stage of explicitness. Treated as symbolic, not of transcendent life but of man's moral experience in the present life, it ceases to be that Gospel or Good News which alone makes life bearable for those to whom instinct, experience and reflection have revealed the shallowness of the gospel of progress and the promise of salvation by development. Doubtless these despairing idealists are a minority, but they are what all men tend to become in the measure of their spiritual development. And, after all, five hundred millions of Buddhists share their pessimism, though not the hope that alleviates it. None should be so ripe for the Gospel; though not for the Gospel of Liberal Protestantism, with its bland faith and hope in the present order, its refusal to face the incurable tragedy of human life—a tragedy that grows deeper as man rises from the hand-to-mouth simplicity of mere animal existence, extends his knowledge and control of experience and wakes ever more fully to the sense of his insatiable exigencies. The more truly he is man, the more truly he is miserable. If he have no hope beyond earth, he can do no better than contract his desires to the point of extinction, unless his humanity be sufficiently latent to let him live like a gnat in a sunbeam. . . .

Immortality

As true spiritual religion is a development, not of magical religion, but of the moral life, so also belief in spiritual immortality has not sprung from belief in ghosts and shades, but from the same root as spiritual religion. Whether recognized or only implicit, it is a postulate of the moral life. I cannot desire what is not in some sense my own good, my own end; and yet I desire the right, i.e. what is good irrespectively of my own individual and temporal interests and of those of all humanity. *Fiat justitia ruat coelum*, is the dictate of the moral conscience. Everything temporal must be sacrificed to this absolute and imperative good. When we say that righteousness must be disinterested, we only exclude these temporal interests. Were it not our own interest in some sense, it could not be an object of will at all. It is therefore my own interest, because I am a spiritual, super-temporal and super-individual being; because, as such, my interest is identified with that of an eternal and universal Will. Hence I feel that what matters for me absolutely matters for me eternally. This I could not feel were I convinced that, when the human race is wiped out of the physical world, it will not matter whether I have lived well or ill.

Men have lived, and do live, moral lives without any implicit recognition of such a postulate. But even if they explicitly deny it with their reason, it is affirmed by their instinct and their conduct. Connecting the doctrine of immortality, in its popular materialistic setting, with a hope of temporal reward, deferred in this life, to be bestowed in a continuation of a similar order of experience, they rightly feel it a nobler thing to love justice for its own sake, and not for the sake of a lower happiness. To say that this love or satisfaction is, in itself, a reward, and that such men are, therefore, self-interested, is a mere quibble. The self-interest that spoils moral purity is the interest of the individual organic self, not that of the universal and spiritual self; it is that which belongs to our consciousness of being identified with all. The desire of an immortality, which means the persistence and expansion of that very love of justice, cannot sully the purity of the heart. It is objectively inseparable from such a love, which implies the desire to be with God, and therefore to be with Him always.

As we have said before, the transcendent and universal end, that justifies the imperative and absolute character of Right, is hopelessly unimaginable for us who command but a moment of duration and a point of immensity. We can only present it to ourselves under symbols drawn from our present experience. So, too, our symbols of the life immortal, drawn largely from animistic and magical religions, imperil the spirituality of the belief, and propose it to us as an object of vision rather than of faith. And this not less but more, when, discarding the symbols of the imagination, we have recourse to those of the understanding and try to conceive the when, where and how of life eternal. . . .

The desire for this spiritual immortality is, then, totally distinct from that desire for a perpetuation of the present life which fits in with magical religion, and has for its object, not eternal life but an endless prolongation of temporal life. To a great extent these desires vary inversely. To the young, vigorous, fortunate and inexperienced, the thought of death is as intolerable as the thought of sleep to an active man in the bright freshness of morning. But night brings a change and a desire for rest and unconsciousness. Men live their fill and want no more of this life. Its endless prolongation would be hell. But in the measure that they have seen through the illusions of this outward experience they are more likely to wake to the need of another sort of experience. As the eternal life that is in them asserts itself, the thought of its extinction grows more intolerable and the faith in its perpetuity more imperative. The immortality that spiritualism strives to establish experimentally is simply a prolongation of this temporal life, in the absence of that environment out of which it is utterly meaningless and positively inconceivable. Moreover the quest is vitiated by the animistic conception of the soul, as a sprite that enters the body at birth and leaves it at death—i.e. as something spatial and material, a shade of the body. Of spiritual immortality there is not, and cannot be, any sort of experimental or philosophical demonstration. Like our belief in God or in other personalities, it is a matter of faith; an inevitable, though not logically inevitable, interpretation of spiritual experience.

That this faith comes late in the history of religion is no more surprising than that a purer morality and more spiritual religion should be similarly delayed. It is none the less natural, for man's nature unfolds its potentialities gradually, the deepest and most fundamental being the last to appear. . . .

Resurrection

The belief in spiritual immortality is, then, inseparable from spiritual religion; though, like such religion, it will clothe itself in the visible and imaginable forms of our present experience. If in some sense it is Christ who "brought life and incorruption to light", yet immortality, or resurrection (for they were not then distinguished) was already implied in the apocalyptic conception of the Kingdom of Heaven. It was the belief of the Pharisees, as opposed to the philosophical scepticism of the Sadducees. It had permeated the uncritical multitude. Jesus did not reveal it, but almost took it for granted. Men, who were not His disciples, were ready to believe that He Himself might be John the Baptist, or Elias, or Jeremiah, or one of the great prophets risen from the dead. It was not from Him that they had learnt this doctrine. According to the Gospel He Himself was not the first to rise. He and the prophets before Him had raised the dead, and at the moment of His own death, before He had risen, we are told that the graves were opened and that the bodies of the just arose. If St. Paul speaks of Him as the first-fruits of the dead he means first in dignity and causality, not first in time. Our modern apologists, with their idea of natural law and of miracle as a conquest of the power of nature by a Higher Power, by which conquest the existence of that Higher Power is proved, miss the meaning which Christ's resurrection had for those who had no idea of natural law or of any other power in nature than that of God. They speak as though the Apostles had doubted whether God could break through the determinism of nature and raise the dead, and as though their faith had been re-established by finding there was a power stronger than that of nature. This is to read later ideas into an earlier age.

In the first place, where there is no conception of nature as a rigid autonomous system of uniformities, there can be no conception of the preternatural. God was the sole mover of the physical world, which had no power of its own to oppose to His. . . .

The Apostles had no doubt as to the resurrection of the body at the last day—a belief that they had not derived from Jesus. They did not regard it as a miracle in any sense, but, like every regular sequence in nature, a rule of Divine action, a part of God's freely chosen plan. In that plan death followed upon sin as regularly as, but not more necessarily than, night followed upon day. With the same regularity resurrection followed upon righteousness. It was only because righteousness came through the conquest of Satan, and the gift of the Spirit by the Son of Man, that St. Paul speaks of Christ as the cause and first-fruits of the Resurrection: "For since by man came death, by man came also resurrection of the dead", etc.

For the Apostles, the resurrection of Jesus meant that He who had claimed to be the destined Son of Man had been approved, justified and glorified by the Father, according to the rule by which resurrection is the established and almost natural consequence and proof of justice. What they had doubted was His claim to be the Christ; not the possibility of His resurrection. When He rose, their trust in Him, in their own redemption with and through Him, in His whole Gospel of the coming Kingdom and His own place in it, was confirmed and verified, not by an exceptional, but by a regular occurrence. Resurrection is the fruit of righteousness, and a tree is known by its fruit. . . .

This, then, was the significance of the resurrection of Jesus for the Apostles. They had no doubt about God, or the possibility of super-human wonders, or the coming of the Kingdom, or the resurrection of the dead, but only about the Messianic claim of Jesus; and this doubt was slain as soon as God approved Him in the established and universal way, i.e. by raising Him up.

And what are we to think of this alleged resurrection, which was undoubtedly the whole inspiration and strength of early Christianity, especially as it was considered a guarantee for the speedy end of all? The harvest had begun; the sickle was thrust in; the risen Christ was the first-fruits of the general resurrection.

Here we are on difficult ground. But it is a poor faith that dare not look difficulties straight in the face. If the Apostles were mistaken as to the immediacy of the End (and, of course, they were so in some sense) may they not have been mistaken as to the Christhood of Jesus, on which alone that expectancy was founded; and also as to His resurrection, on which their belief in His Christhood was founded? Might it not be put thus? If He has risen, He is the Christ;

if He be the Christ, the end is near; but the end is not near, therefore He is not the Christ; therefore He has not risen. We have two interdependent facts—the resurrection of Jesus and the immediacy of the End. It is only by the sort of quibble that has made epochs out of six evenings and mornings of creation that we can pretend that the second of these facts has not been disproved by universal experience. Is the proof of the first anything like as strong as the disproof of the second?

The prophetic mind, as we have said, not only embodies its spiri- tual exigencies and desires in terms of present experience, in some glorified image of the visible world, but expresses the impatience and intensity of its desire in a foreshortening of time. It translates its felt spiritual nearness to the transcendental and eternal object of its faith into the image of things visible. So far as the prophet confounds the image with the transcendent that it symbolizes, he is doomed to disappointment. The whole apocalyptic imagery of the Kingdom of Heaven; of the Son of Man; of the coming in the clouds; of the resurrection of the dead; of the Judgment in the valley of Jehosephat; of the immediacy of these events, is but imagery of the transcendent and unimaginable; of infinitely deeper realities. It is an attempt to figure our spiritual requirements in material form; to give them a language in which we can think of them and speak of them. For an embodied spirit they need embodiment if they are to be brought to bear on our present experience. It is the future moth trying to make itself intelligible to the present grub, in which it is dimly self-conscious and preparing for its coming life and environment.

The only manner in which the Christian Apocalypse can claim a greater finality and security than the repeatedly disappointed visions of the earlier prophets is in recognizing the symbolic and inadequate character of all such visions. And this recognition advanced towards explicitness when the temporal interpretation of God's Kingdom gave place to the apocalyptic and quasi-transcendent. It advanced still further with Christ's insistence on the spiritual as the sole eternal reality. It only needed a gradual cleansing of the idea of spirit to complete the distinction between the imagery and the reality of the transcendent.

Now if we agree with Liberal Protestantism in taking symbolically what the early Church took literally, we differ in taking it all as symbolic of transcendental values and not of the moral order in this life. In so doing we only go more deeply into the original thought and get under its enveloping imagery; we do not go off on another line that is merely analogous. We hold to the transcendent Kingdom and, while not discarding the imagery, we recognize that it is an envelope and not the substance. Hence we claim to be true to the "idea" of original Christianity. To this discrimination between substance and envelope we have been forced by the advance of human thought; by the progressive delimitation between the territories of subjective and objective, between vision and fact. . . .

There can be no doubt as to the appearances of Jesus to His Apostles after death. Without them the faith, hope and enthusiasm of the early Church are inexplicable. It is plain that the Apostles intercalated the phenomena into those of the physical series, yet not without some sense of their otherness. He appeared and vanished like creatures of imagination; He passed through closed doors and rose in the air. St. Paul says: "Have I not seen Jesus our Lord?" yet describes that vision as existing for himself and not for those round him, as belonging to the subjective series of phenomena. His whole doctrine of the spiritual body shows the same consciousness. It is not the body that is sown and destroyed, it is not the body of the flesh, it is a transcendental body, though figured in terms of the phenomenal world. He figures it as, in some way, growing out of the fleshly body, like corn from the perishing seed—as related to it in the same way that the transcendent order is related to the present order. And in all this he was answering the question: "How do the dead arise? with what bodies do they come?" He was answering those who mistakenly supposed that the resurrection phenomena had to be fitted in with the physical series. He tells them, in effect, that they do not belong to that series; that they proceed from an inward, not an outward, reality. Yet, however subjective may be the imaginative clothing of that reality, the reality itself is not necessarily subjective and private. The principles of truth and morality are inward, but not subjective; they are valid for all and not for one alone. God's Spirit works in every conscience and, if our various pictures of its workings are subjective, they are pictures of something within us that is independent of us and is the same for all.

Shall we then be very far from St. Paul's thought if we say that the spiritual body is the imaginative embodiment of the spirit, the expression of the transcendent in terms of natural experience; just as the material or fleshly body is that which expresses itself in the phenomena of the physical sequence? . . .

The resurrection of the just is an integral part of the apocalyptic scheme. We cannot treat the two apart; they enjoy just the same kind of truth and reality—either the same literalism or the same symbolic value, be it moral or transcendent. For the Liberal Protestant the resurrection is a symbol of the victorious survival of the morality of Jesus in the Church and the World. For the Liberal Catholic it is a symbol of the survival of the spiritual personality of Jesus in that transcendental world which pervades the visible order.

Those who accept it as a merely physical event in this lower plane of phenomenal reality must, in consistency, accept the rest of the apocalyptic vision in the same sense—must accept the advent in the clouds, the great assize in the valley of Jehosephat as they were accepted by the Apostles and the early Church. What they actually saw could only confirm them in their literalism—they saw Jesus risen in physical form; they saw Him ascend to the physical heavens; they saw those heavens opened, like an awning, and Jesus standing at the right hand of the visible Father.

Now we may ask ourselves what spiritual significance and value could these phenomenal happenings possibly have for faith? Apart from some truly transcendental reality which they figure, and which alone is the object that explains and satisfies our spiritual unrest, what interest can physical phenomena and marvels have for religion? The physical resurrection and ascension could, at most, be signs and symbols of Christ's spiritual transformation, of the fullness of His eternal and transcendent life; they could never be its substance. Is it in physical radiance and power and subtlety and swiftness that our spiritual nature will find its explanation and satisfaction? Is it in the bric-a-brac, rococo Heaven of the Apocalypse of St. John that our souls are to find rest?

Even, then, though the Apostles regarded the resurrection phe-nomena as quasi-physical; even though they grasped the envelope and its content in the same hand; yet the substance was given to them by faith alone. What their bodily eyes beheld was but a symbol of a transcendent resurrection, visible only to the eye of faith. The inward experience, that thus expressed itself, was the recognition that the Divine Personality of Jesus—the Spirit that He was—cannot die; that it dwells in us all as something distinct from ourselves, ever claiming our absolute worship and obedience. In His mortality He had revealed the humanity and loving-kindness of that Spirit; He had clothed it in visible and fleshly form; He had given it a human voice.

Henceforth, in the inward dictates of that Spirit, they recognized the
"I say unto you" of the voice of Jesus of Nazareth; and the mysterious influence bore His human form and features. Plainly the symbol
was accommodated to their apocalyptic ideas, to their belief in a
quasi-physical Kingdom of Heaven, a quasi-physical resurrection of
the just.

They had no doubt that the just would rise from their graves.
There is no valid critical reason for denying that Jesus had predicted
His resurrection as the pendent to His self-sought atoning death. All
the trust and faith with which He had inspired them bade them expect
that resurrection, which was to justify Him and His claim to be the
Son of Man. Their faith in His resurrection was kindled from His
own. Moreover, it was fortified by the Scriptures. Even had He not
appeared to them at all they ought to have, and might have, believed.
This is the meaning of "Blessed are they that have not seen and yet
have believed", and "O foolish men and slow of heart to believe in
all that the prophets have spoken". The appearances seem to be
viewed rather as a reward of faith than as a proof of the resurrection;
to be a consequence, not an antecedent, of faith, in accordance with
Christ's whole attitude towards miracles. While they doubted they
did not see Him; their eyes were held. As soon as they believed they
saw Him.

Have we not, then, every reason to believe that what they saw was
a vision, the spontaneous self-embodiment, in familiar apocalyptic
imagery, of their faith in His spiritual triumph and resurrection, in
the transcendental and eternal order—a vision that was externalized
by the very intensity of their faith, that seemed something given from
outside; a vision that was divine, just because the faith that produced
it was divine?

Of course criticism will not accept all the details of these appearances; but it cannot deny their possibility and likelihood in relation
to the mentality of the time and place; and it must admit enough to
account for the birth of Christianity. Moreover, we may not look for
consistency of detail between subjective expressions of transcendent
facts, as between accounts of the same physical fact. Visions, besides,
change even in the first telling; still more in the second and third. But
they can remain true to the inward fact they symbolize.

Thus, as visions, the resurrection phenomena take their proper
place in the Apocalypse of the Kingdom of Heaven. The alternative
is to give physical value to the whole Apocalypse. The Resurrection

thus becomes a visionary presentment of the truth of spiritual immortality; of the eternity and plenary expansion of that super-individual life that lies hid in the depths of our being; that strives vainly to express itself in terms of our psychic and organic life; that is the root of our discontent, not only with all that the world gives, but with all that it could ever conceivably give. . . .

That the world passes away for each and for all—not only for man but for all humanity—is the motive for that Christian detachment which sets its affections on things above and not on things of earth. As a truth of reason and experience we do not doubt it. But only in rare moments, when we realize it, does it exercise its due influence on our affections and conduct, and show us life's true values and its illusions in a flash of light. Many a change in our character dates from such moments and is sustained by their repetition. Apart from them, we are tangled in dreams and throw our whole interest into them; and, if there be no transcendent life, we do well, for we are then but dreams ourselves. If we look to a waking; if we take our dreams with a question and a reserve, we shall spoil the little that we have. Let us rather try to believe that our race is eternal, and that its final beatitude on earth is the justification of all our moral endeav-our—that conscience is no more than the specific instinct which com-pels us to work for the survival of the species *Homo sapiens*.

It was, then, the conviction that the Kingdom was at hand, even at the very door, that the harvest was ripe, the first-fruits already gath-ered in, that brought the multitude of believers face to face with the illusions of time and the realities of eternity, and transformed their whole outlook and sentiment. . . .

Yet this emphasis on the other world, however necessary as a corrective, needed to be checked and balanced by a just estimate of the meaning and value of time in relation to eternity. He who said "Blessed are the poor, the hungry, the suffering", spent His life in relieving their needs; He who said "The night cometh", gave it as a motive for working while it was yet day; He who said "The Kingdom is at hand", was urging men to repentance and righteousness. At the Judgment the reward is not for those who have successfully turned earth into paradise and accomplished the impossible, but for those who have striven to alleviate its miseries; who have fought a despair-ing battle against the overwhelming forces of evil. It is not so much the actively evil, as the slack and apathetic, that are excluded from the Kingdom. Life, therefore, gains a new importance as the arena of the great "temptation"—of the conflict between the forces of Darkness and Light, Death and Life, Earth and Heaven; a conflict where Satan must first be victorious in the present order before God shall arise to scatter His enemies and establish His Kingdom. It is not so much by their efforts, as by their consequent failures and sufferings, that the saints are to hasten God's final intervention. In a way they are indifferent to success or failure, so long as they have striven with all their might. In that striving their spiritual personality is created and deepened; their union with God strengthened; their place in the transcendent order determined.

Far, then, from relaxing moral effort for the alleviation of earth's misery, the Christian faith, rightly apprehended, intensifies and purifies it. Those who fight only for victory grow slack when victory is hopeless. Those who fight for hate or for love will fight till they drop. Such has been the desperate energy with which typical Christian saints have combated life's evils, moral and physical—the energy of those who are masters and not slaves of their purpose; whose provisional attachment to life's interests is subordinate to an ultimate detachment; who use the world as not using it; who strain for success and smile when they fail. Like Christ they serve; like Him they are lords and masters of what they serve. They are not immersed in the clay which they are moulding but stand well outside it and above it. . . .

The truth, then, that Christianity symbolizes, under the temporal nearness of the End, is a fundamental principle of the best spiritual life—the principle of an attachment to the world's highest interest, at once strengthened and subdued by an attachment to an eternal and transcendent life, symbolized by the Kingdom of Heaven. . . .

The Son of Man

The necessity of finding in Jesus a German Liberal Protestant, guided entirely by the light of a sweet, nineteenth-century reasonableness, requires us to ignore everything in the Gospel that suggests the visionary or the ecstatic, even though to do so make the narrative incoherent and unintelligible. When He called Himself the Son of Man, we are told it was because He felt Himself so entirely human— the Man par excellence. When He called Himself the Son of God, it was because all men were sons of the common Father; and the Man par excellence was, therefore, the Son of God par excellence. A more drastic and objective criticism has shattered the beautiful simplicity of this tidy little system, obtained by a liberal use of the pruning-hook.

We do not need the Johannine and Pauline writings, we need only to read the Synoptics in the light of contemporary apocalyptic conceptions, to learn that Jesus considered Himself as of a superhuman nature, and as differing in kind from other men. It was a secret He eventually shared with His Apostles; it was the secret of His ascendancy over them; it was a faith with which He inspired them. If the least in the Kingdom was above the greatest born of women, above the chief of prophets and saints and martyrs, He who knew Himself to be the greatest in the Kingdom could hardly regard Himself as a mere prophet—a man among men.

The "Son of Man" was a heavenly being, mediatorial between God and man. He was the Power of God, by which Satan's power was to be broken and the Kingdom of Heaven to be established on earth. To Him all judgment was committed by nature. Like the Spirit of God, He was conceived vaguely and, without prejudice to the Divine unity, as an emanation from God; the Arm of the Lord. What trouble later theology had with these emanations is testified by the Athanasian Creed—which attempts to satisfy reason while preserving the apocalyptic vision in its integrity, and which presents no difficulty when we remember that our rational concepts of the Divine are not less symbolic than our imaginative visions.

Jesus believed that He was destined to be revealed to all the world in the clouds of heaven, as the Son of Man. Probably, if not certainly, He understood this destination as more than moral or decretorial, as an inherent potentiality of His spirit. Already He spoke and acted as God's plenipotentiary. He forgave sins, because He knew Himself to be the "Son of Man" to whom all judgment had been committed; He judged the sacred Law; He called Men to Himself; He bade them imitate Him; all this points to a sense of present, not merely of prospective, super-human dignity. Not till He was glorified, however, would He be technically the Christ and assume the full functions of the Son of Man.

Now it is idle to contend that this was something secondary in the self-consciousness of Jesus; a little touch of the megalomania so frequently attendant on genius and on the realization of unusual influence and power; a fiery tongue of fanaticism, shooting up from the pure flame of faith. He does not begin as an ethical teacher or a prophet, and then warm up to new and astounding pretensions. His

attitude is the same throughout, and is just such as consists with the
secret consciousness of His Messianic dignity. That consciousness is
the cause, and not the effect, of His soul-compelling power. His belief
in Himself makes others believe in Him. The saint, the prophet, is
ever self-obliterating. His strength is God's, not his own. He draws
men to God, not to himself. He says "Thus saith the Lord", and not
"But I say unto you". He claims to be only the servant of all, not also
their Lord and Master. If Jesus believed Himself but man, He was no
saint. But He felt He was more. And even those who did not share
His Messianic secret felt and yielded to the authority with which He
spoke. They asked themselves: "What manner of man is this?" What
won their love and affection was the lowliness and gentleness of one
whom they felt, through an irrepressible emanation of His own self-
consciousness, to be mysteriously great and strong and holy.

We must recognize, then, that Jesus was conscious of Himself as in
some way mediatorial between the transcendent world and the souls
of men; that He felt, not merely His own union with God, but the
power of uniting other souls to Himself and, through Himself, with
God; that this mission was imposed on Him from above; that He was
set as a magnet for souls, which, magnetized through Him, should
draw and magnetize others, till the whole of redeemable humanity, in
Him, with Him, through Him, should be drawn back to God. This
was the nature of His spiritual exigency, the bread for which He
hungered—to accomplish the great atonement; to overthrow sin and
Satan; to establish the Kingdom of Heaven; to banish the night of
time; to bring in the day of eternity. No doubt this desire to redeem,
this power to draw and magnetize, belong to the spiritual nature as
such, and to every man in the measure that his spiritual life has
become explicit. Its source is the Divine nature itself. But no ordinary man, however possessed by the Divine Spirit, could feel himself
to be the sole redeemer, mediator and source of redemption and
mediation, in no need himself of redemption and atonement. Of this
inward experience of Jesus, in which He felt Himself identified
immediately with the Divine Source of Redemption, we can say
nothing. We may rest satisfied that, when He claimed to be one with
the Father, it was in no merely moral sense of accordant wills; but
had reference to some mystical experience, some intuition of same-
ness in otherness.

Every such spiritual experience tends to translate itself into symbolic ideas and images and, where strong and intense, to invest these

images with the objectivity ascribed to dreams and visions. And the nature of the vision, as is proved by a thousand examples, depends on the religious ideas and images already to hand. These make the religious language of the seer; the words in which he must embody his experience for himself and for others. The current religious language in which Jesus thought and spoke was that of the prophets and apocalypses. The Kingdom of Heaven; the Son of Man, the Messiah; the Kingdom of Satan; the final catastrophe—these were the categories, under which His spiritual experience had to be ranged. Hence His sense of universal and supreme mediatorship between God and Man, of identification by love and sympathy with each of the terms to be united, could find no apter symbol than that of the prophetic Son of David, united to and "possessed" by the Heavenly Son of Man, or Son of God.

To transfer to the transcendental order the relations that obtain between the imaginative symbols of spiritual experience, is the same sort of fallacy that projects our scientific hypotheses into the physical world; or gives a real existence to our abstractions and general ideas. All we can say of such fictions is that they are founded in fact and reality. But where that reality is transcendent and spiritual, our fictions have only the truth of analogy—of parallels in another order of reality. Hence all our theology of the Incarnation deals, not with transcendent realities, but with the visions or revelations in which they are symbolized. Its purpose is to preserve the original force and usefulness of that symbolism; to secure its correct rendering for other ages and peoples; to make it coherent with itself and with the equally symbolic ideas of rational theology. We simply do not know what our own spirit is, or what the transcendent world is to which it aspires, or its relation to that world and to other spirits. What we do know is the impress they leave on a mind adapted to the world of physical phenomena.

The value of all these symbols and hypotheses is in the extent to which they anticipate and control that order of experiences on which they are founded; and every new success deepens that foundation and strengthens our faith. The faith in His own Christhood that Jesus, by the power of His personality, was able to plant in His Apostles, has been continually reinforced by the experience of those who have found Him, in effect, their Redeemer, the Lord and Master of their souls, their Hope, their Love, their Rest—in short, all that they mean by God. For them He has become the effectual symbol or sacrament of the transcendent, through which they can apprehend the inapprehensible—the Eternal Spirit in human form.

The Messiahship of Jesus is, then, the symbolic expression, in terms of apocalyptic imagery, of certain transcendent realities—of the spiritual experience of Jesus as to His own relation to God and to men; and of the experiences of Christians as to their own relations to God and to Jesus. It is a visionary presentment of a transcendental truth, which we can present to ourselves in no other way; which we see *per speculum et in aenigmate,* but not *facie ad faciem.*

Theology is right in trying to make our symbolism coherent with itself and to preserve it from corruption. But when it strives to make it coherent with rational knowledge and outward experience, it forgets its symbolic character, and tends to pervert either revelation or knowledge, or both, in the interests of an impossible synthesis. In the orthodox and metaphysical formula of the Godhead of Christ we find, at most, a negative intellectual value combined with a positive pragmatic value. According to the latter, we are to bear ourselves towards Christ as towards a person possessed at once of a perfect human and a perfect Divine nature. According to the former, we are not to think of Him as two persons in only moral agreement; nor as a human person with extraordinary supernatural endowments; nor as a Divine person under the illusory appearances of humanity; nor as the Divinity substituted for a human soul in a human body. In short, the formula excludes every previous attempt to find a positive conception of the relationship of human and Divine in Jesus and to justify, intellectually, the Christian sentiment and attitude in regard to Him. There is little doubt but that those previous formulas, with all their incoherency and inadequacy, were attempts to justify Christian experience and feeling. It is plain that the disciples felt the strange and superhuman in Jesus as well as the human; that they feared as well as loved; that they found Him irresistible in His authority and power over their souls; that they reverenced Him as an incarnation of conscience, as a source of conversion and spiritual strength; that He possessed and governed them as a lover is possessed by the beloved.

It was some experience of this sort that the early Church strove to understand and explain. But the finally accepted formula is rather a statement of the problem than a solution. It insists on factors that the earlier formulas had neglected, and shows their insufficiency. But its solution, by way of a distance between Nature and an unknown something called Personality, to which we can give no more positive

content than to an algebraic *x*, simply leaves the metaphysical problem open and forbids further useless discussion. It prescribes a way
of speaking and a way of acting in accordance with traditional sentiment and practice.

THE RELIGION AND PERSONALITY
OF JESUS*

There is a lower mysticism that is content to wrest the soul from the
tyranny of the external by ascetical self-isolation, by forgetting the
world and the historical process, in which the Divine Will reveals
itself; that lives for rare moments of almost sensible contact with the
indwelling Divinity. However narrowly indifferent to ethics, science
and history, this mysticism emphasizes one-sidedly the great truth
that conscious union with God is the fullest realization of humanity,
the secret of that personality which sets man above nature. But it
fails to recognize that this means union with a Will that is at work in
the whole process of history and in every human soul. It is, as it were,
a form without content.

Not such was the mysticism of Jesus that, in embracing God,
embraced the whole world and all its spiritual interests—truth of
feeling, truth of conduct, truth of knowledge; that forced Him into
conflict with evil, reckless of reward or success, by the mere impetus,
the imperative necessity of the Divine Nature—"driven by the Spirit".
"A new creature", a spirit, a personality, a Son of God—this is the
full fruit of Christian Mysticism.

Jesus did not despise or turn away from the law of God, or the
temple of God, in putting above both the Spirit that had created
them and had revealed itself through them—as it were through sacraments and beggarly elements. At most He desired to supplement
and fulfill the necessarily ever-imperfect expressions of the spirit; to
push the letter down to its proper place of subordination and instrumentality; to carry religion to its final phase; to deny the static immutability and perpetuity of the external embodiment of the spirit, and
to make it a living and growing organism.

When he opposes "But I say unto you", to "Moses said unto you",
it is plain that He regards Himself as the Spirit incarnate, possessed
of a human frame and soul, and uttering itself within all the natural

*From George Tyrrell, *Christianity at the Crossroads* (1909), 261–73.

limitations of local thought and language. It was through Him that
Moses had spoken; what Moses *had,* He *was.* St. Paul is a true interpreter when he identifies Christ with the Spirit; when he speaks of
the indwelling of Spirit as the indwelling of Christ. So mastered and
enslaved was Jesus, that His life was simply the life of the Spirit; His
words the words of the Spirit. Against the Spirit He had no freedom,
but only within the limits of the Spirit. If He could not sin it was
because the Spirit cannot sin.

In this sense we can deny Him a human personality. Man can
progressively subject himself to the Spirit, but with the liberty of
rebellion. He is not overmastered by it in spite of himself. But the
personality, the "I" that speaks and acts in Jesus, is the Spirit, though
it speaks and acts through the limitations of a human organism. It is
the Spirit made man. The Word which enlightens every man is made
flesh; what works within us stands before us, to be seen and heard
and handled. In Him we have seen the Father—not in His fullness,
but so far as God is inclusively the ideal image of man; so far as God
reveals man to himself in a Divine Humanity. He comes, so to say,
and lives our life Himself.

Thus it was that, for Christianity, Jesus and the Spirit became
interchangeable terms; that the birth of the Spirit in man's soul
became a birth and indwelling of Jesus. The inevitable anthropomorphism of man's conceptions of the Divine received a sanction:

> So, through the thunder, comes a human voice,
> Saying: O heart I made, a Heart beats here.

"My little children", says Paul, "of whom I am again in travail
until Christ be born in you"—all the instructions, precepts and
exhortations of the Christian religion fall short of their purpose if
they but make a man an obedient imitator of Christ, as it were of the
first founder and example of a new religious system; if they do not
evoke that Spirit which was incarnate in Jesus, and therefore *is* Jesus.
Jesus was not merely a revealed ideal of human personality, but a
forceful, living, self-communicating ideal; a fire spreading itself from
soul to soul. It is only personality that works on personality. We can
take precepts and instruction impersonally; we can obey and follow
them and build them into the structure of our mental and moral
habits. But we can sometimes apprehend the whole spirit and personality of a man through his words and acts and manner. We can
feel him as an overwhelming personal influence; we can catch the

concrete living spirit from the broken letters and words in which it utters itself. We can feel him living in us as a masterful force. We know his way and his will in a manner that no instruction could ever import.

This it is that distinguishes Christianity from the following of a teacher or prophet. It teaches the precepts of Christ as a means to a birth of Christ in the soul—to the constitution of a divine personality within us; of a spirit that shall supersede all law and precept, as itself the source and end of all law. Jesus Himself was the great sacrament and effectual symbol of the Divine Life and Spirit. He worked on His disciples, not doctrinally as a teacher of the understanding, but with all the force of a divine and mysterious personal ascendancy, transmitted through every word and gesture. He was not a prophet speaking in the name of the Spirit, but the Spirit itself in human form. He spoke as only conscience can speak. Men heard and obeyed, they knew not why. He entered into their souls and possessed them and shaped them to His own image and likeness. When He left them externally, He was still with them internally. Conscience took shape and it was the shape of Jesus. Struck down by conscience Paul cries: "Who art thou, Lord?" and the revealing answer comes: "I am Jesus, whom thou persecutest". To this he refers when he says it was good pleasure of God "to reveal His Son *in me*; I live, and yet no longer I, but Christ liveth *in me*". In what other religion do men so speak of their founder, however loved and revered and followed? Personality is the end, and personality, mediated no doubt through external signs and symbols, is the means. Fire is kindled from fire. The Spirit of Jesus uttered in the Church, in the Gospel, in the sacraments, is apprehended by His followers, not as a doctrine but as a personal influence, fashioning the soul to its own divine nature.

It is impossible for spirit or personality to find adequate expression in terms of another order of experience. It is by a sort of internal sympathy that we read the personality of another out of the meager shorthand of words and acts and gestures, and only so far as we are latently capable of realizing a similar personality in ourselves. The vehicles and sacramental symbols, through which the spirit communicates itself, are no part of the Spirit. The human frame and mind of Jesus, His local and temporal limitations of thought and knowledge, were but the sacramental elements through which the influence of His Divine Spirit was mediated. To our age He would have spoken differently, but the spirit would have been the same. A great artist, who makes the most of the poor materials and methods to hand, can reveal his spirit to a sympathetic apprehension as well as in a richer language; it is the spirit that quickens, the flesh profiteth nothing. The material imitation of the historical Christ tends to extinguish His Spirit. In us Christ, the Spirit, lives and utters Himself in the ever-changing forms of thought and language. In this sense St. Paul says that, if we have known Christ after the flesh, we shall know Him so no longer, but only after the spirit as the Heavenly Adam, the Son of Man, the Spirit of God. We have long since outgrown those apoca-lyptic forms of religious thought in which the Spirit of Jesus first uttered itself as the Son of Man—the Jewish Messiah. But the spirit itself we have not outgrown, and in us it seeks ever new forms where-in to clothe the same revelation.

This, then, is the special characteristic of Christianity. It does not look back upon Jesus, as a Franciscan might look back upon St. Francis, or a Moslem on Mohammed, as being the founder of the society to which he belongs and the first example of that system of spirituality which has been handed down to him. It looks back on Jesus as being the Divine Spirit revealing itself in human form; as Himself the revelation of God; as communicating, not His ideas or His doctrines, but His very self, His spirit and personality to the soul, through the sacramental power of the Gospel and the Church; as constituting the salvation of the soul, its communion with God, its eternal life, by His personal indwelling. To be, as it were, "possessed" by Jesus is to be possessed by the Spirit of God. Those who lay hold of Him, who cluster round Him like swarming bees round their queen, become His very members, quickened by that Spirit which He was; they in Christ and Christ in them, Christ in God and God in Christ, "that they may be perfected into One".

This is what we find from cover to cover of the New Testament. If it be more explicit in the Paulo-Johannine writings, it is fully implicit and partly explicit in the synoptic Gospels. This is what we find in the great Christo-Catholic tradition—"Christ in you, the hope of glory"— a quickening Spirit, an overwhelming personal influence, killing self and sin by a filial and self-sacrificing love of God, and of all the world as in God and from God and for God. This, too, is what we find in those Protestant bodies that, in breaking with the integrity of the Catholic tradition, have retained its central value, and for whom the name of Jesus is not merely that of a founder and teacher, but of a sacramental, self-communicating personality, to be laid hold of and appropriated; of One who reveals Himself in each several soul as He did in the soul of St. Paul; of One through whose intermediating humanity the soul is united to God.

This is what we do not find in that Liberal Christianity for which Jesus is to the Christian only what Mohammed is to the Moslem— the founder and teacher of a society, revealing and exemplifying a doctrine and method. Hence a philosophic chill, which increases in the measure that criticism puts Jesus back in His own century and surroundings, and forbids us to read into His human mind the ideas and presuppositions of our own day, or to see in Him a practicable example of what we now mean by life.

Those for whom He is a living indwelling spirit, a fire kindling from soul to soul down the long centuries, who see the expression of that spirit, not merely in the mortal life and thoughts of the Galilean carpenter, but in those of His followers who have been possessed by the spiritual and eternal personality of Jesus, have no such trouble in the face of criticism. It is no more to them that He was a first-century Jew in His mental outlook than that He was a man and a carpenter. What they live by is not His human mind but His divine spirit and personality, revealed in conflict with His human limitations and with ours, and with those of all generations to come. Had He spoken the language of the twentieth century, would He be intelligible to the fortieth, were it His language and not His personality that He had to communicate and reveal?

Is it any depreciation of the great military geniuses of the past to say that, if suddenly plunged into the midst of a modern engagement, they would be worse than worthless; that, without the requisite knowledge and experience, their genius would be useless? Yet do we not desiderate that same genius for our own leaders, without which all their knowledge and experience is of no avail? What are the categories and concepts of Jesus to us? Are we to frame our minds to that of a first-century Jewish carpenter, for whom more than half the world and nearly the whole of its history did not exist; to whom the stellar universe was unknown; who cared nothing for art or science or history or politics or nine-tenths of the interests for humanity, but solely for the Kingdom of God and His righteousness? And even in regard to this supreme interest is it His religious ideas, His apocalyptic imagery, that we are to take over, and not rather the spirit of which they were the inadequate embodiment—the best possible just for that time and place and no other? Would the military genius of the past tie us down to his weapons and methods of warfare? Would he not have desired and hoped that every generation should, while retaining his spirit, improve on his methods? And would not such improvements be the work of his own spirit?

To demand that Jesus should have had all the knowledge of Solomon is on a par with demanding that He should have had all the earthly riches and glory of Solomon. The note of the Gospel is that God has not chosen the great things of this world, but the small; not the rich, but the poor; not the learned, but the simple. The elect of the world are not the elect of the Spirit; Solomon in all his glory was not arrayed as one of these. Why, if God did not disdain the role of a poor man and a tempted man, should He disdain that of an ignorant man, wherein to reveal the Spirit victorious over the very commonest human limitations? It is not from the human mind that He *had*, but from the Divine Spirit that He *was*, that man has drawn strength to conquer ignorance and wickedness, however costly, however interminable the conflict. To fill us with this Spirit was the mission of Jesus; not to teach us metaphysics or science or history or ethics or economics. The love of truth, the spirit of truthfulness, is the living root of all mental progress. This the most ignorant man may have and communicate.

This idea of Jesus as the Divine indwelling and saving Spirit seems to me the very essence of Christianity. Faith in Christ never meant merely faith in a teacher and His doctrine, but an apprehension of His personality as revealing itself within us.

There is no special difficulty in admitting that the dawn of a new epoch should be associated with the name of some individual who, however much the product of his time and sensitive to its spirit and needs, creates a new synthesis of all he has received, with some new and original contribution of his own. That, after all, is the law of spiritual development. Each spirit is evoked and shaped by the collective spirit of the day and shapes it in turn; as a rule imperceptibly, because in the straight line of its actual development.

But there come periods when a change of direction or of level is the condition of progress, and such new epochs are associated, whether in art, science, invention, politics, or religion, with the name of some individual who, conscious of the *impasse*, discovers a way out and draws the whole world after him. It is no scandal to us that only those who come within the sphere of that man's influence enjoy the advantages thereof. But it seems intolerable that only those who have heard the name and the teaching of Jesus of Nazareth should attain eternal life; that two-thirds of present humanity, and nine-tenths or far more of past humanity should fail of salvation.

Yet this would follow were the personality that spoke in Jesus that of a man, and not that of the Spirit which speaks to every man in the mysterious whisperings of conscience; were Jesus not simply the incarnation of conscience, the manifestation of that ideal humanity which conscience is striving to reveal to, and realize in, every human soul. So He is interpreted in the Paulo-Johannine writings and in Catholic tradition. Because He did not merely possess, but *was* personally the true Light that enlightens every man, the indwelling Logos or Word of God, He could say: "I *am* the Way and the Truth and the Life, no one cometh unto the Father but by me"; "He that hath the Son hath the life".

Hence all who are saved are saved through Christ, whose personality is that of the indwelling Spirit. Christianity has but brought the universal principle of salvation to its highest degree of force and explicitness. Conscience, that is first dimly felt as a mysterious influence interfering with and transcending the natural self and its laws, is revealed at last as the Spirit or Personality incarnate in Jesus.

10

God, Evil, and Eschatology

LETTER TO L. D. (1908)*

. . . I should be inclined to say that pantheism is true as faith, and is false only when it pretends to be knowledge. The attempts to define our relation to the divinity as identity, diversity, to determine it as one or many, as within or without, all assume that God is "a thing"; that He is apprehensible or comprehensible in terms of object or subject, of the world or ourselves. Goethe said that he was theist, monotheist, polytheist, pantheist by turns and moods; i.e. that he accepted none of these theories as knowledge, but only as phases or aspects of the inaccessible truth. I think the old scholastic solution of the controversy between realists and conceptualists very applicable to our religious ideas. The universal, they concluded, is *"formaliter in intellectu, fundamentaliter in re"*—founded in reality, fashioned by the mind; a fiction based upon fact. Our religious ideas are not subjective fancies, nor objective realities, but a little of both. The transcendental and unknowable which, as the principle of our spiritual life and growth, becomes for us, so far, immanental and knowable, seeks to express itself in terms of our understanding and language. Like our expression of the beautiful in poetry and art, this expression of the divine has its relative truth, its objective criterion, its development in

*From *George Tyrrell's Letters*, ed. Maude D. Petre, 31–35.

the individual and collective mind. There is a lower and a higher, a less true and more true, never a finished truth. The would-be finished truth is a lie, and an idol. What saves our "theologia" from being an "eidolopoea" is the sense of its infinite inadequacy to compass the transcendental. Religion dies with the sense of mystery, and worship becomes mere servility. That is why our theologians are so irreligious. Their treatise *De Deo* is as definite as their treatise *De Romano Pontifice*, and they worship God merely as an arch-pope. If, as they teach, God is at once simple (or partless) and incomprehensible, He must be wholly incomprehensible. Yet they speak as though the inadequacy of our God-idea were merely quantitative; as though He were comprehensible up to a certain point. The experimental foundation of our God-idea is our own God-needing, God-seeking, God-making instinct. We give it intellectual form in the explanation or cause by which we account for these spiritual perturbations and attractions. These ideas, as fashioned by the understanding, are fictions founded on fact. If we take them as more, they are idols; if we realise that they are but adumbrations—shadows cast by a ray of the Light Eternal struggling through the thick fog of the human mind—then they are "mysteries of faith." Not arbitrary symbols, for they are natural formations and correspond, not to the Light Eternal, but to the form of that which intercepts it. Finitude is of the very essence of everything we can ascribe to God. We can *say* "infinite goodness," "infinite wisdom," "infinite power," but the adjective destroys the substantive and leaves the mind vacant of any meaning. Only because our God or Eternal Spirit is always surreptitiously humanesque and finite can we give Him an indefinite measure (but still always a measure) of these essentially finite attributes. These names bear the same value as applied to the transcendent as "birdie" or "blossom" applied by a mother to her little child. It is plainly man's religious instinct and duty to find the worthiest possible idea and name for God: "*Quantum potes tantum aude; Quia major omni laude; Nec laudare sufficis.*" The higher will always be nearer the truth; the highest still indefinitely short of it. Every article of the Christian creed is subordinate to and illustrative of its central and governing article—"I believe in God"— and is similarly a mystery or adumbration of superhuman truth in human terms. When I speak of our God-idea I include our whole construction of the world and life in relation to God. Religious creeds are the expression of the collectively elaborated God-idea of a whole people. They are to be valued by the elevation of their conception of humanity and of the meaning of life;[1] by their degree of divine inspiration and moral fertility. They are not mere dreams or poetic fictions, for they are checked by those experiences of which they are the religious interpretation—experience of the inward life, of Nature, of human history. They may idealise, but they must not contradict such experiences. They must be *fundamentaliter in re.* They are of divine and not of human origin in so far as these experiences are God's language of self-revelation; inadequate, as all language is, to the reality it symbolises, and needing a sympathetic spirit for its right interpretation. Monotheism, pantheism, polytheism have reference only to the humanesque images of God; referred to the transcendent reality they are senseless. Monotheism and polytheism save the idea of personality; the former seems to satisfy the craving for unity, the latter admits of a greater fulness and variety of human excellences than are compatible in the structure of a single character. The Jewish and Christian God has no aesthetic or artistic sympathies; no joy or laughter; is, on the whole forbidding and unattractive. The garment of love with which He has been clothed fits ill. He is still the angry, jealous, volcanic Javeh. An Apollo would lack the sterner stuff of humanity. A whole pantheon is needed to display the many-coloured varieties of our nature; not to speak of our collective and social life. Here Christianity, with a wise inconsistency, has discovered a trinity in unity and given us three gods, which it asserts are not three; while in the saints and angels it has found room for the divinisation of every phase and form of the ideal humanity, individual and social. Pantheism sacrifices humanesque personality, but thereby is more conscious of the divine sort of otherness, and finds room in the Deity for every sort of created excellence besides the human. Universal immanence means a transcendence of the human, though falling short of absolute transcendence. So, like Goethe, I admit the truth and therefore the untruth of all of them—as applied to the Reality. As part of the same creed or God-idea I admit they are incompatible; but the Christian revelation represents the best compromise, as being sort of "limited monotheism," tempered by certain polytheistic and pantheistic tendencies.

My private revelation is naturally a simple affair. It gives me the image of a sort of indwelling Christ-God—my conscience, my judge, my other and better self, with whom I converse silently much as I

---

1. Have we not here a suggestion towards a "religion of humanity" of deeper reality and fuller spiritual substance than the various forms of Positivism can offer us?—M.D.P.

converse with my own mind, and with whom I am often at variance, never at peace. This being, I know, is a construction of my understanding and imagination inspired by and explanatory of the Power within me that makes for righteousness, and of whose real nature I have no idea. . . .

DIVINE FECUNDITY*

At first sight it might seem that the impression made upon us by a collective calamity, like an earthquake or shipwreck, is largely irrational, or is, at most, the sum of the impressions that would have been created had each life been separately destroyed. It may be argued that every individual has to die once; that there are more painful and lingering deaths than drowning or crushing; that if all death is a curtailment of possible pleasures, it is also a curtailment of possible pains; that those canceled years were pregnant with evil as well as with good; in short, that reason does not justify the disturbance and horror of the imagination.

There is something in all this. To some extent the curtailment of any individual life, prior to its exhaustion by old age, offers the same problem as the sort of collective catastrophe we are considering. But we cease to attend to a riddle that is put to us every day in the same terms, and that the whole world has given up long ago. A collective catastrophe puts it to us in new terms and more insistently; it forces us to pause and guess again. But to a great extent it is the same riddle: "Wherefore hast Thou made all men for naught?"

But the collective catastrophe is often much more than a sumtotal of individual catastrophes. It differs in kind as well as in degree. It implies a frustration, not merely of individual lives, but of social life. For a state or city has a life of its own, a history of its own. It has its aspirations, ambitions, ideals. Though history shows us that kingdoms perish, yet, for them, the law of death is not an apparent *necessity* as it is for the individual. They live, act, plan, design, on the assumption that they will last for ever. And so of institutions, associations, and other collectivities. They allow for, and are not perturbed by, the gradual elimination and replacement of their individual members. But for collective catastrophes, that interrupt their history or threaten their very existence, they do not allow.

*From *Essays on Faith and Immortality*, arranged by Maude D. Petre (1914), 245–77.

For every loyal, true-hearted citizen the future, the honour, the prosperity of his state or city or country is the cause of God—a cause to which he owes the ready sacrifice of his own life. That he himself should be cut off in the flower and promise of his days, before he has rendered his fruit, would be a scandal and mystery, were it not so familiar an occurrence. But that the state, whose welfare has been for him a divine cause, one with which God was identified, should come to naught, and that all its toil and aspiration for the future should be frustrated, is a mystery of a new order. If God seemed careless of the individual, it was only because He cared for the type, the race, the cause:

> But no,
> From scarped cliff and quarried stone
> She cries: "A thousand types are gone;
> I care for nothing."

The more extensive and socially destructive such a catastrophe, so much the more does it bring home to us the possibility of what may happen, nay, of what must happen, though it has never happened yet; namely, the extinction of the human race in the midst of its career; the frustration of its collective hopes, ideals, and aspirations. Religion has probably only canonised and authenticated a spontaneous and perhaps useful illusion of the mind, in teaching us to believe that human history is working towards some definite and attainable goal in which its destiny will be accomplished; that, like an individual organism, its evolution has a certain inherently determined limit; that the process is to end in some "Kingdom of God" on earth, some socialist millennium, in which the wheels of life will spin round monotonously and without progress—where the order and the regular routine of the bee-hive shall be the solution of all our strivings after perfection. But, manifestly, collective humanity is in no way predetermined inherently to any such fixed goal. As far as it seems designed for anything, it is for an eternal process of ever expanding and deepening life. Not only to man, but to every living species, Nature says: "Increase, multiply, fill the earth and subdue it"; nor is there any inward principle limiting that increase and expansion. The Posterity we work for is not some final generation that is to enter into the fruit of all the tears and sorrows of the Past. Every future generation, even the most distant we can imagine, will have tears and sorrows of its own. If it will look back on our present with a sense of filial gratitude, it will look forward to the generations of an illimitable future with a sense of responsibility and shortcoming not lighter than our own. Relatively, the joys and sorrows of one epoch are no greater than those of another. New supplies create new demands; new answers raise new questions; new attainments breed new discontents; new ideals raise new aspirations.

The quest of happiness, as the older East has realised, should rather restrain than accelerate the march of progress. It should lead men to contentment; to a minimising of their desires; not to the feverish creations of new necessities.

We really progress, not in pursuit of a freely chosen end, such as an earthly paradise, but in obedience to a dire law of our nature, and because we must. Under pressure from behind and from around we are constrained to live better in order to live at all; to advance, in order not to perish. Apart from such pressure we are inert, and even retrograde. We kick against the goad that spurs us on to effort and conflict. Once forced into battle our love of conquest may become a passion, which we put down to our own credit. We prefer to think we are actively pursuing an end, rather than passively obeying an impulse. Yet the only intelligible end we can put before ourselves is either some mark on our ever-receding horizon, some definite point of progress beyond which our foresight fails us; or else it is progress itself, viewed as life and happiness, in contrast to stagnation and death. The latter is, strictly speaking, not an end at all, for by an end we mean that to which progress is a means; that which is being built up by our labours. Building is not the end of building; though it may be good exercise and interesting work. It may be a necessity of our nature, as it is with beavers; we may ever foresee the fairly remote results; but whether there be an ultimate result, and what it is, we do not know.

Yet it is just because we assume that we are building up some final earthly paradise, some Kingdom of God that we are perplexed by those extensive social catastrophes, that suggest the possibility of a racial catastrophe such as a universal plague, or earthquake, or cosmic collision. Our God is in our image and likeness; He is the embodiment and guarantee of our highest; we have no higher aspiration than the welfare of humanity. Can God be indifferent to this?[1]

Indifference! that is the problem. Nature, or God, is so evidently careful, so evidently careless, about one and the same interest. Dual-

1. Let me say, in passing, that in the present context I use God and Nature indifferently, i.e. I speak of God so far as God is immanent in and coincident with Nature, and not as supernatural and transcendent. Sometimes Nature sounds too inhuman for my purpose, at others God sounds too human.—G.T.

ism offers a tempting solution for an apparent conflict between two
principles—one constructive, the other destructive. But no! Construction and destruction are two plainly dependent factors of one
system. Nature destroys in creating and creates in destroying. Death
is but an economy of life in its higher forms; by no means necessary
in the lower. The fly and the mouse perish that the spider and the cat
may live. Yet Nature is on both sides at once. She pounces with the
cat and she runs with the mouse; she rejoices with the conqueror, she
mourns and struggles with the conquered. Is it not the same throughout the whole world? Everywhere forces, impulses, instincts of self-
assertion, self-preservation, self-expansion, whose frustration is
apparently as much the intention of Nature as is their realisation?

Nor can we say that it is the lower that yields to the higher; man
may be the prey of a microbe. Nor again that the lower is wholly
designed for the use of the higher; no plant or animal is designed for
food, but only for its own life and self-expansion. While many are
designed to prey on and infest others, not one instinctively yields
itself to be eaten. All Nature's devices are for conquest or escape.
She has filled the world with feeders, but not with food. Food is
always artificial; it is made out of something that has another destiny
of its own. We *destroy* a plant or an animal to feed on its materials.
But its form or function, all that makes it what it is, is nothing to our
purpose. Nature in each existing individual seems to be wholly on its
side and against all the rest, while, at the same time, the very rivalry
of types and individuals is the condition of their existence and development. Were any one type to fulfil the law of its being without
check it would overspread the whole earth in an incredibly short
time, and in destroying its rivals would destroy the conditions of its
own existence. It is at once intended, and not intended, to prevail.
Therefore man has naively believed, and made his religion teach
him, that he is an exception to this law of life; that the strength and
direction of his natural impulses and aspirations is a guarantee for
their eventual attainment. It was thought reasonable that cows and
sheep should exist only secondarily for themselves, but primarily to
supply him with mutton and beef. Plants (though how few) existed
for animals; animals (though how few) existed for man. As for the
extinct species that preceded man, they were an anomaly.

No; there is no guarantee that man, in obeying the innate law of
his being, in struggling upward and onward out of bestiality to savagery, to barbarism, to grade after grade of civilisation, is a favoured
child of Nature, or is destined to prosperity, or that he may not

fall the prey of some new microbe, or some wild upheaval of the earth's crust.

It is this combination of care and carelessness that constitutes the wastefulness of Nature. She is like some fickle genius who, as soon as he has proved his skill, wearies of his task, and throws it aside, unfinished, to begin another. She loves making, but not the thing she has made; infinitely clever, infinitely heartless.

Newman said that, apart from the phenomena of conscience and man's moral life, he could not see evidence of God in Nature. I would go further, and say that the evidence points rather to a Devil. For a Devil would do good in the interests of evil, like a cat fondling and patting a mouse; allowing it to believe itself free in order to prolong its agony by alternations of hope and despair. But a moral God could not do evil in the interests of good. We can understand how goodness in nature consists with an evil God; we cannot understand how evil consists with a good God.

She takes, not fifty, but fifty thousand seeds—vegetal, or animal, or human—in her careless hand, and flings them into space, on the chance that just one may realise some little part of that infinite potentiality with which she has endowed it. For each is pregnant with a whole world of teeming life. We look up and see in the midnight sky white with star-dust, and we recognise her wasteful hand once more. And yet, in our conceit, we are still confident that our own microscopic atom is a favoured world-seed that cannot fail of eventual success. But what are the probabilities that its potentialities will come to anything, or that Nature would deflect by a hair's breadth the course of a destroying comet for the earth's sake, or turn an inch out of her straight path rather than set her heel on our laboriously constructed ant-hill? I think none at all. But we must perforce conceive the eternal and universal labour of Nature in the likeness of some human enterprise, with beginning, middle, and end; and of which every part and step bears on every other and builds up a final and predetermined result. For earlier thought this unity was more static and architectural; for ours, it is that of a building process, where nothing is wasted, where every movement looks to the total result. And if the manifest waste and incoherence of Nature give the lie to this anthropomorphism, we ascribe this apparent difficulty to the limitation of our view. Could we see all, we think we should see thrift and economy everywhere; "toil co-operant to an end."

But, before we go abroad with the stellar universe, let us look at home and see if the history of this earth, or of man, bear out the idea of progress—of an all-embracing plan to which every existence and event is subservient; let us see if we are justified in extending the categories of the part to the whole; in conceiving the whole (with Fechner) as a vast organism. May it not be a boundless ocean of chaotic potentialities, in which myriad forms of organisms appear, and, by their mere struggle for existence, come at last to constitute that hierarchic world of life, whose unity we are tempted to explain by some sort of finalism—whether that of a governing outside intelligence or that of an immanent idea, or *ratio seminalis?*

The Naturalist school may have been justified in banishing finalism from this region, and only erred (like the Finalists) by their passion for unity; their desire to make one category cover all. Finalism may preside over the living organism, yet not over the hierarchic arrangement of organisms. The Whole Universe is greater than its parts; but it need not be higher, or as high. Its unity may well be of the lowest, most primitive and elementary type—the unity of a cloud or nebula. So too the unity, the intelligence, the experience of a state or society is greater, in some way, but not higher than that of the individual members. It exists for the individual, not conversely.

Are we then justified in supposing that, because progress or development is the innate law of life—of every living individual and type— it is also the law of the world which is the theatre of life; that *the Whole* has been planned with a view to progress? Let us shut up our sacred books, and look at human history as a whole, or in any of its departments as we know it. Can we say that our present civilisation is the steady, orderly outcome of man's past history in the same way that a fully-developed organism is the outcome of its first germ? Can we say that all our past has been co-operant to this end? Manifestly not.

What makes us think so is that, as far as we know, ours is the highest civilisation so far attained. Moreover, it rests on a wider basis than any other civilisation. It is cosmopolitan. It is recorded, and protected against oblivion and extinction, as no previous one. Were it overwhelmed in one hemisphere it would reintegrate itself from the other. Hence there is every reason to think it will last as long as man, and that it will progress and develop without disastrous interruptions. For this reason we are tempted to trace this expanding stream of progress back to the very beginnings of human history, and forcibly to include the whole of that history between its banks. Nothing could be more unhistorical. Only the barest trickle from the Past mingles with its waters. The rest has sunk into the earth or evaporated into the clouds, and affects us as little as the history of Mars or Jupiter. For all that concerns us, the history of Central Africa, or aboriginal America, is mere waste. It might never have happened. I am not sure that we owe anything considerable to Assyria. And when we point to our debts to Egypt and Greece, let us not deceive ourselves. They have not lived on in us, but have died that we might live. We have not steadily built up the structure that they began, but have gathered stones from their ruins to build into a wholly different structure. There is no more continuity of development here than between the beast of prey and its quarry. Let us remember this when we are carried away by the alluring category of religious development, and are told that all the religious history of the Past has been steadily converging towards Christianity as its final form. No doubt Christianity has built into its system many treasures from the ruins of past religions. When Israel came out of Egypt she brought with her more than earrings and jewels. When Christianity went into Egypt, Athens, and Rome she took as much as she gave. But let us not call this "development," or forget that, save for these scanty traces, the vast history of man's earlier religious efforts is mere waste, as far as we are concerned. Like the water bursting from some reservoir, most of it is locked and impeded and absorbed. Only our little stream has chanced to reach us, mingled and lost in waters of a thousand sources.

Each religion has its own internal law of development, according to which it becomes more and more individualised and separate, less and less capable of entering as a member into any sort of higher, all-comprehensive religious organism. If, to-day, various religions and sects are crying out for reunion, it is that their vitality is exhausted; it is that man needs a new religion, that is to be built out of the ruins of the old ones. They cannot grow into it; they can only die that it may live.

Still more futile is it to find a quasi-organic relation between the countless species of life, extant and extinct, that have appeared on our globe; to see them all co-operant and convergent towards some grand final unification. Such order as we find is the result of struggle and competition. "The strongest eel," says the proverb, "gets to the top of the pot," the weakest gets to the bottom; and between the top and the bottom the others are hierarchically arranged, according to the degree of their efficiency. The history of species and genera is

that of a process of division and subdivision in no way subordinated
to some higher complex unity. Each goes its own way independently,
as if it were the whole; and its relation to the rest, if not indifferent, is
hostile rather than co-operative. Horses do not volunteer to work for
man, nor aphides for ants. As far as present species are concerned,
most of the past might never have existed, so little do they enter into
the present resultant. Life has put forth a thousand branches that
have simply perished without trace—each a separate world that
has lived and died, but not for us. They might as well have flourished
in the most distant stars as far as existing flora and fauna are
concerned.

And those distant stars! Is there the faintest evidence in favour of
Fechner's beautiful dream (described by Prof. W. James in the *Hibbert Journal*, Jan. 1909) of an organic unity in which each has its part
to play, each demands and is demanded by all the rest, in which not
one is wasted, or fails to contribute to the realisation of a fore-
ordained end? Does not all the evidence we have explain this apparent order as the blind resultant of a competition between brute
masses and brute forces? Are they not ever crashing, colliding,
destroying one another in their struggle for free play, senseless as the
furious billows of an angry ocean? Let us not be blinded by our
instinctive craving for unity, understanding, comprehension; which is
only an exigency of our practical life.

We can deal with the world only so far as we can unify it into a
system that will make prediction possible. But for that it is sufficient
that the little fraction of space and time, in which our lot is cast,
should present certain purely relative and practical uniformities. Our
mind can deal with that little fraction; if it would go beyond, it must
divest itself of its practical prepossessions and face a world that is
inhuman, indifferent to man and his interests. Religion has not been
half so anthropomorphic as science, with its dogmatic generalisations
of purely human and practical categories.

As far, then, as our experience goes the organic category—the
co-ordination of parts by a whole, of functions by an end—has no
application in Nature except to the individual organism. I say "in
Nature," for plainly we find it in the works of man and in human
society. It cannot even be applied to the history and development of
the species. For while the organism, left to itself, develops, and that
in a fixed way, the species, left to itself, is inert if not decadent, and,
when forced by external pressure to develop, may do so in any one

of a thousand directions, determined by the more or less accidental nature of that external pressure. It accommodates and shapes itself as a river does to its bed; and with as little foresight or design. Its future cannot be predicted from any knowledge of its internal constitution.

Only, then, in the individual manifestations of life do we find anything that looks like plan or finality in Nature. These are, as it were, so many condensations or nuclei in the shapeless, aimless nebula or ocean of the inorganic; each a little world apart, adjusting itself to its surroundings and to its neighbour-worlds as best it may, leaguing with them for common advantage or adventure, depending on them for its very existence and preservation, yet not constituting with them any sort of higher natural pre-established goal. Nature is not working to one end, but has just as many ends as there are living individuals. In each of them the Divine seeks a new self-expression. But its utterances are not connected; nor has their sum-total a separate, an "organic" meaning.

Is the universe then (as we know it) aimless and meaningless? Rather it teems with aims and meanings, although it has no *one* aim or meaning. It is like a great tree, that pushes out its branches, however and wherever it can, seeking to realise its whole nature, as far as possible, in every one of them, but aiming at no collective effect. This is its play, this is its life, this is, if you will, its end.

But the tree grows in the process; it is born and it dies. Have we any reason to think that the universe grows from anything to anything? Not the slightest. All we can find is an endless oscillation, like that of the heaving ocean—a process of making and unmaking, of condensation and dispersion; periods of progress alternating with periods of retrogression. We can see in it only the eternal theatre of those self-manifestations which are, so to say, the pulsings of its universal life. To suppose that God is working out some ultimate end by means of those self-manifestations, that they are not ends in themselves, is to reduce Him to human dependency and poverty, to forget that they are but radiations from the source of life. As well look for plan and system among the blessings that the sun scatters upon our earth. The sun cheers each heart, tunes each throat, colours each flower, fertilises each grain, as though there were no other in all the world.

As far, then, as God in Nature seems at all to care or provide, it is not for the type, but for the single life; not for the Whole, but for a

few of its parts. Plan seems to stop with the individual. He builds a
ship, and provides it for all dangers and contingencies, and sets forth
in it to encounter what storms and rocks chance may have in store
for it. These are no part of the same plan, if of any plan.

Intending to exalt and magnify God, we do so in man's image, and
thereby but narrow and degrade Him. The greatest human creator is
he who carries a work through from a definite beginning to a definite
end, and so orders the means to that end that not one is too much or
too little; while each is valued only for the sake of the end. These
countless billions of separate worlds and ends; this wasteful luxuriance; this lack of any ulterior design in whose realisation the cosmic
labour is to cease; this work for work's sake—all this is perplexing to
us, whose needs and limits alone drive us into action. The artist, the
musician know something of it. We have made our God in the image,
not of the artist, but of the artisan or the man of affairs. "What is He
going to make out of it all?" Perhaps nothing; perhaps the universe is
but His eternal keyboard, His eternal canvas. Perhaps each melody,
each picture, may have a worth in itself apart from all the rest. Lost
stars, lost species, lost civilisations, lost religions—lost as far as any
influence on our own is concerned—may have justified their existence, though they have led to nothing further.

Let us remember this when we think it an injustice that so many
generations should have lived in savagery and barbarism in order
that our civilisations might at last arise. Will not future generations
look back on us, with a like mistaken pity, as having existed only for
their sakes? Do we not feel, and rightly, that we exist primarily for
our own? And did not our savage ancestors feel the same? Are we
not mistaking a result for an end? We conceive progress as planned;
as working for an end, an earthly paradise, into which some far-off
generation is to enter, for whose sake all previous generations have
suffered. And, pray, when? Our just indignation at such a scheme is,
however, wholly wasted if there be no such scheme, and if every
generation, every individual life, has an absolute value of its own,
and constitutes a world apart.

Every animal multiplies, but no animal exists in order to multiply—in order that others may exist about whose existence the same
question recurs. If we live only for posterity we live for nothing; for
posterity, like to-morrow, never comes.

The good of posterity is the result, not the end, of our living as
well and as fully as we can. We should live, not for a posterity that
never comes, but for the present—always remembering that our

present is a little bit of the past, tied to a little bit of the future; the duration of our actual interests; the extent of our clear foresight and retrospect.

If, then, a collective catastrophe, interrupting the course of progress and civilisation, shocks and disappoints our expectation, it is because the expectation was ill-grounded; because we had thought Nature pledged to the development of the social organism in the same way as she is pledged to that of the individual organism— or rather more, since we conceived society as a higher inclusive organism.

Man has, to a great extent, organised society; but Nature has not. She bids the stream of life flow, but digs no channels for it. She increases and multiples, she does not organise. Such order as her ranks preserve derives from external pressure, not from an internal principle. It is man, and not she, that makes the *res publica* an end in itself, superior to the multitudinous ends of the individuals, for whose sake alone it should be valued. The State is but a means, an instrument of the happiness of individuals—a single means common to a multitude of ends, not a single end common to a multitude of means. It is but part of our environment; and we do not exist for the sake of our environment, but conversely. Because we ascribe our own state-worship to Nature we consider her indifference to the State far more criminal than her indifference to the individuals composing it.

No doubt to view the cause of progress as God's cause, and to live and labour for an ideal society or Kingdom of God in the vague future, has been the source of no little inspiration and fertile inventiveness. But it has not been an unmixed blessing. The end is easily forgotten in the means; the means easily idolised into an end. Men come to care more for "causes" than for the persons in whose behalf they are taken up; more for the Sabbath than for man, more for the temple than for Him who dwells in it. Humanitarians may be very inhuman, and Churchmen often put the Church before Christ. We are the victims of our abstractions and personifications. The Church, Society, Humanity, and such abstractions easily become as concrete and separate for us as the living multitudinous units of which they are made up, and for whose benefit alone we may wish them well.

There is a worship of the Future not less pernicious than the worship of the Past; there is a devotion to progress as enslaving as the blindest Chinese traditionalism. Man must never be treated as a means, as a stepping-stone for his fellows. It is not by thinking of remote posterity that we shall do most for it, but by thinking of ourselves and of our children, and making the best of the present, and of that immediate future which is part of the present.

The root of the fallacy is the idea that, because millions of lives are more valuable than one, they combine to constitute a higher order of value; that, because the ocean is greater than all the life it contains, it has a higher life of its own to which its contents are subordinated. And the fallacy is favoured by that hierarchic order which results from competition, and mimics that of a living organism. "As many lives and ends—so many separate worlds." That is the verdict of experience and reflection.

If our problem is thus simplified, if we have only to puzzle over Nature's carelessness as to the individual, it is in some way also intensified. For there was some vague semblance of solution in the idea that the individual was sacrificed to some higher and more universal end, about which Nature was not careless. And even when her indifference to some chosen people or race, to progress, to humanity, to this planet, could no longer be denied, the end was only pushed further away into the darkness of the unknown.

For man's imagination Nature, like space, must be finite, with a centre somewhere; and if there is a multitude of ends and ideas there must be one that unifies and controls all the rest. The infinite, with its centre everywhere or anywhere, an infinity of ends, each of which is supreme for itself, is, for him, a denial of rationality. That the Universe should have no separate meaning as a whole; that its meaning should be uttered in varying aspects and degrees in every particle and every pulse of its totality, makes folly of most of our philosophy. Yet what we see suggests rather the idea of an Infinity that would utter itself to the very full in a million ways, did not such utterances limit and impede each other. As the whole of our knowledge and experience is brought to bear, in varying degrees of distinctness, on every perception and action, so God seems to throw Himself wholly into the very least of His acts and creations, as though it were His sole care and interest. To each microbe He says: "Increase, multiply, replenish the earth and subdue it"; to every force and energy: "Be thou the ruler over thy brethren"; to every soul: "Thou art My Son, to-day I have begotten thee."

Like a forest, the world grows in all senses and directions, in obedience to His pressure from within. Its branches thwart and strangle and overshadow one another. He cares not which prevails. Balked in one outlet, He seeks another. His one end seems to be the fullest and most multitudinous self-utterance, but there is no sign of a general plan, no order but that which results from the very conflict of utterances. There is no arrangement of the garden, only a wilderness of glorious stars, each a world in itself. For us gardeners the universe as a wilderness is a scandal. The seeming wilderness must go to make a pattern in the eyes of God and His angels. We forget that what we call order, plan, classification is only a practical necessity for beings whose experience is limited; who cannot simultaneously apprehend the whole, in all its detail. A man with an unlimited memory would not need to index his books or catalogue his library. For such a being, order—an order that serves no purpose—might not even be beautiful. For whose benefit, for what finite mind, should the whole universe be tidied up and arranged like a Natural History Museum? Are the seas and continents, the clouds and mountains, orderly? What unity have the stellar nebulae?

Shall we not then make a hypothesis more apt to cover the facts, as far as we see them, if we suppose God (or Nature if you like) to be bound by a twofold metaphysical necessity: first, the necessity of producing and creating in all senses and directions, much as a forest does; secondly, the necessity by which such individual productions interfere with and impede one another? What He produces are the individuals; the totality, and its more or less mechanically determined order, *result,* but are not *produced* or intended.

On this hypothesis He cares, and cares supremely, for each individual thing as though it were a world apart. He equips it for the struggle; lives, fights, feels, devises, plans with it. He cannot do otherwise. If He fights against it, on behalf of its fellow-combatants, this, again, is a necessity of His Nature, which utters itself to its utmost in every possible way. He is on the side of the cat and on the side of the mouse; of the oppressor and of the oppressed. He does not will, but He cannot help, the conflict and agony. His will is plainly to minimise and abolish it if it were possible. Here it is that His freedom is exercised—i.e. in dealing with the problem produced, and ever renewed, by His necessary fecundity. Such progress as we see is the work of immanent wisdom and intelligence, striving to make room for the swarming children of life. It is, therefore, a libel to say He is careless of individuals. He cares for them and for nothing else. He does not sacrifice them as means to some far-off, universal, and impersonal end.

What, then, is His interest in man's social schemes and dreams? Just His interest in the individuals that are to benefit by them; just His interest in that problem of life which confronts each of them, so far as, in any degree, they are self-conscious and self-governing—the problem of relieving the pressure and suffering resulting from the fecundity of life, and of finding room for her multitudinous children. At first it would seem to be the self-conserving instinct that leagues them together for a common, or distributive, rather than a collective advantage. But eventually we find a diviner type of life, in which sympathy becomes an instinct of the heart, a principle of the mind; in which the individual shares the divine interest in other individuals— first in its fellows, lastly in "all things both great and small." Then man consciously co-operates with the Divine Will in its care of individuals; in its task of minimising pressure and suffering; in securing the fullest possible conditions of life for all; in wrestling with the inevitable limitations of the finite—with all-conquering death and decay.

The Kingdom of God, the Earthly Paradise, are not ends in themselves, but means to the multitudinous ends of individual happiness. Nor are they terms of an infallible unbroken progress, or ends that can ever be realised; they stand for the direction, not for the terminus, of the Divine effort to minimise the inevitable pressure of its inevitable fecundity. We have here, writ large, the eternally insoluble problem of that over-population, which is at once the source of progress and degradation, of happiness and misery, of life and death. If one people, one species restricts its fecundity, it will only be to the profit of its rivals. Dam the stream where you will, the torrent of life rolls on just the same, only to fertilise some other region.

That evil and suffering are in some way inseparable from the finite, is allowed by orthodox Christianity. The heterodoxy of this view lies in the necessity of universal fecundity which it imposes on God. If such fecundity is not necessary, the pessimist who believes that pain predominates over happiness can hardly forgive God for having produced at all, or for not having accommodated His family to His resources. If, however, it is necessary, we must say that evil is inseparable from the divine fecundity; from the overcrowding of good. No man produces a crowd of children, with all the attendant misery and poverty. He produces the individuals one by one, each for its own sake. The crowd results; and calls forth his efforts to realise an income and position to relieve the pressure.

The theological objection to necessary creation is this: It would make God dependent on something not Himself. He would require the universe, as man requires air. But when we ask: How can God be infinite if creation lies outside His being—if God *plus* creation is more than God? Theology answers that creation is "being" of a different order and cannot be added to God, any more than a point to a line or a line to a surface. And so it is easy to reply that God depends on creation, as on a different order of being, which is a zero compared with His own. The answer is at least as good as the objection. Both are fairly worthless.

We have thus an eternal struggle, without beginning, without end, between being and the inevitable limitations of being; between boundless fecundity and the bounds that result from it. In each particular life or branch of life the struggle is maintained as long as possible by all the devices and contrivances of an inexhaustible wisdom; but sooner or later, as in the individual, so in the race, so too in the cosmic system, the problem becomes insoluble and death conquers. Yet there is no rest or repose in the ocean of being. Again and again, in countless millions of forms, the task is taken up patiently and the riddle is attempted anew.

And now we may consider the religious and ethical bearings of such a view. In the first place, God is exonerated of all that burden of evil and suffering which He is supposed, if not to will, at least to permit deliberately, in the interests of some final scheme, compared with which the individual interest is of no importance in His eyes. Evil is the all-but-inevitable result of His inevitable fecundity. His whole effort is to circumvent and minimise the result. He is entirely and only on the side of life and happiness, and of the fullest attainable expression of His own image and likeness. In all our struggles against evil, in all our endeavours to find room for the greatest possible fulness of life, we are with Him and He with us. It is He Who has gradually raised us to this sympathy with Himself, this sonship and confederacy—to share His joys and griefs. And surely He Himself bears our griefs and carries our sorrows. He is not, then, indifferent to our dreams, nor to our battles for a Divine Kingdom on earth, so far as they are inspired by the highest love of all—love for individuals, not the mere love of ideas and schemes. But this inspiration is no guarantee of an eventual and impossible triumph. All His works perish, from the least to the greatest, He alone abides and works eternally. Is it not enough to be at one with God, Who wills that the battle for life be fought valiantly, and sustained perseveringly, as long as a single soldier is left standing, even though final victory be impossible? Are not the single lives worth *our* care and love, as they are worth *His?*

And I ask whether this view does not enrich our religious sentiment with an element that we observe in the more refined paganism, and miss in the rather crude optimism of our own tradition. I mean, that mute resignation to the futility of man's greatest hopes and enterprises; that sense of a blind fatality that cares not for man, any more than man for the microscopic world that he destroys at every step he takes. Was there not a half truth in all this? Do we not find echoes of it in the great seers of all times?

We have been too long accustomed to a cheap eschatology; to a confident assurance that the whole creation centres round a chance page of human history, that has escaped the moth and mildew of Time and fallen into our hands. We are satisfied that God can have created but one world, that all is directed to but one end; that, could we but see all, we should find everything converging to a rational unity—letters, syllables, words, sentences, all combining to yield one reasoned and connected discourse. The pagan thinker has no such assurance as enables the confident Christian to interpret and justify the ways of God to man at every turn. The sense of dark mystery, of a sad mortality o'erswaying man's largest and loftiest undertakings, of a profound irrationality in the very heart of existence, had taught him more modesty and humility; had made him suspicious of prosperity and the insolence it fosters. We find this note in the wisdom of Job, and its rebuke of the smug exponents of a narrow optimism; or in Ecclesiastes, with its bitter acknowledgment of Nature's indifference to good and evil, wisdom and folly. If, to our ears, this note rings harsh, it is not because it is untrue, but because it is solitary, and needs "a sweet yoke-fellow" wherewith to blend in harmony. The sway of sad mortality is over everything, not only over man, but over humanity; Heaven and earth shall pass away, without a trace of influence upon the heavens and earths that shall succeed them in an endless futurity. We shall not, we have no right to, fare better than the ant-hill built up by toiling generations, to be annihilated by the ox's hoof or the peasant's dog. Its end accomplished? What end? Was not each little life an end in itself? Was the ant for the hive, or the hive for the ant?

But, like the ant, man must obey the life-impulses of his nature, and go on building and toiling as though he were, what in a sense he is, a world apart. He may not sit down in oriental listlessness and despair, with a *vanitas vanitatum* on his lips. The ant does not know, man knows, that he shall die, and that the memory of his race shall at last be obliterated from creation, as a record written in the faithless sand. Here is the pathos, the depth, the dignity of human life and of the struggles of humanity. Here is the blind loyalty of the soldier, who rushes upon certain death in obedience to a command that seems to him folly. The law of his nature is imperative; its purpose is inscrutable. Man knows. There is something of the universal and absolute, that enables him to stand outside and above himself, to measure his relativity, his finitude, his vanity. He looks at himself with God's eyes. Besides his life as an individual organism, he shares a divine life and a divine outlook; a divine sympathy. In him God has given to the work of His hands the power of recognising and understanding its maker, and of freely co-operating in its maker's purpose. Surely man is the son of God by some strange and inexplicable participation in the Divine nature! It is not as a self-centred, self-seeking individual organism, but as the son, the infant son no doubt, of God, that he wakes to a sense of the tragedy and mystery of existence and of the nothingness and unreality of all that is not God. God alone is the substance that gives meaning to all this shadow-play. And thus we are driven back on Kant's great intuition, that there is nothing really or absolutely good, no end on which man may fix his whole heart, but good will. And good will is just God's will. To be at one with that will, to enter into and co-operate with God's struggle in the battle of life, that alone is the inspiring motive, the justifying end, of all our endeavours—that, and not some final resultant in which all these labours are to be crowned with success and rewarded with an eternal Sabbath of inaction.

Thus to the note of Stoic indifference and detachment is wedded that of Christian hope and enthusiasm. So far as God lives in us consciously, we too are sharers of the Divine fecundity and of all the problems it raises. We must, perforce, push onwards and upwards; the love of Christ constraineth us; woe to me if I preach not the Gospel—the Gospel of peace that brings the sword in its wake; the solution that raises a host of new problems; the supply that breeds more demands than it satisfies; life, life, bursting forth on every side, choking, entangling, impeding itself, wave against wave, current against current, victorious for a time, but at last defeated in its endeavour to utter the infinite words.

"But your life is hid with Christ in God." The life of union with the Divine Will is alone the true life, the eternal life. It is exercised, strengthened and deepened by our co-operation with the Divine cause, by our obedience to the law of our nature, that bids us take our part in the eternal problem of the universe, created by the fecundity of God. The true Kingdom of God consists, not in a final solution of the insoluble, in the squaring of the circle, the equation of finite and infinite, but in the multiplication of the sons of God, of wills reconciled and atoned with the Divine Will in its endless joys and sorrows. "He prayeth best who loveth best all things both great and small," for it is by such a love of individual lives, each an end or a world in itself, that we are most closely united to God, and not by the love of collective ends, of states, churches and theocracies, which are but means and devices for individual good; which loom on us from a distance that may make us cold and indifferent to the present whose rights and values are in no way subordinate to those of a to-morrow that never comes.

And perhaps it is not only in the realm of competing existences, but also in that of our own moral and social life, that we may find this problem of the Divine fecundity. Are we not ourselves torn by inward conflicts between impulses that are alike from God? Are we not perplexed as to how He who has given us passions has also given us our reason and our conscience? Can He be on both sides at once? And so in society, are we not faced by conflicting, irreconcilable tendencies and interests, each of which has justice on its side?

Ought we not then to recognise that man, social and individual, is that imperfect solution of a problem that is finally insoluble, and that, apart from external and physical disaster, he, like other species, must at last end in failure as far as this life is concerned? To believe that every moral and social problem admits of ultimate solution may be merely a necessary illusion to protect him from the apathy of despair, until such time as religion has taught him the duty of fighting for victory in the face of certain eventual defeat, and for no other reward than that of eternal life, through union with the Eternal Life.

And shall these sons of God, these Morning Stars, who shout for joy over the glory of creation, shall they, too, vanish like meteors in the darkness? Apart from the desire to live and prevail, which characterises every organism in its vigour, and on which no argument for personal persistence can be based, there is undoubtedly a desire for personal persistence or eternity, and even a hope or conviction of the same, that appears and grows step by step with our diviner life as sons of God. The life into which we then enter, which alone seems to us real and worthful, that life of sympathy with Divine Will, presents itself to us as distinct from and above that physical and organic existence, which is rather its subject matter. In it we seem to belong to the plane of the absolute and universal, and to view the world and its drama, ourselves included, as spectators from the outside. We are simply unable to bring this Divine life under any of those categories by which the mind apprehends and controls everything but itself, the apprehender and controller. We but symbolise it by the "I" of our thought, the object-I, individual and organic. Real, the sovereign reality, for our experience, it remains for our thought and analysis the mystery of mysteries. Let us leave it in the darkness, and trust the larger hope, not faintly but firmly. Man

> thinks he was not made to die, And Thou has made him; Thou art just.

Had a clear knowledge of our *post mortem* state been a strict exigency of our natural and moral life it would have been provided, as is light for our eyes or air for our lungs. We have all the light that we need; light to lead the divine life, to unite ourselves to the divine will, to obey blindly and truthfully the deepest and highest law of our nature, and leave our future tranquilly in the hands of one who is certainly not less just and merciful and loving than those creatures whom He has taught to know, to love, and to trust Him.

May we not then hope that, when the divine spark that is in us has accomplished all that whereunto it is sent, it will return to and merge in its primal source; that, recalled from the outskirts and periphery of the battle, where he fought in blind ignorance of the fortunes of the whole, the soldier will be summoned to the Leader's side to enter into a more universal outlook and interest, into the very centre and source of the world's labour. To be enlarged is not necessarily to be absorbed; nor is the identity of our earlier sense destroyed when it is overclothed with the later and fuller. From that centre of all experience, and as identified with it, we may perhaps look back on the work we have done with mixed feelings of satisfaction with what was done well, and of abiding regret for what was done ill; crowning the former, condemning the latter; at once in Heaven and in Hell, as we are, even now, with respect to our unalterable past. But it is with this Heaven and Hell of the present that we have now to concern ourselves; with that little corner of the battle in which our destiny has placed us. The rest we leave in the hands of God, not asking to see the distant scene.

Note to "Divine Fecundity"

If time allowed it might be interesting to dwell upon the religious and moral consequences of such a *Weltanschauung*. I can do no more than to give the headings of such a chapter.

(1) The exoneration of God from the charge of willing, even permissively, the hurt or destruction of any individual life.

(2) His exoneration from the charge of using such hurt or destruction as a means to some imaginary universal and future end.

(3) The detachment of man from the superstitious belief in and worship of such an imaginary end; and the concentration of his care on individuals, taken distributively and not collectively.

(4) The condemnation of the Gospel of Progress, so far as it promises an eventual millennium, or anything more than an alleviation sufficient to balance the increase of individual suffering that Progress brings in its wake—or, rather, that is itself the cause of Progress.

(5) The need of fighting against evil for the sake of such alleviation, and not in view of ultimate success but rather of ultimate defeat—of fighting because we must and because we ought.

(6) The need of some transcendental other-world hope to oppose to this immediate and provisional pessimism; as the only alternative to accepting that ultimate pessimism which is professed by the largest and oldest religion, or quasi-religion, in the world.

(7) The enrichment of the impoverished Christian consciousness by the restoration of that provisional pessimism to which Christ opposed His message of a transcendental Hope, and which, even by itself, is more respectable than the optimism that looks for a permanent and universal triumph of Progress, and far more respectable than the Christianity that identifies such a triumph with the Kingdom of Heaven promised by Christ.

LETTER TO A FRENCH FRIEND*

The following letter to a French friend is in the nature of an *apologia.*—M.D.P.

January 11th, 1908

You must admit that you set me a difficult task in your letter of December 22nd; the more, because I am so pressed with the same personal difficulties myself, and because circumstances have taken me out of the way of dealing with souls for some years. I can only tell you what I myself feel and aim at in these difficult and soul-starving times. First of all I believe in the Roman Church so far as it is Christian and Catholic; I disbelieve in it so far as it is papal. I see two spirits in it, as in myself, struggling for supremacy—Light and Darkness; Christ and Anti-Christ; God and the Devil. At present Christ is thrown and Anti-Christ is upmost. I believe that the Pope is *de jure* supreme authority in the Church, but his authority, like Christ's, is spiritual and not juridical—the authority of example and sanctity; not of coercion and domination; *non dominante in clero, sed forma facti gregis.* Christ said *Confirma fratres* not *filios* or *servos.* The practical and natural interpretation of the Vatican decrees is for me an intolerable heresy, but, I trust, not quite irremediable. All, then, I allow to the Roman See and Bishop is the *ex officio* duty of being the model and exemplar which it should be the duty of other sees to imitate freely; and I look for the day when Peter, after his boasted fidelity and his manifold denials, *aliquando conversus, confirmabit fratres.* It is a long way off from that blessed cock-crow. So much then for my heresies.

Meantime it is necessary for me to make my personal religion as independent as possible of controversies. I view "religions" as aids to the developments of religion; but it would be perilous to lean too much on such aids in these days of uncertainty. A Quaker repudiates such aids altogether and for everybody. So I am not a Quaker. But I feel each man should aim at an increasing independence of external aids. What I find in myself as the highest law and law-giver of my being, is a Divine Will or Ideal, which struggles to realise itself against a contrary and disintegrating tendency; and does so dependently on my co-operation. I recognise it as the same will which moves every

*This letter and the one that follows are from M. D. Petre, *Autobiography and Life of George Tyrrell* (1912), 2:413–17.

living creature, and indeed the whole world, towards its proper perfection and highest development. Religions can help me to name it,
to imagine it, to understand it, to converse with it. I learn to call it
Conscience, my better Self, the Holy Spirit, the indwelling Christ. As
pervading or transcending all creation I call it the Eternal Father,
source of all being; as working in myself and in the hearts of men, I
call it the Holy Spirit; as giving me an outward rule, model, example
of idealised and divinised humanity in Christ (and in his saints) I call
it the Son of God. And these three are manifestations of one and the
same thing, or Will, or Spirit which I call God. For me the "natural"
is what that Spirit fights against; the "supernatural" what it fights for.
"Forgetting those which are behind (i.e. the natural; the already
accomplished) I press forward to what is in front" (i.e. the supernatural which has yet to be attained, and which when attained becomes
part of the natural; becomes "dead" matter). My "nature" says: "Stop
and rest on your oars"; my "supernature" says: "To rest is to be
dead." In "original sin," "the Atonement," in every doctrine that has
lived and produced life, I try to find some eternal law of the spiritual
life seeking imaginative expression. I know e.g. that my "nature" is
essentially sinful, inert, prone, and is only redeemed when set in
motion by the upward push of conscience or the Holy Spirit. The
"grace of baptism" is a pledge of such an impulse to be mediated to
me through the Church; through the preaching of Christ and His
saints. The Christ Who redeems me is God; the Christ Who is within
me. In the Crucifix He stands outside me that I may see, imaginatively, what I experience spiritually; that I may see how God suffers
Himself to be crucified and dishonoured and persecuted by me rather
than abandon me to my "nature."

You will say all this is very "rationalistic." No; the truths of religion are as infinite and mysterious as the Universe or as God; but it
is only in so far as I can "rationalise" or understand in my own terms
some little corner of that mystery that I can live by it and utilise it;
just as it is only so far as we can press some little fraction of Nature
into scientific form that we can control and utilise Nature. Thus what
I *understand* about the Trinity amounts to Sabellianism. I am quite
sure that Sabellianism is ludicrously inadequate; but it is as much of
the truth as is serviceable to me, and is true as far as it goes; and I am
not defining the Catholic faith but giving the categories of my own
spiritual life—the form faith takes for my own needs. But indeed I
need such categories less and less. It is all reduced to a dialogue with

that (so evidently) spiritual and personal power within me which claims, every moment, my absolute worship and obedience; which is as real and self-evident to me as the most constant impulses of my "nature" with which it is in perpetual and sensible conflict. My imagination is quite cured of the outside God; for I feel that the inward spirit persuades and transcends the whole universe and reveals to me but an infinitesimal fraction of its Will and End and Truth and Nature.

I find most help in reading the Psalms and interpreting them into this immanent view of God, e.g. *In te Domine speravi*—all my hope is in this inward Spirit. *Tu est Deus fortitudo mea*—all fortitude and [sic] strength is the strength of Conscience; all weakness and feebleness is from an abandonment of Conscience. That is our Refuge, our Rock, our consolation in trouble. "Keep me as the apple of Thine eye; hide me under the shadow of Thy wings. If Conscience is on my side, I will not fear what man can do unto me." "Whom have I in heaven but Thee, and what is there in earth that I desire in comparison with Thee?" Owing to counter-habits such meanings will be at first forced and non-natural, but very soon they come at once to the mind, and they are undoubtedly the hidden truth which the writer of the Psalms tried to express in terms of the "outside" God of the childish imagination.

That is my own line of thought and feeling. It may possibly help you to find your way towards what you want. In the most intimate things no two think and feel alike. At all events one must learn enough detachment from the Church to be able to keep one's soul in peace and feel that even if the ship sank one has a lifebelt.

LETTER TO WILLIAM SCOTT PALMER

The following is another, and more mystical *apologia*, addressed to William Scott Palmer.—M.D.P.

August 23rd, 1908

Like you I am ruminating the results of a year's grazing. I can do it best leaning over a gate and watching a cow similarly employed—the most tranquilising influence in Nature. The world is too much with us; Nature, too little. I used to keep a Buddha under my crucifix— to the shock of my *confrères*. Henceforth I shall keep a cow—a

sacred cow, emblem of the quiet weary East with its *Quand même?*
"After all?"

One does not accept that world-wide world-old verdict on life.
But one cannot ignore it. It is a fact that will not be laid; that rises up
in the mad rush and roar of Piccadilly Circus and demands a hearing.
Perhaps the presence of that haunting is the condition of any *positive*
faith in life's value, and the faith of those who are quite free from it is
folly and superstition. Perhaps the crucifix with its call to energy and
suffering and progress is best understood beside the cold comatose
Sakya Mouni. I feel more and more that as regards God and immortality man was made not to know but to hope. Hope, rather than
faith; for faith is so hopelessly confounded with knowledge. There
the Buddha is so right; for we do not, we cannot know. And there the
Christian with his theology-faith is so wrong, so poor, so thin, so
shallow, so provincial. For him the fringe of mystery that lends life
its dignity, its pathos, its humility is torn away, and replaced by a
brick wall with nothing beyond. When I contrast the temper of Job,
xxxviii-ix, with that of the ordinary cock-sure Christian I find it hard
to believe in the steady development of the religious sense. Are our
theologies more than an attempt to give shape and substance to one
Hope? and are they not to be rated by a moral rather than an intellectual criterion—i.e. according to the quality, the elevation, and the
"truth" of the Hope? The gods that we fashion are the measure of
the Divine that is in us, whose face we dream of, but cannot see. I
know we should not be frightened by the star-dust on these dark
nights; that a particle of mind is more than an universe of matter, etc.
But is there not probably some proportion, some relation of analogy? Or is it not merely that our spiritual conceit and self-importance
have not yet been detected by a metaphysical Galileo? We are so
young and cock-sure that from man to God there is but one or at
most two steps—mineral, vegetable, animal, human, (angelic), divine.
Is it not infinity to one that as the earth is, quantitatively, to the
universe of star-dust so, qualitatively, is man's spirit to the divine? All
I dare say is that the divine has a human aspect which alone concerns
man; just as it has a canine aspect which alone concerns dogs; but
that it is as little human as it is canine. It is that all-pervading indwelling Power which moves dogs and men towards their proper perfection; which, for them, is the Divine Will. It is man's privilege to think
of it; to wonder; to hope; to figure it to himself in terms of his own
spirit. It is the Divine Will, because it is human nature, that he should

do so: "He thinks he was not made to die: and Thou hast made him; Thou art just." We do not know nothing about God; but we know infinitely little. We can have no word of God, no revelation, except the ideal or eternal Man; the Christ. That is as much of God as we can ever *see*; but we can have the sense of the infinitely more and other that God is. It is only because He presents Himself to us as the Christ, with a human spirit, face, voice, and hands, that we can speak to Him or deal with Him at all. Mystics think they touch the divine when they have only blurred the human form in a cloud of words. The best mysticism is to submit to the limitation *consciously*; to realise that our best God is but an idol, a temple made with hands in which the Divine will as little be confined as in our Hell—Purgatory—Heaven (*rez-de-chaussee; entre-sol; premier etage*) schematisation. For you and me this is an escape from the prison of theology into the liberty of faith. But for the man in the street God and the idol fall together, thanks to centuries of theologism. Like you, I fear we must look for an "abomination of desolation" a *religio depopulata*, a desert of negation and materialism between the Egypt of the Past and the Jerusalem of the Future. My consolation is to recognise its necessity as a stage of purification. . . .